# Moral Freedom

tial Rc
0196

D1145588

Volume 3 of Ethics

with a new introduction by
**Andreas A.M. Kinneging**

# Moral
# Freedom

## Nicolai Hartmann

*Transaction Publishers*
*New Brunswick (U.S.A.) and London (U.K.)*

Second printing 2015
New material this edition copyright © 2004 by Transaction
Publishers, New Brunswick, New Jersey, www.transactionpub.com
Originally published in 1932 by The Macmillan Company.

This book is printed on acid-free paper that meets the American National
Standard for Permanence of Paper for Printed Library Materials.

Library of Congress Catalog Number: 2002032029
ISBN: 978-0-7658-0594-2
Printed in the United States of America

Library of Congress Cataloging-in-Publication Data

Hartmann, Nicolai, 1882-1950.
    [Ethik. English]
    Ethics / Nicolai Hartmann ; with a new introduction by Andreas
A. M. Kinneging.
        p. cm.
    Originally published: [S.1.] : Macmillan Co., 1932.
    Includes bibliographical references and index.
    ISBN 0-7658-0962-1 (pbk. : alk. paper)
        1. Ethics. I. Title.
B3279.H23 E8813 2002
171'.2—dc21
ISBN 0-7658-0594-4 (Volume 3)

                                                        2002032029

# CONTENTS

## PART III

# THE PROBLEM OF THE FREEDOM OF THE WILL

### (THE METAPHYSIC OF MORALS)

## *Section I*

## PRELIMINARY CRITICAL QUESTIONS

# CONTENTS

## *Section II*

### THE CAUSAL ANTINOMY

## Section III

### THE ANTINOMY OF THE OUGHT

## Section IV

### ETHICAL PHENOMENA, THEIR EFFICACY AS PROOFS

## Section V

## ONTOLOGICAL POSSIBILITY OF PERSONAL FREEDOM

CONTENTS

## *Section VI*

## APPENDIX TO THE DOCTRINE OF FREEDOM

# TRANSACTION INTRODUCTION

ETHICS is concerned with an aspect of the question of what the ancients called the good (*kalon, agathon, bonum*), and the moderns often call the valuable, namely that which we call the moral. It is concerned with the question: what is *morally* good, what is of *moral* value? (And, of course, the converse question: what is morally not good, i.e. morally bad or evil, what is morally without value, or of disvalue?)

But there is a yet another question concerning the moral that also lies at the heart of the subject matter of ethics, even if one were to deny that it is an ethical question *per se*, but rather a question of ontology or anthropology. It regards the freedom of the will. The question is meta-ethical or, to put it more precisely, "critical" in the Kantian sense of the word: it is concerned with the necessary preconditions of morality. The existence of the freedom of the will is precisely that: without it, there is no morality in the full sense of the word.

This is not to say that, without freedom of the will, we would no longer be able to distinguish between good and bad/evil in the moral sense of the word. Quite the reverse is true. We could and would still distinguish between justice and injustice, honesty and dishonesty, courage and cowardice, and so on. It is merely that, *stricto sensu*, an act of, for instance, justice by a person would no longer constitute a moral act, because it would not be the result of a free choice by that person. Without freedom of the will our choices are predetermined, and thus not of our own making. In that case, moral attribution makes no sense, since attribution presupposes that one could have willed and acted otherwise. Only if a person could have done otherwise is it appropriate to speak of guilt, responsibility, merit, remorse, etc. If human action were to be wholly the product of various stimuli, a different approach would be needed, reminiscent of the training of dogs: punishment to deter from unwanted ("bad") action and reward to stimulate wanted ("good") action, sticks and carrots, incentives and disincentives.

Thus, the sphere of morality would remain something external to the human psyche, in the way it is to dogs. A moral *act* would be nothing more than moral *behavior*: induced by various incentives and disincentives. In different circumstances, with different incentives, the same man would behave immorally. Hence, his morality is heteronomous, not autonomous, that is, self-willed. He is not moral in the true, deep sense of the word.

The question regarding the freedom of the will is the subject matter of this third and final volume of Nicolai Hartmann's seminal work, *Ethik* (1926), first published in English in 1932 as *Ethics*. The first two volumes, *Moral Phenomena* and *Moral Values*, dealt with the other ethical problem: the question what moral value is and which moral values there are.

Since these are two separate questions, one might be tempted to conclude that it is possible to read this volume independently of the other two. To a certain extent, this is correct, but diving into the depths of Hartmann's thoughts on the freedom of the will completely unprepared is rather precarious, since they are closely linked to his more general ethical and ontological ideas. One cannot fully comprehend his views on the freedom of the will if one has no knowledge of the latter.

Moreover, most contemporary English-speaking readers tend to find Hartmann a difficult author, having commonly been brought up in an entirely different—analytical—philosophical tradition. Readers with a grounding in contemporary continental—mainly Heideggerian—philosophy, however, are not much better off. Hartmann's philosophy is anchored in other sources: above all in Plato and Kant and, to a somewhat lesser degree, in Aristotle and Hegel. It is the thought of these philosophers that has shaped Hartmann's own philosophy. As a first-rate, original philosopher in his own right, Hartmann has incorporated essential elements of Plato, Kant, Aristotle, and Hegel into his own thought, but is never a mere expositor. In his works, their ideas, though still recognizable, are transformed into something quite new and distinctive, unlike any of its ingredients, both in what it has to say, and in how it is said. The result is a fascinating oeuvre, impressive in its depth and richness, that goes counter to the dominant drifts in contemporary philosophy, as summarized in the notion of "subjectivity." Hartmann's works, on the contrary, are an extraordinary effort to reestablish the idea of "objectivity" at the center of our thought, where it had stood in the great philosophical tradition from Plato to Hegel.

That this does not make for easy reading speaks for itself. It therefore does not seem redundant to start this introduction with a short outline of Hartmann's main ontological and ethical ideas. For a more detailed exposition, the reader is referred to volumes 1 and 2 of *Ethics*, published by Transaction in 2002 en 2003 respectively. These volumes include lengthy introductions, by the present author, on both Hartmann's ethical and ontological thought.

## I. REAL BEING

Let us begin at the beginning: with Hartmann's ontology. After all, this is what the philosophical tradition, which Hartmann wants to reestablish, has always considered the *prima philosophia*. Hartmann's philosophy of being (ontology) is built upon the idea that the world (being) encompasses two different kinds of being (*Seinsweisen*): real being (*reales Sein*) and ideal being (*ideales Sein*).

Real being includes everything, corporeal and incorporeal, that is in or attached to the spatio-temporal world. The entities that partake of this kind of being come into existence and perish, they are impermanent, altering, and singular. Ideal being, on the other hand, is timeless and not spatial.

There are, as far as we can tell, four different, hierarchically ordered strata or layers (*Seinsschichten*) of real being, from the stratum of inorganic being (*anorganisches Seins*) at the bottom, through the strata of organic being (*organisches Sein*) and mental being (*seelisches Sein*), to spiritual being (*geistiges Sein*) at the top. The meaning of the categories of the inorganic and the organic are evident. Mental being encompasses everything that exists within the individual soul, consciously or unconsciously. It is an inner, untransferable, esoteric being of the individual. Animals, al least the higher animals, also seem to have a mental life. Spiritual being is based upon mental being, but it exceeds the mental. Only man is a spiritual entity. It is transferable between different individuals, and for every one of them it is objective. "Culture" is a term that renders the meaning of spiritual being quite accurately, if one defines culture broadly, as including language, morality, law, politics, historical consciousness, ideology, the arts, religion, and philosophy.

All four strata exist separately. The higher strata cannot be reduced to the lower, nor the lower to the higher. Materialist or idealist monism fails to do justice to the irreducible multiplicity of the world. Yet, separate existence does not imply complete independence. The various strata are all connected. The relation between them is governed by several ontological laws, the most important being the law of substance (*Gesetz der Materie*) and the law of freedom (*Gesetz der Freiheit*). The first law stipulates that the lower strata are the ontological base of higher strata. Higher strata are dependent on lower strata, in the sense that the lower strata are the matter out of which being at a higher stratum is formed. Thus, many categories of being (*Kategorien*), that is, characteristics, typical of the lower strata return in the higher strata. However, in each stratum some new categories are added, and others disappear. Hence, each stratum has its own nature and its own determinants. It is not entirely determined by the lower strata, but partially "free." This is the law of freedom.

Take, for instance, the three categories of temporality, spatiality, and causality. Temporality (*Zeitlichkeit*), i.e. being-in-time, is characteristic of all four strata of real being. The real world is a Heraclitean world, in which all things change and no one can cross the same river twice. Spatiality (*Räumlichkeit*), i.e. being-in-space, on the other hand, is a characteristic only of inorganic and organic being. Mental and spiritual being are not spatial, although both are attached to, and carried by, spatial being.

More important even for our purposes is the category of causality. The causal nexus is the principle of motion characteristic of inorganic being, and it reappears in all the higher strata. But other, supra-causal (*überkausale*) determinants are added there. Already in the stratum of organic being, the vital sphere, a preexisting *telos*, a system of predispositions, somehow molds the causal process. The organic process is in some way directed towards a goal (*Zweckmäßigkeit*). In the stratum of spiritual being, this teleological tendency becomes a full-fledged purposiveness. Here, and only here, we find what Hartmann names the finalistic nexus (*Zwecktätigkeit*).

## II. IDEAL BEING

In addition to the sphere of real being, the world encompasses a sphere of ideal being, according to Hartmann. This sphere consists of ideal entities, such as mathematical units and laws, the laws of logic, the essence (*Wesen*) of concrete, existing things, acts and occurrences. And it includes values. These entities have no spatio-temporal being.

With this notion of ideal being Hartmann reintroduces a traditional idea. "In ancient times, it was seen that there is another realm of being than that of existence, than that of 'real' things and of consciousness, which is not less 'real.' Plato named it the realm of the Idea, Aristotle that of the *eidos*, the scholastics called it the realm of *essentia*. After having been long misunderstood and deprived of its right in modern times through the prevailing subjectivism, this realm has again come into recognition with relative purity in that which phenomenology calls the realm of *Wesenheiten*. *Wesenheit* is a translation of *essentia*. It means the same thing, if we disregard the various metaphysical presuppositions which have attached themselves to the idea of essence. But on its part *essentia* is a translation, although a very faded one, of the Aristotelian phrase *ti èn einai*, in which the past tense *èn*, understood as timeless, points to the sum total of the structural elements that are presupposed—that is, of that which in the concrete thing, act or occurrence constitutes the objective *prius* and on that account is always contained in it." The kind of being peculiar to this *prius* is that of an *ontós on*, that "through which" everything participating in it is just as it is.

Hartmann's indebtedness to Plato is obvious here. But, contrary to Plato, who believes that the sphere of Ideas is the sphere of true being, and real being is merely an imperfect reflection of it, he regards ideal being as "a 'thinner,' floating, insubstantial being, half-being so to speak, which still lacks the full weight of being."[2]

The case of mathematics is instructive. In the units and laws of mathematics man first discovered ideal being. Mathematical units and laws are beyond time and space, beyond genesis and disintegration, which are typical of everything in the real world. But although mathematical being differs fundamentally from real being, it pervades the latter. The principles of mathematics are the principles of reality. Things, acts, and occurrences in the real world necessarily comply with the principles of mathematics. It is possible, by eliminating or adding one or more axioms, to develop a mathematics that has little to do with the real world, but it is not possible for the real world to escape from the grip of mathematical principles.[3] The real contains and is molded by the ideal.

The real world is suffused with mathematical principles, but these principles cannot be observed empirically. Moreover, the validity of mathematical principles is universal and stringent, whereas empirical observation can only render probable results. Therefore, knowledge of mathematical principles must be the product of a different kind of observation that is not empirical and can claim absolute validity. Plato called it an inner perception, a perception with the mind's eye, so to speak. Kant's synthetic judgment a priori also bears upon this kind of knowledge. Following the latter, Hartmann speaks of a priori knowledge as "an inner grasping of a state of affairs that has immediate certainty, and can claim generality and necessity."[4]

What goes for mathematics goes for all other types of ideal being as well, viz. for the laws of logic, for the essence of concrete, existing things, acts and occurrences, and for values. All of these cannot be observed empirically, but are perceived a priori. Our knowledge of these ideal entities is a priori knowledge.

### III. Value in General and Moral Value

Values are ideal beings. They are therefore part of the world's makeup. We cannot invent them. We can only discover them. Values are thus not subjective, but objective.

From a practical point of view, everything that exists somehow falls under the category of values. Even the most remote and indifferent thing, act, or event either has a positive or a negative value. The world of things and their relations is at the same time and no less a world of goods and evils.

All of these goods are values, and all of these evils are "disvalues" (*Unwerte*), but it would be erroneous to call all these goods and evils *moral* values and *moral* disvalues. A piece of property, for instance, is a good, and has a value, but is not as such a moral value. A book, a vacation, peace of mind, anything may be a good, and anything may be an evil. But this does not make these things morally good or evil, moral values.

There are thus several different species of value. Moral values constitute only one category among many. How many, we cannot know for certain. There might be species of value in the ideal realm of value that are not accessible to man. Being, Hartmann maintains, is much richer and more profound than the phenomena that constitute an object to man. Moreover, of the existence of some species of value, such as the aesthetic for instance, we are aware, but we can hardly be said to have much knowledge.

Two non-moral categories of value are discussed at length in the *Ethics*, "subject-values" (*dem Subjekt anhaftenden Wertfundamente*) and "goods-values" (*Güterwerte*). The moral values are, in different ways, grounded on them. Examples of subject-values are life, consciousness, and mental strength. Goods-values are, for instance, the piece of property, the book, and the vacation mentioned. These values are the material basis of moral values. Without them moral values would be unthinkable. "[W]herein would an honest man be superior to a thief, if the things purloined were not somehow of value? What one man can steal, what another can treasure as a possession, is not merely a thing but a good. Honesty then, if it is a moral value, necessarily presupposes the positive worth of material (i.e. non-moral, AK) goods. It is inherently dependent upon the latter."[5]

It thus appears that, like real being, ideal being is a hierarchically ordered whole of different strata or layers (*Seinsschichten*). Moral values are intrinsically higher than goods-values and subject-values, according to Hartmann. They are in fact, as far as we can tell, the highest values there are.

What else is specific to moral values? First of all, moral values are necessarily affixed to man; primarily to his acts, but also to his character, which is shaped by and expressed in these acts. In the latter case, when values are inherent in a character, we speak of virtues. Moral values are always attached to acts or characters, never to things and the relation between them. Only acts or characters can be morally good or bad/evil.

Secondly, moral value appears "on the back of the act" (*auf dem Rücken der Handlung*), not in the goal that is aimed at. In being truthful one does not aim at veracity itself, but at giving the person spoken to the possibility of learning the truth. "[L]ikewise, the object of the high-minded or loving person is not to be high-minded or loving, but that the other person, to whom something is given or whom he makes glad, may have the gift or the gladness. He gives out of love, but not for the sake of being a loving person. He is concerned not at all with his own moral being, but with the being of the other person, and indeed by no means only with that other person's moral, but with his whole being, bodily as well as mental, that is to say, with conditions (*Sachverhalte*) that are valuable for that person. But these conditions are valuable for him in so far as they embrace goods (i.e. goods-values, A.K.). The knowledge of a truth is as much a good (i.e. a goods-value, A.K.)—or surely intended as a good—as the gift bestowed or the gladness occasioned."[6]

Finally, since, given the above, the moral value of an act does not depend on the value of what is intended (*intendierter Wert*), but on the moral value of the intention (*Intentionswert*), the moral value of an act does not depend on the success of the act, but merely on the moral value of its intention. If one intends to do what is morally good, but for other reasons does not succeed, the failure does not constitute a moral blemish.

### IV. THE REALIZATION OF MORAL VALUES

There is one fundamental difference between moral values and the other species of ideal being, such as mathematical units and laws. Unlike the latter, moral values do not categorically govern real being.[7] They can of course be realized, but they can also remain unrealized. It does not lie in their essence as principles that the real necessarily corresponds to them. Moral values are not inviolable determinants to which everything real is subordinate.

What, then, is the relation between moral values as ideal entities and the real world? At this point Hartmann introduces the notion of "the ought."[8] Moral values and the ought are indissolubly bound together. The ought is not principally an ought-to-do, but an ought-to-be. The ought-to-be is the mode of being of a moral value, and a moral value is the content of the ought. The ought-to-be of the moral values refers to the real world. When the ideal finds itself in opposition to the real, when it is unrealized, the ought-to-be becomes "actual," the ideal "calls out" to be realized.

To be heard and acted upon, there must be in the stream of real existence, in fluctuating reality itself, a point of support upon which the ought-to-be impinges. There must be something or other within the real world, which shares completely in the world's existential mode of coming into being and perishing, and yet, at the same time, is able to hear the call of the imperishable, the ideal.

This point of support is man, writes Hartmann. He, and only he, is capable of grasping moral values. Grasping a moral value is sensing it, or more precisely, being gripped by it (*Erfaßtsein von ihm*). The specific "organ" with which man perceives moral values is his sense of value (*Wertgefühl*). This sense is neither a cognitive nor a conative, but an affective, an emotional capacity. It is a peculiar axiological sense, an "ordre de coeur" or "organe morale," a primary, pre-, or subconscious "response" to the presence of moral values. It is this sense, and the conscious discernment of moral values (*Wertschau*) based on it, that enables us not only to recognize moral values, but also to intuit the ranking order between them.

Of course, the fact that one has the capacity to sense moral values does not mean that one actually senses them. The sense of value of concrete persons is often immature, deadened, or unevenly developed, and consequently they are blind to a part of the realm of moral values, just as some people are blind to mathematical truths. Not everyone has the eye, the ethical maturity, the spiritual level, for grasping the moral meaning of a situation. The sensing of values presupposes devotion and attentive listening. The realm of values needs to be lovingly and carefully hearkened to. Only to the attentive and patient does it reveal its secrets.

Grasping moral values is not enough, however. The ought-to-be is converted into reality only if man, having grasped a moral value, acts upon it. It is at this point that we encounter the issue of the freedom of the will that is central to the present, third, volume of the *Ethics*, entitled *Moral Freedom*.

There are two possibilities regarding the act realizing the ought-to-be. Having grasped a moral value, man is either free to place his acts in its service or not, or the moral value utterly determines his will and he has no choice but to realize it. If the latter is true and the human will is wholly predetermined in making a choice, the moral significance of human acts is nil, even when in these acts moral values are realized, because that which would make these acts truly moral is lacking: accountability, responsibility, guilt, and merit. If that were the case, the world would contain moral *objects*, i.e. moral values, but since it would be without moral *subjects*, morality in the full sense of the word would be impossible.

The concept Hartmann uses to signify a moral subject is "person." A person is a human being (a subject) who possesses freedom of the will. The question that is at the heart of *Moral Freedom* might thus be rephrased as: can we ascribe personality (in this sense) to man? As everyone familiar with Kant's practical philosophy will have noticed, this is exactly the question central to both the *Grundlegung der Metaphysik der Sitten* (1785) and the *Kritik der praktischen Vernunft* (1788). Significantly, the subtitle of *Moral Freedom* is "Metaphysik der Sitten" (The Metaphysic of Morals). Volume 3 of Hartmann's *Ethics* is a continuation of Kant's efforts to establish the freedom of the will. A continuation, that is, not in the sense of "a return to Kant," but in the sense of "having gone through and moving beyond Kant."

### V. Two Antinomies

Almost at the outset of *Moral Freedom*, Hartmann states that, "as the problem of freedom stands today," the freedom of the will cannot be proved.[9] What can be proved is merely that freedom of the will is "ontologically possible."[10] But it is a possibility with a high degree of certainty.[11]

This result might seem disappointing. Hartmann argues, however, that it is philosophically of great importance, since it is a refutation of the determinist view that freedom of the will cannot exist. Moreover, it establishes the likelihood of the freedom of the will. Admittedly, that result falls short of certainty, but ontological *principia* like these can never be proved, for the simple reason that everything we consider as knowledge is derived from these same *principia*. To prove *principia*, we would have to use knowledge that itself depends on the truth of the *principia*. Hence, we are stuck in an insoluble *petitio principii*. With the *principia*, we have reached the outer limit of what can be rationally accounted for. Beyond them lies what Hartmann calls "the irrational," that which cannot be rationally explained.[12]

The aim of *Moral Freedom* is hence more modest than proving the freedom of the will. Its goal is the refutation of the determinist view that there can be no freedom of the will. This leads to the question: what exactly is the determinist view?

The historical roots of determinism go back a long time. It arose in the wake of the religious dogma of God's omnipotence, from which the idea of predestination follows logically. The modern determinist view, however, comes up only in the seventeenth century, with such thinkers as Spinoza, who argue that not God, but the causal nexus leaves no room for freedom of the will. The older, religious determinism had been teleological/finalistic: God pulls us towards his goals. The newer determinism, on the contrary, is causal. "No finalistic purposes of the divinity now paralyze the finite creature. He stands over only against the blind causality of a world, the all-pervading determinism of which envelops even his innermost being, consciousness and will."[13] "[N]ot only the physical world is placed under the law of causality, but also the mental and spiritual world are supposedly governed by it..."[14]

This is the position of ethical naturalism. The crudest species of such a theory is materialism, writes Hartmann, which takes consciousness, will, and ethos as physical functions. A less trivial version is biological evolutionism, which tends to reduce every moral phenomenon, including man's decisions, dispositions, and preferences, to inheritance, influence of the environment, or the conditions of life, and other, similar causal factors.[15]

It is the contradiction between this causal determinism and the freedom of the will that is referred to by Hartmann as "the causal antinomy" (*Kausalantinomie*). Hartmann contends that Kant was the first to give a precise picture of the causal antinomy.[16] And he also solved it. That is to say, he demonstrated that it is not a true antinomy: the contradiction is not real.[17] Both Kant's description of the problem and his solution to it, however, are marred by his transcendental idealism, according to Hartmann. And what is even worse, Kant has completely overlooked a second antinomy, which poses at least as great a threat to the freedom of the will as the causal antinomy. This second antinomy Hartmann labels "the antinomy of the ought" (*Sollensantinomie*).

Section II of *Moral Freedom* is devoted to an exposition of the causal antinomy and Kant's solution to it, while at the same time freeing it of its superfluous and flawed transcendental-idealist trappings. As of Section III, apart from the two collateral chapters at the end, Hartmann is concerned with the problem left unsolved by Kant, because it was not noticed by him: the antinomy of the ought.

## VI. Two Determinations

Before Kant, attempts at refuting causal determinism postulated at least a partial indeterminism. The freedom of the will was thought of as independence, as a gap in the causal nexus, as freedom from it, i.e. "negative" freedom. This was not convincing, however, because we cannot conceive of such a thing within the causal nexus. Consequently, scepticism concerning the freedom of the will had become widespread in ethics.[18]

Kant's great achievement, Hartmann asserts, consists in having shown that freedom of the will is not to be conceived of as indeterminism, as negative freedom, but as an extra determinative force that is brought into the real world on top of the causal force, i.e. as positive freedom.[19] "The causal nexus would be interrupted if anything in it were suspended, infringed upon, cut off—as is required by negative freedom. Now, however, none of its elements of determination is suspended; all causal determinants that are present in the human will (as motives, for instance), and have an effect on it, remain intact. But a new determinant is added to them. And this determinant differs from the others only in that it is not itself the effect of prior causes, but enters the causal nexus from another sphere, a sphere in which there are no causal chains."[20] The causal process is not interrupted by this addition, but only diverted in a different direction.

This theory does away with the difficulty inherent in the notion of freedom of the will as negative freedom, but brings in a new one: how to conceive of this "sphere without causal chains"? Kant tried to solve this difficulty by contrasting the world-as-it-is (the intelligible/noumenal world) with the world as it appears to our senses (the empirical/phenomenal world), and arguing that causality is a mere feature of the latter. Causality is in the eye of the beholder, so to speak. It is characteristic of how we perceive the world, not of the world itself. Applying this theory to man himself, Kant concludes that, although to our senses his doings appear causally determined, man as-he-really-is is not determined. We cannot help empirically seeing man as causally determined, but at the same time our reason is capable of understanding that this is merely an appearance. Man, considered as part of the world-as-it-is, must be taken to be self-determining, i.e. as possessing free will. Hence, Kant essentially solves the problem by reducing the causal nexus to the status of an "ideal" entity—something merely in the mind of man.

Hartmann rejects Kant's idealism. That the causal nexus is only appearance, and that behind it lies an intelligible world that is real, but does not appear to our senses, is "metaphysical construction."[21] However, it is not essential and can be dropped. What is essential is merely the insight that there are two layers, two sets of laws, two ways of determination in the world, the world in which man exists, that both manifest themselves in him. The first layer is causally structured. From the second layer heterogeneous determinants enter into this causal nexus.[22]

What is the nature of these heterogeneous determinants? To Kant, this second way of determination is the determination by the moral law (*das Sittengesetz*), which commands the individual to aim only for what he can will to be a universal rule. This law does not determine causally, like genes or social background. Since it pertains to aims (*telos, finis*), it follows that the moral law is a teleological/finalistic determinant.

The moral law is not part of the empirical/phenomenal world, where we find only causal determinants, such as genes and social background. But we can rationally deduce its nature and being. Hence, it belongs to the intelligible/noumenal world. As a result, we get the picture that, by obeying the moral law instead of causal forces, we introduce a heterogeneous, finalistic element into the causal nexus: the element of morality.

Dropping the idealist metaphysics, Hartmann argues that the second layer of determination should be seen not as the moral law, coming from the intelligible world, but as the moral values, coming from the sphere of ideal being, and thus independent of all the causal forces present in the real world. Once adopted by man, moral values enter into the real world and hence into the causal process without difficulty, changing its course, but not breaking it off. They determine finalistically, not causally, since they are intrinsic to, or in any case behind all aims, and, as we already observed, aims constitute a finalistic determination.[23]

Hence, we get the following picture. The finalistic nexus is introduced from the ideal world into the real world through man, on top of the causal nexus that pervades the real world. The finalistic determination inserts itself without conflict into the causal, because the course of its realization is itself causal. In the achievement of the goal, the actual process is a causal process, in which the means are real causes that, step by step, bring about the good aimed at. This implies that the causal nexus is not antithetical to the freedom of the will. Indeed, "a free will with its finalistic efficacy is possible only in a (real, A.K.) world that is entirely causally determined."[24]

"Here," Hartmann concludes, "man's freedom shows itself to be an ontological function of his unique position within the hierarchical relation (*Schichtungsverhältnis*) between the two types of determination. It is a dual position; he stands under a twofold determination. As a natural being, he is determined causally, even in his desires and aversions, a plaything of the eternal forces of nature, overpowering him and working irrespective of him and through him. But as a 'person,' he is the carrier of another determination that comes from the ideal realm of values. In his sense of value he finds himself also determined by the ought-to-be (*Sollensforderung*) of the moral values. And it is this determination that manifests itself in his purposive activity (*Zwecktätigkeit*). He can only make his goals what he senses to be of value. But in making it his goal, he transforms it into reality. Thus, he positively creates what causal necessity could never bring forth, a world of moral reality within natural reality."[25]

If one of the two determinant forces were absent, and man were wholly determined by only one of them, freedom of the will would be non-existent, and hence morality would be impossible. "If the causal nexus in him controls the positing of goals (*Zwecksetzung*), mechanicism rules uninhibitedly, and man becomes, as Lamettrie had it, a 'machine.' But if the finalistic nexus controls the natural processes, all-powerful, controlling, macrocosmic goals of the world (*Weltzwecke*) stand over against the weak, finite purposive activity of man, for whom he is no match. He is hamstrung, fettered, predestined even in the most secret movements of his heart, indeed, in his sense of value."[26] In both cases, man would possess no freedom of the will. "The laws governing real being (*Seinsgesetzlichkeit*) and the laws governing the ought (*Sollensgesetzlichkeit*), causal and teleological determination, must so to speak have the seat of their cosmic struggle in him. And only as long as this struggle continues is there a free being."[27]

## VII. FREEDOM AND ONTOLOGY

How does this ethical dualism fit into Hartmann's wider ontological views? As has been set out above, Hartmann's ontology rests on the idea that being is twofold: it is either real being—being in time and space—or ideal being. Real being is, as far as we can see, split up into four different, hierarchically ordered strata or layers (*Seinsschichten*), from the stratum of inorganic being (*anorganisches Seins*) at the bottom, through the strata of organic being (*organisches Sein*) and mental being (*seelisches Sein*), to spiritual being (*geistiges Sein*) at the top. (There might be more strata, but if so, we have no knowledge of them.)

These strata are connected by various ontological laws, most importantly by the law of substance and the law of freedom. The first law stipulates that the lower strata are the ontological base of higher strata. Higher strata are dependent on lower strata, in the sense that the lower strata are the matter out of which being at a higher stratum is formed. Thus, many categories (*Kategorien*), that is, characteristics, of being of the lower strata return in the higher strata. The law of freedom lays down that, notwithstanding this dependence, in each stratum some new categories are added, and others disappear. Hence, each stratum has its own nature and its own determinants. It is not entirely determined by the lower strata, but partially independent. Hence, the law of freedom. The question at issue here is how the dualism of causal and finalistic determination, which is central to Hartmann's ethics, fits into this general ontological framework.

The causal nexus is the type of determination distinctive of the stratum of anorganic being.[28] Beneath it, and thus included in it, are two other types of determination we know of: mathematical determination and, below that, logical determination. These even more fundamental types of determination than the causal are included in the causal nexus, as categorial elements.[29]

The finalistic nexus is typical of the stratum of spiritual being. One has often taken finalistic determination as something that is introduced at the level of organic being, but this is not strictly true. Of course we find processes of self-preservation and self-development in this stratum, and even more so in the next higher stratum of mental being, but these processes are not in the full sense of the word teleological. What we find in these strata is functionality (*Zweckmäßigkeit*), not purposiveness (*Zwecktätigkeit*). On top of the causal nexus something else has appeared, but that something is not yet purposiveness. Purposiveness is the prerogative of the stratum of spiritual being, and hence of the human person.[30]

Thus, looking at the problem of the freedom of the will from the wider perspective of general ontology, Hartmann concludes, "is only a special case of the categorial freedom, which appears from stratum to stratum."[31] "In its own way, an animal (organic being, A.K.) is free as compared with inanimate nature (anorganic being, A.K.), which is clearly manifested in its self-movement, its sensitivity to stimuli, and so on; consciousness (mental being, A.K.) is free in relation to the organism to which it is bound in time and space."[32] In the same way, a person's will is free in relation to his consciousness. The former is not entirely determined by the latter.

More generally, we can conclude that the ethical dualism of causal and finalistic determinants is merely a specific aspect of a more complex ontological whole. This whole, however, is not a part of the subject matter of moral philosophy. It belongs to the field of general ontology, and is the topic of Hartmann's great ontological trilogy, *Zur Grundlegung der Ontologie* (1935), *Möglichkeit und Wirklichkeit* (1938), and *Der Aufbau der realen Welt* (1940).[33]

## VIII. The Antinomy of the Ought

Section III of *Moral Freedom* begins with a summing up of the result achieved. "'[F]reedom in the positive sense,' i.e. the autonomy of ethical-teleological determination of the will by principles of value...is obstructed neither by the causal nexus, nor by any other kind of lower determination (such as functional determination, A.K.). The autonomy of the moral principles in the sphere of ethical real life (i.e. in man as a being in the real world, A.K.), may consequently be considered established."[34] "It is a different question, however," Hartmann then continues, "whether the problem of freedom is already solved with this, indeed, whether it has been completely thought through and set out from top to bottom."[35] The answer is: no.

This becomes clear, if we take another, closer look at Kant's solution to the problem. "The moral law is the principle of a 'transcendental subject,' of practical 'consciousness in general,' to the same degree the twelve categories are principles of theoretical 'consciousness in general.' *Hence, transcendental freedom is not at all freedom of the moral person.* For such a person is only the real individual."[36]

The problem of the freedom of the will is not about the question to what extent a "transcendental subject" is responsible for man's acts, but about the question to what extent he himself is responsible. "Kant wants to prove the freedom of the will, and does not notice that he actually proves something altogether different—something, to be sure, that is essential as a presupposition of freedom of the will, but is surely not that freedom itself: the autonomy of the principle."[37] That is to say, Kant proves the possibility that man is governed not by causal determinants, but by an entirely different and independent principle. In Kant's transcendental-idealist makeup, this is the principle of "practical reason." Shorn of these specific metaphysical overtones, and in its new Hartmannian dress, it is the principle of teleological determination by values.

This proof, however, leads to the paradoxical conclusion that man, to the amount that he is free from causal determinants, is subject to another type of determinants, viz. moral values. This would leave him as unfree as he would have been if he had been completely subjected to the causal nexus. Man turns out to have a different master, but he is a slave all the same. Whichever is the case, there is no freedom of the will and morality is therefore nonexistent.

Thus, "what is decisive is that freedom exists not only as against the law of nature (i.e. the causal nexus, A.K.), but also as against the principle of the ought (*Sollensprinzip*) (i.e. moral values, A.K.)."[38] If the will (*Wollen*) necessarily coincides with the ought (*Sollen*), it is still unfree. Here we have a new antinomy, transcending the causal antinomy: the antinomy of the ought. Kant completely overlooked it. But the possibility of the freedom of the will is established only if this antinomy can be solved as well.[39]

This is not a new and original insight, writes Hartmann. It goes back to the scholastic philosophers. They already recognized that the problem of the freedom of the will has two sides. In their conception the omnipotent God not only rules causally through the laws of nature, but also by way of moral commandments. In this view, we recognize the two ways of determination we distinguished. It is not surprising then that we also find the question of human freedom—and responsibility—discussed in their writings, with reference not only to causal, but also to moral determination. In the scholastic view, the individual does not necessarily adhere to God's moral commandments. On the contrary, he is free to go against them, that is, to "sin." If he does, it is his responsibility, and he is guilty of the transgression. The question then arises: how is this possible, given the fact that God is omnipotent? This is exactly the antinomy of the ought, albeit in a religious clothing. It is this second side of the traditional problem of the freedom of the will that has been snowed under by Kant's theory, and has to be unearthed again.[40]

This analysis, in all its apparent simplicity, provides a fundamental critique of Kant's ethical thought, without returning to a naive pre-Kantianism. It establishes that Kant's positive conception of freedom is what is crucial to his solution of the problem of the freedom of the will, whereas his transcendental idealism, on the other hand, comes out as redundant. Moreover, it lets us see clearly the mistake at the heart of Kant's argument, a result of not proving what he thinks he has proved: the freedom of the will. Kant has solved only one half of the problem, the causal antinomy. The other half—the antinomy of the ought—still has to be solved. That is what Hartmann aspires to do in the remainder of *Moral Freedom.*

If man were inescapably determined by moral principles, he would not on that account be morally good, for he would not be free. Such a will would be neither good nor evil. It would be subject to the moral values, as a natural process is subject to causal laws. Thus, "[i]t is a fundamental mistake to regard a person's mere compliance to moral values as morality.... Only the compliance of a free being, a being who 'can also do otherwise' in the face of these values, is morality."[41]

This gives rise to the two following questions. First, why should we believe in the freedom of the will with regard to the moral values? Are there good reasons for thinking that it exists? Second, if freedom of the will vis-à-vis the moral values exists, how is it to be conceived? The first, "existential" (*quid*) question constitutes the subject matter of Section IV, "Ethical Phenomena, Their Efficacy as Proofs." The second, "modal" (*quomodo*) question is the theme of Section V, "Ontological Possibility of Personal Freedom." Only if both the existential and the modal questions can be substantiated, only if can be established *that* and *how* the freedom of the will exists, the antinomy of the ought will have been solved.

## IX. The Phenomena of Moral Life

How to tackle the question of existence? Hartmann insists that we have to start with a description of relevant empirical phenomena. It is true, of course, that phenomena cannot, *stricto sensu*, prove the existence of the freedom of the will. Phenomena indicate what something appears to be (*Schein*), not what it is (*Sein*). But by reasoning back analytically, like Kant, from the appearances to their presuppositions, we might be able to draw some conclusions as to the real being of freedom as well.[42]

Three phenomena of moral life are singled out by Hartmann as the most important empirical indications of the freedom of the will: the consciousness of self-determination (chapter XII), responsibility and accountability (chapter XIII), and the consciousness of guilt (chapter XIV).

"I can do it this way, but also differently. That is the consciousness of self-determination (*Bewußtsein der Selbstbestimmung*). Characteristic of this phenomenon is its permanent, invisible presence—as an unspoken of, dark, unacknowledged conviction.... And every time, wherever and whenever one directs one's inner gaze towards this point, self-determination appears simply to be a fact, a certainty...."[43]

Hartmann admits that "from the consciousness of a thing we cannot infer the real existence of just that thing."[44] The consciousness of self-determination might also be an illusion; we might be determined by factors we are not aware of. On the other hand, the thesis that the consciousness of self-determination is merely a semblance cannot be proved, and it has the additional disadvantage that, contrary to the first thesis, it is not supported by any phenomena. So the real existence of self-determination seems more likely, even though it cannot be definitely demonstrated.[45]

This conclusion is strengthened by the consideration that in the consciousness of self-determination there is no natural tendency to falsify the facts, as there is, for instance, in our moral depreciation and condemnation of other people. The latter meets a very elementary tendency in our nature, and must therefore be regarded with suspicion, because the truth is easily distorted.[46] This is not the case with the consciousness of self-determination. It is true that there is in man a wish to regard himself as morally free, but at the same time he has the propensity to relieve himself of the burden of responsibility and possible guilt by considering himself unfree. Indeed, this propensity is probably the more forceful of the two conflicting tendencies. "Hence, if the consciousness of self-determination nevertheless exists ubiquitously, a perfectly firm and clean-cut power must lie behind it in the constitution of man, that balances out all such tendencies. The real existence of the freedom of the will would be such a power."[47]

Turning from the consciousness of self-determination to the phenomena of taking responsibility (*Verantwortung*) and holding oneself accountable (*Zurechnung*), Hartmann argues that in them we have an even stronger indication of the real existence of freedom, "because this claim runs counter to every natural interest, all indolence, and the all-too-human weakness of shirking one's responsibility."[48] Moreover, these phenomena are not just something in consciousness, but real acts. They exist not only for the individual person, but have an intersubjective validity. Of course, they might nonetheless be illusory, in the sense that no real freedom of the will lies behind them. But such skepticism again does not match with the phenomena, and there is no other evidence for it. Therefore, the view that these phenomena do reflect reality is undoubtedly preferable.[49]

Finally, Hartmann discusses the consciousness of guilt (*Schuldbewuβtsein*). This phenomenon is, he thinks, the most significant empirical indication of the freedom of the will. "What was already inherent in responsibility, the inner tribunal, in which a person is twice represented and so to speak divided, that is drastically manifested in the consciousness of guilt, the most convincing inner reality. Everyone is acquainted with this phenomenon as the voice of conscience (*Stimme des Gewissens*), and with its moral influence as 'remorse' (*Reue*). Both are morally elemental phenomena, independent of reflection. With an inner necessity, they follow upon the act, as soon as its moral disvalue is sensed. This necessity and inescapability—the ancients characterize them in the mythological form of the persecuting Erinyes— renders the consciousness of guilt a testimony of self-determination of even greater significance than responsibility and accountability. Here, something primary, unfalsifiable speaks, from the depth of the human constitution, directly to the moral consciousness, something over which man has no control.... Here a fact of moral life is at hand, that contradicts every natural inclination of

man. Thus, the possibility of a subjective falsification of the phenomenon is out of the question. No one will acknowledge guilt, as
long as he can somehow avoid it, as long as he can say to himself,
for example, that the matter is not so serious, or that he is not the
originator."[50]

Again, this phenomenon does not provide absolute certainty.
But it does give the highest possible degree of "hypothetical"
certainty achievable in metaphysical subjects. We cannot get
more. Here we reach the limit of what is empirically knowable.[51]

### X. MORAL CONFLICT AND DECISION

As a second approach to the question of the existence of the freedom of the will, Hartmann returns to an issue already discussed in
the earlier volumes: the essence of moral conflict, i.e. of the relation between the ought (*Sollen*) and the will (*Wollen*) (chapter
XVI).[52]

Two different kinds of moral conflict are possible. On the one
hand, there is the antagonism between moral and immoral, or even
non-moral impulses in man, between "duty" and "inclination."
This is a conflict between natural instinct and the sense of values.
Here, behind the opposition between the ought and the will lies
the more general opposition between "ought" (*Sollen*) and "is"
(*Sein*), between the ideal realm of value and the real, factual world.
In the will, the axiological and ontological determinations meet
each other, that is, the moral values and the natural, causally determined inclinations. Often, they clash. Hence, moral conflict
type one.[53] It is obviously closely tied to the Kantian problem of
the causal antinomy, set out above.

But there is also a moral conflict of another kind, the conflict of
moral values with one another. Admittedly, not all moral values
are exclusive of others. Many go together quite harmoniously.
"But among them there are some that contradict one another, which
in concrete cases by their contents exclude one another and which
nevertheless, in one and the same situation, ought all to be realized. Here arises a conflict of another...kind, not between moral
and immoral or non-moral, but between moral and moral."[54] In this

case, the opposition between the ought and the will is not in essence an opposition between "ought" (*Sollen*) and "is" (*Sein*), but
between "ought" (*Sollen*) and "ought" (*Sollen*).[55]

. The first type of moral conflict does not give us any clues regarding the freedom of the will. The conflict here is a clash between the two determinations within the individual. But whatever
the outcome of this clash, we can think of the individual as remaining determined throughout, either by the causal forces of
nature alone, or by the moral values as well. With the second type
of moral conflict it is a different matter. That does provide evidence for the freedom of the will, at least where there is *a conflict
between moral values of a similar ranking*. When that occurs, and
only when that occurs, the need for a decision (*Entscheidung*)
becomes acute.[56]

To explain this we must briefly return to a subject central to
volume 2 of *Ethics*, *Moral Values*, viz. the gradation of moral
values. In the realm of values, as pictured by Hartmann, not everything is equal. On the contrary, there is a clear and elaborate stratification of values. Goods-values, for instance, stand lower in the
hierarchy of values than values attached to the human subject,
and both of these are less elevated than the moral values. These
Hartmann proclaims to be the highest type of value, as far as hu-
mankind can tell at least. There might be even higher types, but
they are "irrational"—beyond the bounds of what the ratio can
grasp.

Within the category of moral values there is a ranking as well.
Some have a higher moral value than others, although this does
not mean that they naturally take precedence. In fact, the lower
moral values often do, because they are the more fundamental, the
more urgent values. Realizing them is not meritorious; it is simply
our duty. One deserves merit only for the realization of the higher
moral values. Only through them we can become morally excel-
lent. An example of a lower moral value is not to murder anyone,
brotherly love an example of a higher moral value.[57]

When two or more moral values conflict, it is thus often clear
which of these values takes precedence and what must be done.

The decision is, as it were, given by the structure of the realm of moral values. But that is not always the case. Now and then the difference in rank between clashing moral values is just not clear. An example would be a situation in which truthfulness and trustworthiness/loyalty conflict with each other. If the choice is between lying and betraying a friend, the decision can become notoriously difficult. It is far from obvious which of the two moral values mentioned should take precedence.

This is precisely what Hartmann has in mind when speaking of a conflict between moral values of a similar ranking. It is here that we must look for evidence concerning the freedom of the will. It is exactly the evident impossibility of solving these conflicts of value by reference to the hierarchy within the realm of moral values that is the definite and surprisingly straightforward solution to the question of the freedom of the will. If a conflict of moral values cannot be solved by reference to the realm of moral values, and thus not on the ground of our sense of value, this means that it cannot be solved at all—at least as far as we can see. There is no given solution to the conflict in the nature of things. And precisely because of that, such conflicts have to be and are decided upon by man, by what must be a free ruling of his will.[58]

## XI. MORAL VALUES AND FREEDOM

Having given an account of what he considers the most important reasons for believing that freedom of the will vis-à-vis the moral values exists, Hartmann than turns to the question how freedom of the will is to be conceived. How must we picture the freedom of the will of the person, considering that he is determined as much by moral values as by causal forces? At a first glance, it would seem that this double determination rules freedom out, since the person is determined one way or the other. Yet, we have seen above that there are compelling reasons to believe in freedom. How to solve this paradox?

The answer lies in the way moral values determine. Moral values do not determine the will directly, compulsively, and inescapably, as causal forces do. They appeal to the person as something he ought to realize, they do not control him as something he must necessarily realize. "Whether teleological determination of the will by (moral, A.K.) values comes about or not, is rather a question of the decision of the will of the person itself."[59] No determination springs from the moral values, unless a person freely commits himself to them. Of themselves, moral values do not have the power to have an effect on the real world. Such power they can acquire only if a person commits himself to their realization. Thus, "in truth, determination by values is not only no obstacle to personal freedom but rather is conditioned by it."[60]

This implies that the teleological determinant is more complex than was presumed up to this point. It consists not only of the ideal component of moral value, but also of the real component of the will. It is only with the help of the latter that the former becomes a determining principle, on top of the causal laws of nature. Neither can the will determine itself without having before it and sensing the demands of the autonomous moral values. The will can only decide in confrontation with these values. Hence, the two components are complementary. The two of them together—the autonomous principle and the autonomous will—constitute the teleological determinant.[61] It is the autonomy of the will vis-à-vis the principle (i.e., the moral values, A.K.) that allows us to speak of a free will.

Contrary to the freedom from the causal nexus that, as we have seen, can only be conceived of as an extra determination—as positive freedom—this second and conclusive aspect of the freedom of the will has two sides. It is yet another, third, type of determination, and hence a positive freedom, but it also presupposes a negative freedom—an indetermination—of the person as against the various moral values that can be chosen. Thus, the older—and common sense—view of freedom as negative freedom, the rejection of which was central to Kant's solution of the causal antinomy, by whom it was replaced by a positive conception of freedom, is partially reestablished by Hartmann. Negative freedom does have a place in the world, though not with regard to causal forces, but with regard to moral values. That Kant overlooked this is not surprising since he, as we saw, had reduced the problem of the freedom of the will to its incompatibility with the causal nexus.[62]

That leaves us with one, final problem: what exactly is the ontological place of this third determining power, this will that is free as against the moral values? "[H]ow is it ontologically possible?"[63] To answer this question, we must return once more to Hartmann's general ontology. Up to this point, a dual determination by values and causal forces had been the frame of thought. It had been found that this duality is possible, because it accords with the hierarchical order of real being. The teleological determination by values, typical of the higher stratum of spiritual being, is added to the determination by causal forces, typical of the lower stratum of anorganic being. The higher determination is dependent upon the lower. It can only exist where the lower type exists as well. This is the law of substance. At the same time, the higher determination is something new and partially independent. It has an autonomous influence on the world. This is the law of freedom.

It now becomes clear that this picture has to be modified somewhat, for the teleological determination by values is in itself a complex determination. (Not unlike causal determination, which includes mathematical and logical determination.) We have three instead of two determinants. The question consequently arises whether this fact can be squared with Hartmann's general ontological framework. He is in no doubt that it can: the relation between the free will and the moral values is exactly equivalent to the relation between the teleological determinant as a whole and the causal determinant. In both cases, the former depends on the latter, in the sense that it cannot exist without the latter, and can only work through the latter. And in both cases, the former is independent of the latter, in the sense that it freely enters into the latter type of determination, and bends it into a preferred direction. Thus, the hierarchical order and the laws of substance and freedom are respected in a tripartite state as much as under dualistic conditions. We are not confronted with any anomalies.[64]

Can we now say that we truly understand the freedom of the will, that we comprehend what personal autonomy means? No, we cannot. But that, Hartmann argues, lies in the nature of things. The question of what something really is can never be answered regarding the ultimate foundations, such as the freedom of the will, simply because what something really is, is ultimately explained in terms of these foundations. What they are cannot be taken hold of rationally. Here we stand at the limit of what is rationally conceivable.[65]

## XII. CONCLUSION

Summing up and concluding, Hartmann states that freedom of the will is both morally necessary—without it there can be no morality—and ontologically possible. More cannot be said. We cannot prove the ontological necessity of the freedom of the will. Yet, the case for the freedom of the will is a strong one. Both the empirical phenomena and a set of fundamental, ontological arguments speak for the freedom of the will. Scepticism remains possible, but it can only cast doubt upon the evidence given for freedom of the will. It cannot itself come up with any positive evidence for its claim. "Thus the door remains open to scepticism. But it stays outside. Of itself, it cannot cross the threshold. And whoever in the field of ethics does not, dazzled by its work of delusion, extend his hand to it, and hauls it in illegitimately, will remain unimpressed by it."[66]

## XIII. EPILOGUE: ETHICS VERSUS RELIGION

With these words the discussion of the main subject matter of *Moral Freedom*, the freedom of the will, is closed. By way of an appendix, however, Hartmann has added two final chapters, the second of which, entitled "Ethical and Religious Freedom", should be accorded some space in this introduction, if only because Hartmann's renown is based to a disproportional degree on what he puts forward in this chapter, where he discloses himself as an staunchly anti-religious thinker.[67]

What is it that he puts forward there? In the opening passages of the chapter, Hartmann states that there is a close connection between ethics and religion. Most of the ethical problems are also religious problems: good and evil, value and disvalue, commandment and prohibition, responsibility and guilt, freedom of the will and determination, etc. Long before philosophical ethics began to ponder these things, religion dealt with them and it has continued to do so. The concerns of ethics and religion are thus overlapping. Their subject matter is to a substantial degree the same. Yet, the perspective from which ethics and religion look at the issues, questions and problems they share, is often completely different. Indeed, their viewpoints time and again contradict each other. In Hartmann's terminology: there are several antinomies between ethics and religion. It is to a discussion of these antinomies that the last chapter of *Moral Freedom* is devoted.

Of the many antinomies, according to Hartmann five need to be specifically highlighted, because they are the basic antinomies and behind all the others. All five of them are true, insoluble antinomies. The human mind finds in them an irreconcilable "either, or." Two of the five antinomies—the most glaring, in Hartmann's opinion—relate to the problem of the freedom of the will. We will discuss them last.

The first antinomy concerns the tendency towards this world (*Diesseits*), inherent in ethics, versus the tendency towards the beyond (*Jenseits*), inherent in religion. All genuine religion, Hartmann writes, inclines towards something better that transcends our existence in this world. Its firmest defenders contend that this world contains no moral values at all, if not as a preparation to the beyond. To strive for the moral values of this world for their own sake is evil. Good within this world is merely what has a tendency towards the beyond. The consequence is a depreciation of this world and a turning away of man from this life.

Ethics, on the contrary, is wholly focused on this world. All moral values relate to man's actions in this world. From this point of view, the tendency towards the beyond is as contrary to moral value as is the concentration on this world's moral values from the standpoint of religion. "It is a waste and a diversion of moral potency, away from the true values and their realization, and therefore immoral. For moral endeavor, all transcendence is a deceptive phantom."[68] Even where the two tendencies materially concur, as in the sacrifice of oneself for a morally good purpose, from the ethical point of view the religious impulse to do so has no moral value, as it is coupled with longing and hopeful glances towards a better lot in the beyond.

The second antinomy concerns the focal point of everything. For ethics that is man; for religion, it is God. From the ethical viewpoint, it would be morally wrong to let anything in the world take precedence over man, to consider anything more valuable than man; from the religious point of view, God is the aim of all aims, and the devotion to Him the true concern of man.

The third antinomy pertains to the ontological status of the moral values. It is most famously set forth in Plato's *Eutyphro*, in the passage where Socrates asks his interlocutor: "Is the holy loved by the gods, because it is holy, or is it holy because it is loved [by the gods]?"[69] The thesis that moral values are autonomous, that they are valuable not on the authority of and for the sake of something else, but entirely of themselves and for themselves, is a necessary underpinning of any ethical view that deserves the name, Hartmann asserts. Neither an authority, nor a command, nor a will, nor human opinion lies behind the moral values. They are an irreducible, independent presence in the world. Against this thesis religion puts forward the antithesis that what man senses as a moral value is at bottom God's command, the expression of His will. Accordingly, from this perspective moral values are heteronomous, and metaphysically of a secondary importance.

The fourth and fifth antinomy Hartmann deems the most important. Both are "antinomies of freedom," because they are linked to the problem of the freedom of the will. The first is named the "antinomy of providence" (*Vorsehung*), the second the "antinomy of redemption" (*Erlösung*) or, as the translator has it, "the antinomy of salvation."

In ethics, the will stands facing the causal laws of nature and the moral values, both of which, as we have seen, allow for the latitude that is necessary for the will to be free. In the religious view of the world on the other hand, the will is also confronted with divine providence. And that is a determining force of quite a different weight. Divine providence entails finalistic determination. God foresees everything that will occur, even the most inconsequential impulse in the human soul. But if that is the case, there is no room for self-determination. Every initiative and teleology lies with God. The moral freedom of man is nullified. If, conversely, moral freedom is granted to man, finalistic determination by divine providence is ruled out.

This antinomy exists not only between the ethical and the religious approach, but also within the domain of religion itself. For religion cannot do without the freedom of the will. The responsibility, accountability, and guilt of man are central to it, as is proved by the principal role accorded to the notion of sin. One cannot rationally have it both ways, however. There is either divine providence or freedom of the will. To assume that both exist is possible only by a *sacrificium intellectus*, Hartmann argues.

The final antinomy discussed by Hartmann is the antinomy of redemption, that is, salvation. The relation of man to God, in the religious view, is not limited to man's providential dependence on Him, and his sinfulness before Him. It culminates in man's deliverance by God from sin: his redemption. (Sin refers to what ethics names moral guilt. Sin, however, is principally guiltiness before God, whereas moral guilt is guiltiness before one's own conscience and the moral values.) Redemption is the taking away of the burden—guiltiness—that results from committing a sin. It is this burden that, in the religious view, makes man evil and incapable of doing any good. Hence, Hartmann contends, "from the point of view of religion, evil does not really inhere in the evil deed or the evil will, for these cannot be made undone, and are not retracted by redemption. They are merely 'forgiven.' The real evil is the burden, the necessity of having to carry it, and the state of being morally cramped by this burden."[70] From that, from the consequence of having sinned, man is liberated by redemption.

Ethics has no room for such a conception. From this viewpoint, only an act or a will (including a disposition) can be morally evil.

There is no state of being evil from which there is no escape without divine assistance. Man always remains free to do wrong, but
also to do right. It is up to him every time. In this, ethics is more
optimistic than religion. On the other hand, for ethics there is no
redemption. Guilt, once brought upon oneself, is eternal and irre-
trievable. It is possible that one is forgiven, of course, but if that
happens it is due to someone else's moral virtue. It does not eradi-
cate one's own guilt. In this ethics clearly is less optimistic than
religion.

   Indeed, from an ethical point of view, redemption, the taking
away of guilt, is not only impossible: it is morally wrong, asserts
Hartmann. Even if it were possible, through the grace of God, it
would be an evil, because it would mean a degradation and a
humiliation of man. It would mean that he is not morally free.
Self-determination implies that man is willing to accept that he is
guilty, and is prepared to bear the burden. If one recalls that it is
precisely this complete humiliation and mortification of man that,
from the religious viewpoint, has value before God, it is obvious
that we face a fundamental antinomy here. Religiously, redemption is the elevation of man; ethically, it is his degradation.

## XIV. POSTSCRIPT

The question of free will belongs to the most important philosophical issues there are. The answer given to this question has
major implications for one's view of man, society, and the world.
Ultimately, there are only two options: either man possesses a free
will or he does not. Today, the Enlightenment view, fathered by
Hobbes and Spinoza, that no such thing exists and everything is
causally determined, is clearly predominant, both among scien-
tists and in society at large, where due to the decline of the influence of Christianity, beliefs are more and more exclusively shaped
by science. As a consequence, it now seems self-evident to many
people that man is nothing but an animal who, like apes and dogs,
responds to the stimuli of pain and pleasure. This view has had
disastrous effects on our moral sensitivity, not only with regard to
what we owe to others, but also concerning what we owe to our-

selves. Thinking of human beings as apes and dogs, we have more and more started to treat them like apes and dogs, and behave like apes and dogs.

Ever since the rise of the Enlightenment view, there has been opposition against it. From various quarters, counter arguments have been and still are put forward. Whatever the exact position taken, all serious contributions to the defense of free will as of the late eighteenth century start from the views of one and the same author: Immanuel Kant.[71] Hartmann stands squarely in this Kantian tradition. Not as an acolyte or an expositor, but as an independent philosopher who, standing on the shoulders of this giant of the mind, is able to look even further than he did. As a result, the defense of the freedom of the will that is presented in *Moral Freedom* is among the best, most thought through vindications we possess of this vital notion.

ANDREAS A.M. KINNEGING
University of Leiden, Faculty of Law

NOTES

1.  *Ethics I*, pp. 183-184. The wording of the Hartmann quotes in this introduction may differ from the wording in the text. In such cases, the present author has made his own translation from the German original.
2.  *Grundlegung der Ontologie*, ch. 50d.
3.  Cf. on the philosophy of mathematics in general, e.g. Stewart Shapiro, *Thinking about Mathematics*, Oxford etc.: Oxford University Press 2000; specifically on Platonism in mathematics, Julius Moravcsik, *Plato and Platonism*, Oxford etc.: Blackwell 1992, ch. 7 and Mark Balaguer, *Platonism and Anti-Platonism in Mathematics*, Oxford etc.: Oxford University Press 1998.
4.  *Grundlegung der Ontologie*, ch. 45c
5.  *Ethics II*, pp. 24-25.
6.  *Ethics II*, p. 31.
7.  This goes for non-moral values too, but they are not relevant here.
8.  It is not entirely clear whether Hartmann reserves the notion of the ought for moral values. Sometimes he seems to apply it to other values as well. But can we really say that, for instance, a piece of property ought to be bought, in the way we say that one ought to be honest or temperate? I don't think so.

9.    *Ethics III*, pp. 38-39.
10.   *Ethics III*, p. 246.
11.   *Ethics III*, p. 246.
12.   *Ethics III*, pp. 137-139.
13.   *Ethics III*, pp. 29-33.
14.   *Ethics III*, p. 63.
15.   *Ethics III*, p. 63.
16.   *Ethics III*, p. 29. It is introduced as "the third antinomy" in the *Kritik der reinen Vernunft* (1781), and fleshed out in the *Grundlegung der Metaphysik der Sitten* (1785) and the *Kritik der praktischen Vernunft* (1788).
17.   *Ethics III*, p. 101.
18.   *Ethics III*, p. 65 ff.
19.   *Ethics III*, p. 62.
20.   *Ethics III*, p. 55.
21.   *Ethics III*, p. 56.
22.   *Ethics III*, pp. 57-59.
23.   *Ethics III*, pp. 59-61.
24.   *Ethics III*, p. 78.
25.   *Ethics III*, p. 80. Hartmann's phrasing is somewhat loose here. As he himself has set out, moral values appear "on the back of the act" (*auf dem Rücken der Handlung*), not in the goal that is aimed at. Nevertheless, they are constraints on goals, and thus directly influence them.
26.   *Ethics III*, pp. 84-85.
27.   *Ethics III*, p. 84.
28.   *Ethics III*, p. 90.
29.   *Ethics III*, pp. 88-89.
30.   *Ethics III*, pp. 90-92.
31.   *Ethics III*, p. 89.
32.   *Ethics III*, p. 96.
33.   Cf. the list of Hartmann's main works at the end of the Transaction Introduction to *Ethics I, Moral Phenomena*, pp. xxxv-xxxvi.
34.   *Ethics III*, p. 101.
35.   *Ethics III*, p. 102.
36.   *Ethics III*, pp. 102-103. Emphasis added.
37.   *Ethics III*, p. 103.
38.   *Ethics III*, p. 104.
39.   *Ethics III*, p. 105.
40.   *Ethics III*, pp. 108-110.
41.   *Ethics III*, p. 106.
42.   *Ethics III*, pp. 129-130, 142.
43.   *Ethics III*, pp. 145-146.
44.   *Ethics III*, p. 148.
45.   *Ethics III*, pp. 146-151.
46.   *Ethics III*, pp. 144, 152.

47.  *Ethics III*, pp. 152-153.
48.  *Ethics III*, p. 160.
49.  *Ethics III*, pp. 163-166.
50.  *Ethics III*, pp. 173-174.
51.  *Ethics III*, pp. 176, 169.
52.  Cf. Transaction Introduction to *Ethics II, Moral Values*, pp. xxiv-xxvi.
53.  *Ethics III*, pp. 184-185.
54.  *Ethics I*, pp. 300-301; *Ethics II*, p. 76.
55.  *Ethics III*, pp. 185-187.
56.  *Ethics III*, p. 190.
57.  Cf. Transaction Introduction to *Ethics II, Moral Values*, pp. lvii-lix.
58.  *Ethics III*, p. 200.
59.  *Ethics III*, p. 210.
60.  *Ethics III*, p. 212.
61.  *Ethics III*, pp. 219-221.
62.  *Ethics III*, pp. 221-230.
63.  *Ethics III*, p. 234.
64.  *Ethics III*, pp. 240-246.
65.  *Ethics III*, pp. 236, 238.
66.  *Ethics III*, p. 247.
67.  *Ethics III*, pp. 260-274.
68.  *Ethics III*, p. 263.
69.  Plato, *Eutyphro*, 10e
70.  *Ethics III*, p. 271.
71.  Much of the twentieth-century discussion on free will in the Anglo-Saxon world does not seem to have thoroughly thought through Kant's views, and thus appears to remain stuck at a somewhat mediocre level of reflection. Cf. e.g. Gary Watson (ed.), *Free Will*, Oxford etc.: Oxford University Press 1982; Derk Pereboom (ed.), *Free Will*, Indianapolis and Cambridge: Hackett 1997.

# PART III

# THE PROBLEM OF THE FREEDOM OF THE WILL
## (THE METAPHYSIC OF MORALS)

## *Section I*

### PRELIMINARY CRITICAL QUESTIONS

# THE CONNECTIONS OF THE PROBLEM

## (a) MAN'S POWER TO CHOOSE

THE table of values is only one half of the ethical problem. The other half is the metaphysic of moral acts. In the centre of this stands the problem of the freedom of the will.

Morality is not merely one among other values. It is something entirely different: it is real human life, man's fulfilment of values. But as this can take place only in human conduct, a new question comes to the front: what power in man decides his conduct in relation to values?

This power is not the discerning or sensing of values. It is not at all a power of comprehending, but is one of deciding, of taking up an attitude towards what is comprehended. If it consisted of comprehending, the proposition of Socrates would hold good, that virtue is knowledge. But knowledge is far from being virtue—not to mention the fact that we cannot arrive even at knowledge without an orientation which rests upon a more fundamental and inner attitude. If one penetrates deeper into this matter, one finds in the spiritual life a swarm of powers both of outward and inner origin, and in their own way determinative of a person's real conduct. Even inner conduct, the mere disposition, is itself real behaviour. Certainly values, being felt, also directly bring about an attitude of mind favourable to the value discerned or adverse to the disvalue; but this element in determining the attitude is only one among many, and by no means the most elemental.

What then gives direction to real conduct, in so far as it lies in the power of man to decide for or against a felt value?

This something in man is precisely what we mean by "free will"; and in this sense the proposition is to be understood that moral values are essentially bound up with freedom of will.

By this statement is meant that they appear only in acts in which such a decisive power somehow participates.[1] It is the peculiarity of moral value and disvalue, that these are attributed to the person, that upon him fall guilt, responsibility, merit. The person is not simply marked by the value (or disvalue); he is also accounted to be the originator of its fulfilment or of the failure to fulfil it. By this origination we mean something quite definite: whoever does wrong could just as well have acted rightly; whoever tells a lie or breaks his word could nevertheless have done otherwise; he was not constrained; he was in a position to tell the truth and to keep his promise. And only in so far as this was possible for him is there any question as to a real lie or a breaking of his word. In the same way, whoever does right, whoever speaks the truth, and so on, is only in so far actually just and truthful as it was possible for him to do otherwise.

In all this of course we may immediately see that the expression "freedom of the will" is too narrow. Moral values by no means attach only to the phenomena distinctive of the will. The concept of the freedom of the will, by which a whole group of problems is indicated, was adequate for an ethics concerned only with the Ought and with ends. In such an ethics conduct and the will are the basic phenomena. But in the attitude of mind, prior to all volitions proper, decision and disposition are manifest. Indeed all behaviour, whether manifesting itself outwardly or not, all taking of sides, direction, bearing, fall under the same moral standards of value, and are therefore connected in the same way with freedom.

Hence the question does not concern freedom of the "will" alone as literally understood; it concerns the freedom of every inner attitude and tendency. In the following pages the term "freedom of the will"—it has once for all to be sanctioned and no substitute for it can easily be found—is to be understood in the larger sense. But this will not at all obscure the fact that the most conspicuous phenomena are none the less will and conduct.

[1] Cf. Chapter XIII (*a*), Vol. II.

## (b) MAN AS THE MEDIATOR BETWEEN VALUE AND ACTUALITY

There is still a second line of investigation which leads to
the problem of freedom. It is found in the metaphysic of the
Ought.[1] The essence of values is such that, unlike categories,
they do not directly determine the actual, but only express an
Ought-to-Be which everywhere becomes positive, when the
actual is not in harmony with it. Values do not, like ontological
laws, irresistibly force their way through, subjecting everything
actual to themselves; their ideal Ought-to-Be subsists quite
independently of fulfilment and non-fulfilment. Of itself it
has no real power to execute itself. Only where a being is
found which takes hold upon the requirement of the Ought
and commits itself thereto, does the ideal law begin to press
into the realm of the actual.

Now the distinctive attitude of man to values is precisely
this, that he is such a being. He is such, as a personal subject,
by virtue of his peculiar qualities and capacities as a person, by
virtue of his sensing of the realm of values, by virtue of his
activity, foresight, capacity to decide and purposive energy.
As one may easily see, these are the characteristics of a subject,
which exalt him into a person, and constitute in him the valuational bases of his acts.[2]

Among these it is the ability to decide, in which the element
of freedom is most conspicuously contained. This ability is
especially essential to the metaphysical situation. If the person
were constrained to follow the requirement of the Ought in
regard to all apprehended values, he would indeed still be a
mediator between value and actuality, a pivot of the Ought in
the real world, but he would be a passive pivot, a forced mediator. He would not be an entity in which the distinctive valuational qualities could manifest themselves; he could very well
actualize situational values beyond himself, but not moral
values in himself. Man would then be without will as regards
the values apprehended.

[1] Cf. Chapter XIX (b), Vol. I.    [2] Cf. Chapter XI (b–g), Vol. II.

Such is not in fact the mediation which falls to man. He is by no means an absolutely faithful mediator. He does not act under valuational points of view as under some necessity. Even if he possessed complete insight into values and unlimited power, he would not make the world perfect. For every single issue which to him is clearly of value he must commit himself with his own person, in so far as the issue is to become actual through him. But it is precisely this, to which he is never necessitated by the mere fact of his discernment. Hence, although he is the only being which mediates between the Ought and life, he is a highly imperfect mediator. An automaton—if it could assume such a function—would be more nearly perfect. But such perfection is not morality, but merely utility; it could possess only the value of a means. Precisely the deficiency of man in respect to this great gift which falls to him in the world, is his superiority. For solely thus is he a moral being; imperfection is his freedom. It consists in this, that he, unlike an automaton, is not forced to do what is laid down for him beforehand—even if it be prescribed by the highest values —but always retains at least in principle the possibility of doing the opposite.

## (c) FREEDOM INDEPENDENT OF DECISIONS IN SINGLE CASES

Evidently this metaphysical concept of freedom is exactly the same as that which was manifested in the nature of a mental attitude. Thereby the two fields of investigation in Volumes I and II of this book coincide. Although on different lines, both lead to the view that freedom is a fundamental condition of the possibility of all moral phenomena. The metaphysical nature of a person depends upon it no less than does the meaning of morality. But in this its existence is not yet proved. For there is a long series of difficulties which adheres to it. To analyse and overcome these difficulties is the task now before us.

For instance, if it be proved that the condition is not fulfilled, everything which has been built upon it falls to the ground; moral values, then, are not properly moral; their specific difference from situational values vanishes. Man then is not a moral being; what seems to be morality in him consists simply of certain useful and otherwise valuable qualities which adhere to him, or do not adhere, according to the confluence of ontological relationships—just as valuational qualities adhere to things, or do not adhere, according to their constitution. But these qualities could no more call forth disapproval, contempt, indignation, or acceptance, respect, admiration than could the qualities of things. In a word, the whole significance of morality is abolished, if freedom be proved to be an illusion.

This has been again and again controverted by those who make little of the question of freedom—and many a famous name has been mentioned among them—, and even to this day it is controverted by them. Indeed concerning no problem has the technique of brilliant formulations which cover up what is not understood, had a more misleading and distorting effect than concerning this question. And perhaps concerning none is man so predisposed to be misguided. To this emotional predisposition must be added the circumstance that it is much easier and more satisfactory to yield place to a solution that is intuitively longed for, than to pursue steadfastly a line of investigation without rushing to conclusions, and without knowing whither the arguments are leading. Indeed, to many a one it may seem unnecessary to stake the greatest problems of life upon a single Either-Or. But one forgets that it is not man who makes the problems, but that it is precisely life itself, whose riddle he cannot solve, which imposes them upon him.

For the understanding of ethical phenomena it is absolutely necessary in this matter to pursue the consequences with rigid exactitude, not to exaggerate them, and yet not to be satisfied with any half-way thinking.

In connection with freedom of the will the appearance and disappearance of moral phenomena—as moral—are not to be understood as if there would be no justice, brotherly love, truthfulness and so on, if there were no freedom; rather would these phenomena exist without exception and without diminution, except that they would not be, in the proper sense, moral. Ontologically, the quality of personal conduct is plainly quite independent of whether the person could, or could not, do otherwise. But morally the quality of the conduct is not independent of this. Justice is a virtue only in so far as the person, at least in principle, had before him the possibility of being unjust; brotherly love, only in so far as he had been able to be without love. This by no means signifies that the moral value of love is so much the greater, the greater the person's temptation was not to love. That would completely invert the meaning of moral value. On the contrary, the more fixed a man is in a virtue, so much the greater is his moral value. But this means that the less he is in need of a special "free" decision of the will in any single case in order to do right, so much the higher does he stand morally.

The freedom which we are now discussing therefore does not refer to the momentary conflict of motives. It subsists even where no moral conflict at all is at hand, where no distinctive decision is made. It subsists singly in the fundamental possibility, in the fact of not being constrained. But this essential basis must perdure. Without it, one's moral being, even in its highest perfection, becomes completely transformed into a state of moral neutrality; yet evidently not into a state of neutrality towards values in general—for the qualities of human conduct in their situational value (their goods-value for others) remain unaffected—but only into moral neutrality, wherein no accountability, no responsibility, no guilt, no merit, can be attributed to the person.

The relation between freedom and moral value may be compared to that between a conditioning goods-value and a moral value. This also is not quantitative. The height of the moral value does not increase or decrease with that of the goods-value;[1] nevertheless, the latter is the valuational basis of

[1] Cf. Chapter I (a), Vol. II.

the former, and with it the moral value stands and falls. *Mutatis mutandis*, in regard to freedom and morality, the case is similar. It is only in principle that moral value is connected with freedom; the person must in general have the possibility of behaving either way. The amount of his conflict, the strength of the opposing motives, are irrelevant. Of course a man becomes most quickly conscious of his freedom when he is confronted with an actual decision. Yet in principle his state of freedom does not consist in his consciousness of it, but is evidently independent of such consciousness. And his moral value is so much the higher, the less he is in need of making a special decision and the more stable his basic attitude is. But the fundamental disposition itself, which is the carrier of his moral value, is based upon freedom; the disposition in itself could have been different. And, if one traces back the chain of actions in which the disposition has evolved, one comes somewhere unconditionally upon a primal attitude. That the latter as an act does not generally permit of being discerned psychologically is of as little significance as is the psychological lack of evidence concerning cognitive conditions in the problem of knowledge.

From this point of view it can be seen how entirely un-psychological is the ethical problem of freedom, and how great must be one's error if one seeks in the domain of psychic events for a point of contact with it.

## (d) Extreme Cases as a Test

One loses insight into this matter as soon as one either over-refines or foreshortens the problem. The principle that morality is based on freedom applies unrestrictedly to all moral values, but it looks highly suspicious, if one sees in it more than is really contained in it; if, for instance, one asserts that there are special acts of freedom that can be pointed out. There are moral values which directly prove such an interpretation to be false.

Of this kind are purity and everything related to it, like innocence, simplicity, straightforwardness, frankness of nature and the like. A resolution on the part of a man to be pure is indeed not an impossibility; and it can show itself in many of the phenomena of moral conversion, or change of spirit (even, indeed, in repentance). But never does the conversion bring again the purity that once has been lost, nor does one who is really pure know of such a conversion. Not only does purity not permit of being striven for; in general it does not permit of being actualized.

If now, on the other hand, one asks where the element of freedom is to be found in it, or whether, as it were, it constitutes an exception and cannot be at all referred to freedom, one shows by the very question that one misunderstands the meaning of moral freedom. For purity can be lost, and is lost, the moment it comes in question as a moral value of the person or is even in danger of being questioned. It is in the preservation of purity against moral guilt that the element of freedom lies disguised within it. For, even in its perfection, the purity of a being who did not at all have the possibility of moral transgression, would still be purity, but not a moral value. And such purity would stand on the level of the innocence of an animal.

The value of personality is misleading in another way. At all events, a man does not choose the uniqueness of his individual ethos; he finds it at hand along with everything else which belongs to his humanity. Indeed, he cannot even convert the personality, which he finds as a value, into an object of volition. He would thereby be most liable to miss it. Nevertheless he bears the responsibility of fulfilling or falling short of this value. He misses it, for example, if he loses himself entirely in the uniformity of general moral requirements, or falls under the tyranny of single values; likewise if, in the imitation of another's qualities, he overlooks his own, or if, in striving after originality, he tries to give himself a quality which he does not possess. In all these cases he incurs the guilt of failure to actualize his own essential character. He could have done otherwise. And even where in a special case he could not have actually willed otherwise, it still holds true that in general, and on principle, he could have been different. It is not at all necessary that his ideal ethos in any way should have stood clearly before his eyes, or could have been the goal of his effort; it is sufficient that he somehow has inwardly the sense that there is in him a determining power not different from other discerned values. Everything here depends upon the existence of this power. Whether and in how far a man gives scope to it—indeed, he can easily do too much, to the disadvantage of the general values—, must somehow or other rest with him, and also whether or not it is a matter of reflection and deliberate choice.

But herein is found the element of freedom which even in personality is tacitly presupposed.


## (e) THE PROBLEM OF FREEDOM, ITS METHODOLOGICAL POSITION

These extreme cases show that the question of freedom extends along the whole frontier of ethical investigation. Without the foundation of freedom, moral values as moral acts lose their distinctive meaning. In principle, they are the values and acts of a free being. If man is not such a being, his acts possess neither moral worth nor its opposite, and he himself is neither good nor bad.

Thus the question of freedom once more reverts to the primal foundations. It opens up the problem of the first basic condition of moral existence. Hence, if it were possible in ethics to follow simply the *ratio essendi*, the question of freedom would need to be investigated quite at the beginning; and when it is not investigated at the beginning, all that follows, any research into the essence of value, of the Ought, of the person, of will, of action, of disposition, indeed even any analysis of moral values, is in reality based upon the presupposition of freedom.

That our investigation has pursued another route, that it has had to postpone the fundamental metaphysical problem to the last, has solely methodological grounds. The problem of freedom is the most difficult problem of ethics, its distinctive *exemplum crucis*. In order rightly to understand the very concept of freedom, we must presuppose an orientation along the whole line of concrete problems. Hence in fact one first arrives at the question of freedom, after one has the subject-matter throughout before one's mind, but especially after one has attained lucidity in regard to the nature and content of moral principles. But these principles are the values, and this is why the table of values needed to be elaborated beforehand —even at the risk of its being illusory, in case afterwards its metaphysical basis should not permit of being proved.

Thus then it is an inner necessity that, with a backward glance at the fundamental problem, we should again subject to question everything thus far considered, and examine whether or not it is to be justified. Every embarrassing difficulty—ultimately metaphysical—can be analysed only on the basis of a survey of the phenomena. But in this connection a survey of the phenomena is the most that the first two volumes of this book have furnished. All theoretical outlooks have hitherto been only surmises, anticipations. In the nature of the case they are all so constructed that the positive concept of freedom, in case it permits of being justified, needs only to be introduced into them in order to give them inward support. Then of itself the remainder falls into place.

Whether this support be forthcoming is now the question.

# HISTORICAL DEVELOPMENT OF THE PROBLEM OF FREEDOM

## (a) PRELIMINARY HISTORY

FROM the point of view of freedom it makes no difference whether we can accept a single moral law or a whole realm of values as the principle of moral appraisement. Every single moral value, purely in itself and independently of all others, is dependent upon freedom. Hence the presupposition of freedom is, in fact, common to every moral system, irrespective of which value is selected as its standard. Of course not every value can be cast into an imperative form—not every Ought-to-Be has a corresponding Ought-to-Do, and commandments can be expressive only of an Ought-to-Do—, but behind every Ought-to-Do there stands an Ought-to-Be, behind every wise imperative, a mass of values. Hence, so far as it was rightly conceived, what Kant maintained concerning the question of freedom on the basis of the categorical imperative must hold good for every treatment of the question on the basis of every variety of value.

This is of importance, in so far as the Kantian philosophy for the first time set forth the problem of freedom in distinct outline. Kant's presentation of the problem is independent of the kind of solution which he offered. We may reject the solution or regard it as inadequate, and yet at the same time accept the presentation as valid. The service which Kant rendered in the mere exposition of his "third antinomy" was a turning-point in the history of philosophical ethics. What has since been done on the question of freedom falls, in comparison, quite into the background. Accordingly it follows of itself that the point of departure taken by Kant must also constitute our starting-point.

The older ethics was astonishingly superficial in treating the question of freedom. Ancient thinkers took freedom for granted as something self-evident, which clearly shows how little they knew of the metaphysical difficulties which they passed over in so doing. They rightly felt that without freedom nothing avails, that it is imperatively involved in the meaning of moral qualities, of virtue, approval, disapproval; and they reckoned with this intuited state of the case, in that they simply allowed it to be accepted that man is free. But they did not see that the actual existence of his freedom is not by any means thereby proved. For in itself the contrary has indeed been the case; the meaning of virtue and approval was a mere assumption. Of course morality itself would then fall away and ethics would be exposed to scepticism. But this tremendous alternative, in which everything fundamental is at stake, is precisely what the problem of freedom deals with.

All such undebated assertion of the freedom of the will is naïve. It does not know the depth of the difficulties which it conjures up; on that account it gives no further thought to the question. Such is the freedom of choice which Plato proclaimed in mythological form;[1] such also is Aristotle's statement that man is free to know what is good and to be virtuous.[2] Somewhat nearer to a consideration of the difficulties is the rigidly defined Stoic concept of the ἐφ'ἡμῖν (that which it is in our power to do or not to do): to it the motive of συγκατάθεσις can be referred, which signifies an inner assent.[3] Nevertheless, even with the Stoics these passages are only sporadic; bound up with them are other lines of thought of a far more superficial kind which entirely distort the concept of freedom. Also unconnected and side by side

[1] Plato's *Republic*, X, 617e.
[2] Aristotle, *Nicom. Eth.* III, 1113b. 2–1114b. 25.
[3] Cf. Arnim, *Stoicorum veterum fragmenta*, II. frg. 1006 and 1007. Here is found a fragment of an entire dialectic concerning the metaphysical contrast between divine providence and human freedom. The passage is directed against a radical, sceptical, atheistic interpretation of freedom.

with the ἐφ'ἡμῖν is found the concept of a freedom from the affections, or even a freedom in obedience to "Nature," that is, to the universal cosmic law (λόγος), which, more closely examined, is seen to be the very opposite of freedom. Even Plotinus is under the spell of the latter conception, although he gives it other names.

The Church Fathers and the Scholastics had a firmer grasp of the problem; but it was not so much moral as religious freedom that they had in mind, not freedom in relation to the course of the world, nor in relation to moral requirements as such, but freedom as over against God. Where Providence and infinite power prevail, how can man retain self-determination?

This question is in itself of importance, but it is a different one. To introduce it into ethics is particularly unfortunate, because moral freedom exacts far less than religious freedom, that is to say, because over against an all-powerful and all-knowing Being the question of scope for choice on the part of a finite entity is much more unfavourably placed, than merely over against commandments and values which as such exercise no foresight whatever. But among the Church Fathers and Scholastics the problem of ethical freedom as such remained undebated, indeed unknown, although it is included in religious freedom.

It needed to be carefully extricated from metaphysical entanglement with the relation between God and man, in order finally to become purely ethical. Such separation has taken place only in modern times, and indeed on the part of those thinkers who sacrificed freedom to the causal nexus of the cosmic process. Spinoza—and no crude Materialist—was recognized by later philosophers as the classical champion of such a theory. According to him everything (the series of the *modi*) issues from the necessity of absolute substance; nothing therefore can be otherwise than as it is. Even the will of man cannot act differently. It also is only a *modus*, and stands within the unalterable sequence of the *modi*. If at every moment man knew all the real causes that determine his actions, it could never occur to him to imagine that he was free in his decisions. But he does not know the causes, and so believes in his own freedom.[1] That Spinoza, together with this determinism (but scarcely bound organically to it), recognized a freedom of the mind, which when correctly interpreted was little more than the Stoic freedom from the emotions, does not at all detract from his principal thesis. For this kind of freedom is evidently not the moral kind.

## (b) THE DETACHMENT OF THE ETHICAL FROM THE RELIGIOUS PROBLEM OF FREEDOM

The carrying over of the concept of freedom into the sphere of religion nevertheless had indirectly the effect of exposing to view for the first time the depth of the metaphysical difficulties involved in it. When the problem again returned to the sphere of ethics, the analysis which had been made of the difficulties could not but be of service to the ethical concept of freedom.

Divine providence, which threatens man in his independence and which when taken unconditionally (as in the theory of predestination) must logically reduce him to nothing, is nevertheless thought of as prevailing in the very world against whose natural course ethical freedom is to maintain itself. If now the personal divinity in the determining act of providence fades away, if determination becomes secularized into a mere law of nature, the religious antinomy between divine and human efficacy passes over into the ethical antinomy between natural necessity and human freedom. In Spinoza one can clearly recognize the transition. The personal character of God is dropped; God and Nature—the latter pre-eminently in the sense of *natura naturans*—are no longer distinguishable. No finalistic purposes of Divinity now cramp the finite creature. He stands only over against the blind causality of the world, the all-pervading determinism of which penetrates

[1] Spinoza, *Ethica II*, prop. 48, likewise the appendix to Part I.

even into his inmost being, into his consciousness and will. This determinism, at once cosmological and psychological, is what makes it possible to discuss the ethical problem of freedom.

Now all that is needed is to detach the problem from the ambiguities of pantheism, in order to conceive distinctly the antinomy between the blind determinism of nature and the freedom of man. This process of detachment was already accomplished in Kant's third antinomy. The all-oppressive concept of God, with its metaphysical weight, was excluded. It was reduced from an *ens realissimum* to the "ideal of pure reason." By this enfeeblement it ceases to be dangerous. It has itself become highly problematical. Kant has turned the tables. No longer does the moral consciousness need to protect itself against an action of all-powerful Providence; but the reverse is true: if there be at all any certainty as to the existence of such a Providence, it can rest only upon the fact of precisely that moral consciousness itself. Whether the Kantian doctrine of postulates, and with it the notion of a "moral theology," is well founded, is a question by itself, and is not in place here. The detachment of the problem of freedom from that of religion, as Kant purposely brought it about, is independent of the question and may be taken up without discussing the Kantian philosophy of religion as an achievement of criticism.

It is also quite another question—one which indeed lies heavily upon ethics itself—whether Kant in this detachment transferred into his third antinomy the whole of the Scholastic problem of freedom. We shall meet with it in a later analysis. But for the moment we are not concerned with it. For even independently of it the Kantian antinomy holds good.

### (c) The Kantian Antinomy of Freedom

Now in this antinomy there is no longer any reference at all to God, Providence and fore-ordination, but exclusively to causality as against freedom, or (as Kant preferred to express it) to the "causality of nature" as against the "causality of freedom."

For an understanding of the problem the latter expression is extremely helpful. For Kant the question does not concern the wresting of the free entity out of the universal causal nexus—as if there were a cessation or interruption of the latter, whereby there would be scope for free decision—, but concerns the positive intervention of first causes into the causal nexus, of causes which on their side have in that nexus no further prior causes, although a continued sequence of effects. The freedom which we are here discussing takes on the causal form in the chain of causes itself. Kant therefore calls it "a causality through which something happens of which the cause is not itself determined by another antecedent cause according to necessary laws; that is to say, there is an absolute spontaneity of causes, whence issues of itself a series of appearances that proceeds according to natural laws."[1] And in his comment upon the thesis he calls it "a power to initiate a series of successive things or conditions." His setting aside of all metaphysical encumbrances in the question of freedom is especially characteristic of him in this, that he does not find it necessary to say how such a power can be possible; indeed, we cannot properly explain even the causal nexus, since we "do not at all comprehend how it is possible for one existent to bring about the existence of something else."

From this point of view the embarrassment about freedom does not consist in its irrationality. For causality is equally irrational; the embarrassment is altogether due to the antinomic relation to the causal nexus, according to which no cause can be "first."

That this antinomy is one which inheres in the nature of the matter is shown in the elaboration of the proof of the antithesis: "Freedom (independence) from the laws of nature is indeed a liberation from compulsion, but is also a liberation

[1] *The Critique of Pure Reason*, Second German edition, p. 474 f.

from guidance by any rules. For one cannot say that, in place of the laws of nature, laws of freedom enter into the causality of the cosmic process, since, if freedom were determined according to laws, it would not be freedom but simply nature itself." However much the future course of events after the introduction of the "first" cause is a causal sequence and proceeds according to natural laws into infinity, still something takes place at the point of its introduction, that is, at the beginning of the sequence, outside of the uniformity of nature; seen therefore from this point of view, there is an absence of law. Now that has no meaning, for absence of law is indeterminateness; but a first beginning of a sequence brings with it its own determinateness, and carries this over into the whole future causality of the series which it has introduced. Hence the question must be: How is such a determinateness to be understood, in so far as it for its part is not in turn causally determined?

Thus far, Kant's conception of the problem. Compared with all previous conceptions it is a radical reduction, a narrowing down of the problem from an almost limitless question embracing the whole structure of the universe into a quite modest and special question concerning a single metaphysical point. We shall see how this limitation certainly goes too far, how in the problem of freedom something more is contained than the relation to natural causality. But this is a matter for later consideration. It must first be noted that Kant's achievement was to bring into the problem definiteness and comprehensiveness of survey. In this way the problem can be dealt with philosophically. No limit is thus set to the taking up of further points of view, just as little as a definite mtehod is prescribed for the treatment of the question. But at all events further stages of the problem can be clearly grasped, only if Kant's causal antinomy is investigated as to its solubility. Accordingly this investigation must take precedence of any further difficulties.

But before we enter into it we must once more grapple

with the concept of freedom itself. On the basis provided by Kant it is for the first time possible to measure how great a variety of obscurities and ambiguities attaches to the concept. At the outset we must secure our investigation against these.

# ERRONEOUS CONCEPTIONS OF FREEDOM

## (a) The Three Typical Sources of Error in the Treatment of the Problem

THERE are so many theories which attempt to furnish a metaphysical proof of the freedom of the will that it is impossible to pass them in review. Their number sufficiently illustrates the importance of the matter. But the lasting benefits derivable from them are few. Almost everywhere a clear grasp of the matter is lacking, the most popular prejudices hold their own undiscussed. Sometimes they prove too much, sometimes too little, not to mention the arbitrary methods and presuppositions of the reasoning. Indeed, even the concept does not remain the same. It is changed sometimes in one way, sometimes in another, according to what suits the theory under discussion.

In these theories three kinds of error can be distinguished. They may appear singly or all together.

First, the concept of freedom, that is, of free-will as it is implied in moral values, may be lacking, something else outwardly similar being substituted for it. For even in the domain of the ethical problem there exists another freedom than that of the will. Now if a theory tries to "prove" such a misunderstood freedom of the will, it proves something else than what it meant to prove. It commits the error of *ignoratio elenchi*. But if in the argument a displacement of the concept eludes notice, if it substitutes in the theory the something else which it "proved," it radically falsifies its own contents.

Secondly, one may permit the rightly understood concept gradually to slip away, because one loads it with metaphysical or psychological by-products which do not pertain to it, but which one mistakenly connects with it. If one draws conclusions from such an overloaded concept of freedom, these conclusions naturally will not stand the test and will not be in agreement with the moral phenomena. They are consequences drawn from a phantom and are themselves phantoms. We have here a case of a πρῶτον ψεῦδος.

Finally, along with the correct concept and with a critical disburdenment of it the argument may still be defective. Most defects of this sort consist in presupposing in a disguised form what was to be demonstrated and in furnishing a plausible proof. In this case one commits the error of the *circulus vitiosus*. When the circle is not completely closed, there is always a *petitio principii*.

Although in metaphysics these three typical errors are everywhere difficult to avoid, the problem of the freedom of the will is especially threatened by them, because of the pressure of the extraordinarily strong interest which the moral consciousness has in the assertion of freedom at almost any price. A procedure based on a sense of insoluble difficulties is always most exposed to danger when one's interest is attached to a definite kind of solution. The anticipated result forces its way to the front, prescribes to the investigation the goal it ought to attain and thus falsifies its impartial course. It is impossible in this case to demand that the philosopher should rid himself of all interestedness. The interest is natural and is profoundly justified; and whoever is without it either misses the import of the question or surrenders himself to a sceptical indifference. To do either is incompatible with a genuine apprehension of the problem. Hence the most difficult thing is required: a combination of the most positive interest in the establishment of the freedom of the will with a calm observation of objective facts undisturbed by one's interest. Hence the laying bare of the facts cannot be undertaken too cautiously. It hovers step by step on the brink of metaphysical illusions.

Only a strict adherence to the ethical phenomena can do justice to the undertaking. The investigator must keep his mind open to both possibilities, to positive and negative.

But at the outset let it be noted that, as the problem of

freedom stands to-day, we cannot attain a real and complete solution of it. Even where the positive chances rise so high that every doubt involves improbability, still we never advance so far as actually to lift scepticism off its pivot, just as little as we succeed in doing so in the problem of knowledge, where likewise the vein of scepticism is never quite eradicated. It is important that we should be quite clear upon this point from the start. The exalted expectations which one naturally brings with one must all be dropped at the threshold of the investigation. Inevitably they would force one sooner or later into the trodden paths of falsification, which are more dangerous than any scepticism.

### (b) MORAL AND LEGAL FREEDOM. CAN AND MAY

At this point only the first of the three sources of error cited above can be considered. Not till later (after the appraisement of Kant's doctrine of freedom) can the second and third be examined. Accordingly the question now is: Which concrete conceptions of moral freedom must be set aside as erroneous?

Of the many which are current in ethics only one at most can be right. But naturally we cannot know beforehand whether the right one is precisely that which permits of being demonstrated metaphysically. The falsest of all false tendencies is that which at the outset accepts a concept of freedom because it can be proved; that is the tendency so to conceive of freedom that its contents can be verified. Such a short-sighted opportunism—not to say self-deception—has shattered many a brilliant theory. It is very possible that the genuine freedom of the will does not permit of being proved. This possibility must be kept open. If we knew at the outset what the result must be and had only to shape the concept of freedom, all further investigation would be idle pretence.

In the first place there is a series of crude misunderstandings. Only one of them need be mentioned, the confusion of moral with legal freedom. This is natural, in so far as the latter has throughout an ethical character. Legal, including political and civic, freedom consists in this, that the law within the sphere of its commandments and prohibitions allows the individual a definitely limited scope, and protects this scope against infringement. Now it is perfectly evident that what is here secured to freedom is neither the will nor any determinative power of the person behind the will, but is his outward activity, his opportunity in life.

Yet the confusion does not lie in this alone. Legal freedom does not say what one can but what one may do. Its domain is not that of what is preferred by the person but of what is permitted to him; it is the domain of that in which the person has the protection of the law. But freedom, in the sense of what one may do, is by no means restricted merely by the legal standard, but by every standard, whether imposed by the arbitrary command of the stronger or by the sense of moral value. Every moral value of a general kind draws a circle of the permissible about the man who comprehends its commands. Yet even in regard to a moral value the sphere of what is allowed is anything but freedom of the will. Much rather does this begin only with the capacity to transgress what one can, not as regards what one may, do. It may be consistent with the latter; indeed only through what-one-can-do does what-one-may-do receive any actual significance. But in this relation of Can and May it is evident that freedom of the will is something different from legal freedom. Free will is precisely that ability of man about which the permissible as a norm draws the outer boundary.

## (c) FREEDOM OF ACTION AND FREEDOM OF WILL

Even freedom of action, which is so often mistaken for freedom of will, is altogether different from legal freedom. In it there is no question as to what one may do but as to what one really can do. It means that a man can do what he wills to. Hence it presupposes the will, including the direction of its determinateness. It refers only to the carrying out of the will, not to the setting of its direction; accordingly it is not the freedom of the will itself but only freedom to actualize the will.

In life the question concerning it is important enough; within certain limits it even reacts upon volitional decision, in so far as no rational being can accept, as the goal of his striving, anything which is not within his power to achieve. Even a strong will, when with a perverted estimate of its own power it has once turned to something unattainable, cannot hold steadfast to its goal for very long. But still for that reason the power to carry out a plan is something altogether different from the decision of the will, and freedom of the former is not the same as freedom of the latter.

For the distinctive quality of freedom of action, as compared with other kinds, it is a matter of indifference whether the freedom inheres in a man's physical, mental or social capacity. As the limits of his muscular power prescribe the bounds to his bodily capacity, so those of his mental abilities restrict the scope of what he can achieve mentally; in the same way an individual's social status or a nation's place in world politics sets limits to what can be done. Yet social freedom of action has nothing to do with legal freedom. It is exactly in social life that the limits of what can be done differ from those of what is permissible. One is allowed to do much which one cannot do, and one is not allowed to do many things which one is very well able to do. If one were not able to do anything beyond the limits of what was permitted, to do wrong would be an impossibility for man. To this extent the relation between these two kinds of freedom is ethically of deep significance. But neither of them coincides with freedom of the will. Whether after a decision the will has the power to execute its purpose, and whether in executing it the will is doing what is allowed or not allowed, are matters of indifference as regards the question whether in its decision it was itself free or not.

It is evident that freedom of action is just as irrelevant to freedom of will as is legal freedom. The will can be free where there is no freedom of action, and action can be free where there is no freedom of the will. The extreme case of the former situation is where there is an impotent yearning for the unattainable, the extreme case of the latter is where there is a paralysis of the will, an incapacity to decide or a moral cowardice in face of what is in itself easily attainable. Freedom of action is only a question of strength in the face of outward conditions. On the other hand, freedom of the will has no relation to the strength or weakness of the will itself.

### (d) "Outward" Freedom, as Misunderstood

Freedom of action is a kind of outward freedom, but not the only kind. One may very well apply the term outward freedom to the will itself. This gives another conception of freedom, not less false, but one which nevertheless stands nearer to the distinctive freedom of the will.

What is meant is freedom from the course of outward events, of circumstances, situations and the possibilities which are actually at hand. And indeed it is the will itself, the decision, the attitude assumed, to which this freedom is ascribed, in contrast to the bondage of action to just these outward circumstances, situations and actual possibilities.

This contrast as such has a valid significance. As a matter of fact, by virtue of the mere circumstance that human foresight cannot survey the multiplicity of real possibilities, the will is not limited to actual possibility alone. Ordinarily, a man's decisions are held within certain limits of what in general passes before him as possible; but these limits are elusive. The actual limits of possibility may be altogether different and in fact are almost always so. Hence the decision is made much more upon a chance; and the weaker the chance, the greater are the adventure and the requisite moral strength in making the solution. Now it is exactly the venture which is characteristic of the phenomenon of moral freedom; for ordinarily the real possibilities disclose themselves only gradually, often enough only in the sequel. Upon this gradual and certain disclosure of the possibilities the resolution has already reckoned and must reckon—consciously or unconsciously. But this means that the limits which restrict the decision are not the actual limits of free action.

Yet it is at the same time clear that the expectation of such an outward freedom of the will is a false expectation. Indeed, it is false ontologically. The decision cannot be independent of the situation—the actual possibility. Moreover it is ethically false. For the decision ought not to be independent in this respect. It ought rather to take particular cognisance of the real possibilities; it ought to grasp them, so far as it is at all able to do so. The will ought to be provident, it ought from the outset to take thought of the means to its goal and to estimate the possibilities which are offered. A will which did not allow itself to be determined by the structure of the given situation would be blind to actuality, it would be childish. In fact there is no such will; the real will always grows in the first place out of the immediate situation, and from the very start moves only within what in general comes into question according to the nature of the situation. The scope which this allows to it is naturally always a limited one. But it is precisely this limitation which the person must take into account. Not to recognize it is blind self-conceit.

But the picture of it is entirely wrong, so long as one interprets the complex of outward circumstances in the situation as being merely a limitation. In truth it is precisely these circumstances which first offer to the will its positive concrete possibilities of direction. No one constructively "invents" for himself his concrete goals; but the full reality in the midst of which life places him holds up before his eyes the directions of possible striving. Of course there must somehow still remain scope for decision—otherwise it would not be free—but such freedom can be reasonably thought of as selective only in respect to the varied contents of the given possibilities. Without a specific situation before it there never could be a will at all, not to mention a free will. Adaptation to what is before it is always its presupposition.

Hence freedom of will cannot and ought not to consist in such adaptation. If it be anything at all it must be something different from "outward freedom." The circumstances, the situation, the conflict, the wider connection of cosmic events, in which all these are embedded, in short the whole given "case" with all its ontological and ethically actual determinations, are precisely what ought to determine the will throughout. Accordingly the moral will ought in this respect to be unfree—however paradoxical this may sound. Whether in some other sense freedom still exists is the problem.

It is easy to see that hereby the answer to this problem is by no means anticipated. It would indeed be necessary that in addition to the determinants of the outward situation still another, unique, coming from another quarter, inward, peculiar to the will itself, should be added in order to bestow upon it the character of freedom. But thus much is to be held fast: If man is creatively free in volitional decision, his can never be a creation outside of the actual course of the world, having no basis there, but must always be a construction inside of and upon the cosmic process.

### (e) "Inner" (Psychological) Freedom, as Misunderstood

If we have once seen this and are convinced that inwardly freedom can exist only together with an outward unfreedom which prevails at all times, it is natural to seek in the inner world, in the life of the soul, for that independence of actuality which we fail to find in the outer world. But at this point one immediately falls into another error, not less fatal. For the inner world has its uniformity of sequences just as much as the outer world. The concept of psychological freedom is exactly as false as is that of physical freedom.

One conceives "inner freedom" to be a kind of independence of the course of inner events, for instance of the coming and going of emotions, impulses, motives, affections and the various psychic powers, of which the origin is deeply concealed but which at all events defy all arbitrariness on the part of man. It is a matter relatively of indifference, how one interprets the sequence of the psychic process. The widespread mistake of accepting the analogy of outward events, even down to the single structures of the process, is only an extreme case of such an interpretation. But what, in fact, irresistibly forces itself upon one's mind after a closer investigation is the view that the inner process is altogether as thoroughly regular as is the outer. Whether we trace back this determinateness to a single type of psychic dependence, perhaps to a psychic causality, or conceive of different kinds of determination imposed upon the psychic nexus, makes no radical difference. The important point is solely this, that the inner psychic situation at every moment is also one which is given, which is present and can in no way be displaced, and that every actual volition always grows out of the situation, is from the outset born into it and never exists apart from or in independence of it.

Whoever expects that psychology, as a science of the orderliness of psychic connections, processes and events, will provide a solution of the problem of freedom in the positive sense fundamentally deludes himself. Long before scientific psychology proper could elucidate this matter, men of critical insight clearly anticipated the result of such efforts. We need only to recall Spinoza's doctrine of the "mathematical sequence" of the *modi* in the attribute of *cogitatio*, or Kant's statement that a human act could be calculated beforehand just as well as an eclipse of the moon, if we could know all the psychic factors which determine it.

Hence of whatever kind the uniformity of inner events may be, we can entertain no doubt that such a uniformity exists. But then the question of freedom is exactly the same in regard to inner as to outer events: the will is in no wise free from the course of the inner process. And naturally there ought not to be such a freedom. Together with the outward there is always at the same time an equally determined inner situation. And a man can no more extricate himself from the one than from the other. He bears within himself the whole sphere of unfreedom. He carries it with him into his decisions, his mental attitudes, the inner conduct of his soul. This conduct is always determined thereby.

It is not at all inconsistent with this view that men do not discern the inner situation in its elements, that to them the swarm of motives which lead to decisions is anything but clear. This obscurity may delude them with an appearance of "inner freedom"—for where the grounds of decision are not known and cannot even be suspected beforehand a man cannot but regard himself as independent of them—; but such an appearance of freedom can have no effect upon the actual psycho-physical unfreedom. It is, however, only an epiphenomenon of self-ignorance, a state of blindness in regard to one's dependence.

The attempt has been made to reduce this dependence to a single formula under the law of "motivation," which declares that everything, even the most minute, in our decisions is "motivated," that it has its grounds for determination. When a man stands, for instance, before a given alternative—as it were, at the parting of the ways—there is something beforehand in the apparent balance of motives which finally gives the decision. But the decisive factor is just as much a "motive" as are the two sides of the alternative, whether it be a natural inclination, the sensing of a value or anything else. The word "motive," of course, says very little, and is far removed from offering a solution of the complicated psychological questions which one wishes to solve by it. But if one disregards the obscurity of the term, the law of inner determination, which one crudely describes by it, strikingly resembles the law of cause and effect. "Motivation" is a kind of "psychic causality," and is evidently derived from an analogy to physical causality. This is the weakness of the concept of motivation.

Nevertheless there is something psychologically more

specific in it. For the will at the parting of the ways is undoubtedly by no means undetermined, but is very decidedly
determined. Otherwise it could not make a decision. If the
analogy to the physical nexus extends only so far that in
general a thorough-going determination in the inner life must
be assumed to prevail—whatever the type of determination
may be—it is not unjustifiable, since it fundamentally rests
upon a universal law of ontological determination which applies
just as much to psychic as to physical existence. If a man could
ever in face of an alternative stand in complete indeterminateness, and therefore in the position of an ideal *liberum arbitrium indifferentiæ*, he would, at all events in this position,
have no free will. Much rather would he have no will at all.
But as soon as a volition set in, it could set in only as a volition
which was determined and which decided according to the
one or the other side of the alternative; hence it could not in
any case be indifferent. In the sense of so-called "motivation"
the will would again be unfree, there would be a motive for
the decision. In general terms: if one thinks of the will as
freed from one "influence," it forthwith falls under other
influences; but if one thinks of it as freed from all "influences,"
one has also set aside the determinateness of the will, and has
therefore in fact set aside also the will itself.

Accordingly the case of the inner situation is exactly the
same as that of the outer. It is meaningless to say either that a
man could will independently of the inner situation or that
he ought to will independently of it. In every respect only a
volition within the inner situation and determined by it is
conceivable. Every barring-out of the situation, whether inward
or outward, falsifies its positive meaning, its necessary concrete
attachment to the determinateness of the will. A man ought
not to be at all independent of it; he ought to reckon with it.
But this is not to say that he ought to be wholly its slave.
Rather ought he to control the inner situation just as much as
the outer; within it he ought to be creative. Hence his freedom
can only consist in his having together with the inner situation

still other determinants in himself, which he introduces from himself into the inner situation, and in his throwing them into the scales of the alternative before which he is placed both inwardly and outwardly.

But in this it becomes even clearer that the concept of freedom—the only one that is tenable and ethically intelligible—is essentially transformed. Freedom cannot consist in negative indifference, but only in a positive determinateness of a unique order, in a determination peculiar to the will itself, in an autonomy of the will.

### (f) THE FUNDAMENTAL ERROR IN NEGATIVE FREEDOM OF CHOICE

It has become clear from what we have been saying that a still profounder mistake is concealed both in outward and inward freedom. It is the error of negativity, of the claim of independence. Negative freedom as mere "freedom from something" is altogether a false concept.

But precisely the same blunder is contained in all "freedom of choice." It is exactly this, to which the moral consciousness clings most tenaciously. Is it, then, possible to discard all freedom of choice and still hold fast to moral freedom? Where does the error lie? Or are we here perhaps confronted with an antinomy?

If one entirely ignores the question from what precisely the will is said to be free, if one only requires in general a certain scope which remains open to it—and which is, after all, compatible with wide-reaching inward and outward determination—, then the minimum of scope consists formally in a duality of possibilities which must remain open. Between these at the least the decision must also remain—so one involuntarily believes. If a decision is still contained among the given determinants, the will is not at all free.

This reflection takes up a position on the higher side of decision. It fixes attention upon the still undecided will, that is, upon that will which does not yet know how it is about to decide. This not-yet-knowing is a rightly conceived phenomenon. But it is still questionable whether the will at this stage can be regarded as a free will, of the kind which we are considering in respect of decision itself.

One needs only to bear the full import of this question in mind, in order to see that it must be answered in the negative. For it is clear that all that is needed is the addition of a specific determinant (which perhaps is already present in a latent state) in order to give to the will its decision on one side or the other. After the decision has been made, if the attitude of reflection itself is excluded, one sees it clearly—most clearly if the motives of the case are discernible, and if one knows the reason for the decision. Still the being held by a value—and commonly valuational perspectives are the decisive factor—appears as one motive among other motives.

When the will has chosen, it presents itself unmistakably as determined. The act of choice itself is clear evidence of unmistakable determinedness. If the decisive factor is lacking in the will, it does not choose. Hence if it chooses, one can no longer say it is free in the sense of negative freedom of choice. The choice itself consists in the introduction of a decisive determinant. On this point it is a matter of indifference whether this determinant be inward or outward, whether it is provided by the character or consists of "influences."

The conclusion is startling: evidently negative freedom of choice is not at all the freedom of the will for which we are seeking, concerning which alone there is any question in the ethical problem and in which moral values and moral judgment are involved. There is no tenable meaning in the "will," not to mention the deeper disposition or attitude of mind, if one connects it with negative freedom of choice. Free will is not undetermined will, but precisely a will that is determined and chooses determinately. Now in a positively determined will there is always a decision made. That the will subsequently accomplishes its choice "freely" is evidently a perverse notion which is easily explicable subjectively—because of the man's own ignorance of the factors which determine the choice. The positively determined will has in reality already chosen. Hence it has no more choice, it has no longer any alternatives before it. The one who chooses in the sense of *arbitrium indifferentiæ* stands on the hither side of the determined will, hence on a summit anterior to volition proper. He is not willing at all, therefore he is not willing freely. He can just as well be unfree and choose unfreely. The latter case would then signify nothing more than that the process of the decision of the will in favour of one side of the alternative is carried out in rigid dependence upon certain determining factors, and is therefore necessitated. But that is exactly what must be rejected as unfreedom of the will by anyone who mistakes negative freedom of choice for moral freedom.

Plato's expression, αἰτία ἑλομένου, when understood in the sense of negative freedom of choice, is false. If the man who chooses were to blame, then it would rather be God who would be to blame. But Plato says: θεὸς ἀναίτιος. Hence even for Plato the guilt of the man who chooses is not that of one who is undetermined in his choice, but of one who is determined. But then we must abandon the negative concept of freedom altogether as contrary to sense. Not he who chooses has the guilt, but he who determines the choice. Yet determination is accepted as the contrary of freedom. How is this contradiction to be resolved?

*Section II*

THE CAUSAL ANTINOMY

# CHAPTER IV (LXVIII)

# THE SIGNIFICANCE OF KANT'S SOLUTION

### (a) The Projection of the Intelligible World into the World of Appearance

THE contradiction to which the postulate of the freedom of the will leads can be solved only if determination and freedom are not opposed to each other. But then moral freedom must originally mean not independence, indeterminedness, that is, not at all "freedom from something," but precisely a determinedness *sui generis*. And the obvious point in this change of position is the transformation of the concept of freedom from a purely negative into a purely positive one.

This transformation Kant achieved in his solution of the causal antinomy. It is accordingly in place here to examine his solution as regards its philosophical import.

Kant starts from the presupposition that the totality of the cosmic processes is throughout causally determined. The antithesis in his antinomy gives clear expression to this. To the regularity which prevails in this unmistakable nexus there is no exception, not even in man. Man belongs to the natural world as a part of it. His doing and his leaving undone are entirely drawn into it and into its regularity. Hence in this sense at all events he is not free. This means that he is not free from the causal nexus. There is no freedom "in the negative sense." That would mean a gap in the causal nexus of the world. But according to the entire meaning of cosmic regularity, such a gap cannot exist.

If moral freedom consisted in "negative freedom," the whole question would thereby be settled in a negative sense. It is otherwise if there is a "freedom in the positive sense," that is, if there is a positive order of the will together with the order of nature, a determinant which itself is not contained in the causal course of the world, but which in the will of man enters into the world of appearance. Now under what condition is this possible? Evidently only if man does not belong to nature alone, but at the same time rises into a second realm with a law of its own, if he, therefore, is not only a natural being but is also as Kant says a rational being. The latter expression may be ambiguous on account of the note of idealistic rationalism which pervades it. One must for a time accept this ambiguity and consider whether it cannot afterwards be removed, without danger to the essence of the matter.

At first glance Kant's doctrine of freedom appears to be purely methodological, hence extremely problematical. "Nature," in which the all-pervasive law of causality offers no room for negative freedom, is itself only an "appearance"; behind it stands the self-existent world of which no experience gives us knowledge, but which manifests unmistakably in all the ultimate problems of knowledge. This self-existent reality is an "intelligible world," which is not subject to the categories of the sensible world, and therefore not subject to causality. Over against the natural world, which only "appears," there is a real world. Now, granted that we could prove that in the world of appearance there is one point at which determinednesses of the intelligible world penetrate it, and call forth in it the beginning of a new (hence a causal) series of appearances, then at this point in the causal nexus itself a power would intervene which did not emanate from it, which therefore would have behind itself no causal series of origins, but would draw such a series after it. This accordingly would be a "causality issuing from freedom," or a "freedom in the positive sense."[1]

### (b) The Causal Nexus and the Something More in Determination

If we accept its methodological presuppositions, we can easily see in how far there is in this a kind of solution. The essential

[1] Cf. Chapter II (c), Vol. III.

thing here is simply to demonstrate that in the causal nexus there is room for a unique determination which is not causal in its origin. This would not happen at the expense of the causal nexus. The general causal interlacement within the cosmic process must go on uninterrupted.

But it is exactly this which Kant's theory effects. The causal nexus would be broken, if anything in it were suspended, violated or cut off—as would be required in "negative freedom." But here no one of its determining items is suspended; all the causal determinants, which accompany the human will (let us say, as "motives") and are efficacious in it, remain unaffected. But to them is added a new determinant. And this is radically distinguished from the remaining factors only in the fact that it is not itself the effect of prior causes, but descends out of another sphere into the causal nexus, out of a sphere in which no chain of causes exists.

Hence "freedom" in the positive sense is here actually achieved. It is not a Minus in determination (like "negative" freedom), but is evidently a Plus. The causal nexus does not admit of a Minus. For its law affirms that a series of effects, once it has entered upon its course, can by no kind of external agency be annulled. It may however very well admit of a Plus—if only there be such—, for its law does not affirm that no elements otherwise determined could be added to the causal elements of a process. If one should make an ideal cross-section through the bundle of causal threads, the determinational items which would be laid bare would produce a total determination of all the ensuing stages of the process and would constitute in this sense a totality. But this totality is never absolutely closed; it does not prevent the addition of new determining elements—if there be such; and the process is never broken by such an addition, it is only diverted. Precisely this is the peculiarity of the causal nexus, that it does not allow itself to be suspended or broken but does permit of being diverted. The further course of the process then is different from what it would have been if it had lacked the new determinant; but no one of the original causational factors in it is on this account diminished; all are just as efficacious and unhindered in the diverted process as they would have been if no diversion had taken place.

The case may be stated in this wise. The human will is an appearance among appearances; it has the same "empirical reality" as have the natural processes. Hence it is subject to complete determination through the total series of causes which permeate it. But by them the possibility of its determinateness is not altogether exhausted. It can be determined over and above them, provided there is a determination of another kind. Now granted that there is such, then the will's total determination is a duplex of what is in itself qualitatively heterogeneous: that is, there is a synthesis of causal and non-causal determinations. The former derive from the infinitude of the causal nexus of the universe; but the latter first arise in the will, and thereby first enter into the cosmic nexus, in which henceforth they work as further determinants. Accordingly there inheres in them exactly what the thesis of the antinomy affirms: "an absolute spontaneity of causes, a series of appearances which, beginning from themselves, take their course according to natural laws." In the former, on the contrary, the antithesis holds good.

### (c) KANT'S TRANSCENDENTAL IDEALISM, ITS SOLUTION

The objectionable feature in this theory is to be found in its methodological drapery. Even the antithesis between a natural and a rational being can scarcely be accepted, unless something else is concealed in it. But finally the presuppositions of transcendentalism are wholly arbitrary. That nature, and with it the causal nexus, are nothing but "appearances," that behind them stands an "intelligible" world which is real but does not appear, and that it is this real world which in positive freedom projects itself into the sphere of appearances,—all this is mere metaphysical construction. That nature is nothing but appearance is the thesis of the idealism which is rooted in the doctrine of the subjectivity of the categories and in the doctrine of "consciousness in general"; that in positive freedom the real world projects itself into the world of appearance is a consequence of the ethical rationalism which sees in the moral law an autonomy of "reason." The intelligible world is then ultimately reason itself, which in its practical activity has primacy over its theoretical activity.

Now the question is: How in reality does the solution given by Kant to the antinomy stand to these methodological presuppositions, upon which they seem to be built? Is it detachable from them, or does it stand or fall with them? If the latter be the case, all further investigation would be wasted upon it.

To-day it is no longer a secret that Kant's systematic construction was from beginning to end not commensurate with the magnitude of the problem he set. Already in his hands the problems burst bounds. Whoever intends to confine Kant's work to its transcendental idealism falls at the first step into contradictions. It is the greatness of Kant that the consequences of his mode of setting the problem are incomparably more important than those of his system. This applies also to the problem of freedom. And in this sense it is not only quite possible to separate the meaning of the solution of his third antinomy from the fetters of his idealistic system, but it is even necessary—at least if one wishes to understand its philosophical, super-temporal and super-historical significance.[1]

The Kantian distinctions between appearance and the thing-in-itself, between the sensible and the intelligible world, natural and rational being, as well as everything which is metaphysically related to these—such as the origin of causal uniformity in the transcendental subject or of the moral law

[1] Cf. Hartmann's *Diesseits von Idealismus und Realismus, von Beitrag zur Scheidung des Geschichtlichen und Übergeschichtlichen in der Kantischen Philosophie, Kantstudien*, XXIX, brochure 1, 2, 1924, especially Sections 1 and 6.

in practical reason—, are evidently not what would produce
the solution of the antinomy. Whether, for example, the
causal nexus is appearance or exists in itself is evidently a
matter of indifference for the question whether it can or
cannot at any point of its course take up heterogeneous determinants together with its own, that is, whether it can take
them up without doing violence to its own. But solely upon this
question depends the possibility of "positive freedom" in a
world throughout determined causally. What is of importance
is not reality or ideality, not the origin of the uniformity or
that of the heterogeneous determinants, but solely the categorial structure of the causal nexus itself on the one side and
on the other side the presence of heterogeneous determinants.
If one insists upon the real existence of the causal nexus, nothing
is changed in the situation. To be sure, the whole structure of
the world is different, but not the problem of freedom in the
causal nexus. Only to this, not to the structure of the world, is
any importance to be attached.

What then remains as the essential part of the Kantian
doctrine of freedom, if one allows the idealistic interpretation
to drop? Only two elements: the categorial concept of the
causal nexus and the double stratification of the world.

In Kant the latter presents itself in the form of a dualism
between appearance and thing-in-itself. In the contrast
between the empirical and the intelligible, this permeates the
double nature of man as a natural and rational being. All these
metaphysical definitions are unessential to the matter. The
only essential point is that there are in general two layers, two
orders of conformity, two kinds of determination in the one
world, the world in which man exists, and that both manifest
themselves in man himself. For if the one layer is entirely
determined causally, there is need of a second layer, in order
that out of it heterogeneous determinants may be projected
into the causal nexus. On the other hand, it is again a matter
of indifference whether this second layer is an "intelligible"
world, whether it is practical reason, whether its uniformity is

an autonomy of reason or is something else. All that is needed is that it should not be a causal uniformity; otherwise it would coincide with the first layer, and the world would once more be a single stratum and positive freedom would be impossible.

### (d) THE TWOFOLD STRATIFICATION OF THE WORLD, CAUSAL NEXUS AND MORAL LAW

In fact behind the Kantian duality of the sensible and the intelligible world there lies concealed a most essential discovery. But it has nothing to do with idealistic metaphysics. Its object was to show that besides the causal order there is another, which we meet with only in the will of man but which we can verify there just as certainly as we can verify the causal order in the process of nature. Kant produced this proof in his doctrine of the moral law. The moral law is a "fact," even if not "empirical." Because it is a fact, it is a power in man's moral life; hence man is capable of determination through the moral law. For Kant this fact is distinct evidence that behind the causally determined stratum of the world there exists that second stratum. And at the same time it is evidence that at least in man the two strata are connected, that is, the order of the second stratum strikes into that of the first. This is what is meant by saying that there exists a self-direction of the human will according to the moral law. For the human will is always causally determined in various ways. But man is positively free in that over and above this determinedness he experiences a Plus of determination, which is not contained in the causal factors, a determination through the moral law.

That this is a correctly discerned relationship we shall soon be convinced, if we recall what sort of a law the moral law is. Of course its content is here as much a matter of indifference as is the ideality of the causal nexus; the whole question concerns its structure. The moral law is an imperative, a law of the Ought. To use non-Kantian language, it is an expression of the Ought of certain moral values—not of all, only of such as can in any case be intelligently demanded. The power of these values to determine the human will is the tacit presupposition of the categorical imperative, a presupposition well founded in valuational feeling. Now this power is evidently of a different nature from that of causal determination. It is not a compulsion as is that of natural laws. It is merely a claim. And the peculiarity of man's moral being is that among the "motives" which inwardly determine him, this claim, purely as such, can weigh very heavily in the scales. To see this, no special metaphysics of the will, likewise no psychology, is needed. The weight of the claim in the conduct of men is simply an actual ethical fact. That in reality men seldom enough fulfil the claim cannot be brought as an objection against it. The very nature of the law excludes the idea of compulsion. And should anyone be inclined to take up a sceptical attitude on the ground that such a defective fulfilment is proof of a lack of determining power there always remains the entirely different but equally incontrovertible fact that human conduct is approved and disapproved from the point of view of the law.

At all events one must concede to the Kantian doctrine of freedom two positive achievements: first, a demonstration of the fact that there is a power in the moral Ought, which as a heterogeneous, non-causal, determining factor, strikes into the nexus of causal trends, and, secondly, a demonstration that the structure of the causal nexus makes such an intervention possible, without any interruption to itself.

On the other hand, Kant's view that the power of the moral law consists in a self-legislation of "reason," that there exists a *homo noumenon* which exercises autonomous activity, is quite subordinate to his achievements and may be discarded along with the rest of his idealistic metaphysics. To discard it is in so far important that then the essence of the Kantian doctrine can without forcing be applied to the table of values. For instance, in the order of the Ought, in the claims which the moral values make upon man, the values are indeed autonomous—and autonomous exactly as regards the order of nature—but their autonomy is not that of reason. Moral commandments do not issue from reason but are directed towards it. This, however, as regards the law of causality, is a matter of indifference, so far as the heterogeneity of the moral claim is concerned. Whether the power which here intervenes comes from reason or from values which are self-existent makes a difference only as regards the nature of moral principles, but none as regards the positive meaning of moral freedom as a Plus of determination in a world which is causally determined throughout.

# CHAPTER V (LXIX)

## DETERMINISM AND INDETERMINISM

### (a) THE RADICAL ELIMINATION OF CONCEPTUAL ERRORS

IF one recalls the swarm of traditional errors which, by a single happy stroke, Kant was the first to avoid, one will be the better able to appreciate the significance of his doctrine of freedom, even with its load of idealistic metaphysics. With him there is no longer any trace of the confusion of freedom of will with freedom of action, or even with legal freedom. Likewise, all blending of moral with religious freedom is avoided. Still more significant is it that Kant grants no place either to "outward" or "inward" freedom, despite their popularity. By asserting the supremacy of the causal nexus he barred out all independence of the course not only of outward events and situations, but also of inner (psychological) events and situations. Finally, his avoidance of all ambiguities concerning "freedom of choice" gives pre-eminence to his theory. In this respect Kant's significance is far from being exhausted in the exposition given above. Of special importance is his coining of concepts which transform popular notions of freedom into philosophic interpretations, and which, in their very terminology, contrary to all expectation, bear upon their face the paradoxes: "freedom in the positive sense," "causality issuing from freedom," "freedom under law."

One may view the matter from another side. Kant's service consists in having shown that the true meaning of moral freedom is not the negative one of choice, but the positive one of an order *sui generis*, which autonomously encounters that of causality and nevertheless adds itself to the prevailing texture of the real world, without rending it.

## (b) The Mistake of Ethical Naturalism and Psychologism

But even now we have not exhausted Kant's achievements. He was also the first to expose to view a further series of failures which are hidden in other theories but which he, by the same happy stroke of genius, was able to avoid. They are the errors of πρῶτον ψεῦδος, which consist in the metaphysical overloading of the concept of freedom—and of other concepts as well.[1]

In fact, even the order of nature, which stands over against that of freedom, can be metaphysically overloaded. No error is more familiar than this. One transforms the category of Nature into a universal cosmic category; one subjects not only the physical world to the law of cause and effect, but the spiritual and the mental worlds are said to be ruled by it, and indeed only by it, or—to speak more exactly—only by laws which, like those of Nature, have their basis in causality. If one applies this notion to the will and to the totality of ethical phenomena, one takes one's stand in the midst of ethical naturalism. One can reduce this theory to the crudity of materialism; in which case consciousness, and with it the will and the ethos, are resultants of bodily functions. This theory is still more common in the form of biological evolutionism, the tendency of which consists in tracing every ethical phenomenon of man, even his resolutions, dispositions and preferences, to inheritance, to the influence of environment or of the conditions of life, and to other similar causal factors.

It is plain that such a causal determinism renders not only negative freedom of choice but even positive freedom impossible. Of itself this would naturally be nothing against causal determinism; for whether there be such a thing as moral freedom is precisely the matter in question. But as such important consequences depend upon it, it would need to be most firmly established. It is, however, far from being so established. Ethical naturalism quite arbitrarily transfers

[1] Cf. Chapter III (a), Vol. III.

the causal nexus from natural events, in which it is at home, to a domain which evidently has a different constitution and manifests other laws. Here the mistake is committed of carrying a single category too far. The metaphysical picture of the world which it presents is indeed astonishingly simple; but its very unity is suspicious, in face of the multiplicity and diversity of phenomena. The very feature of the theory which was supposed to commend it makes it doubtful. And as its very simplicity excludes the possibility of positive freedom, the universalizing of the causal nexus is a highly questionable procedure.

Nor is it any improvement if, instead of incorporating consciousness with the natural process, one confers upon it an equally extensive psychic law of causality, analogous to that of Nature. In such causal psychologism the whole domain of the ethos is referred to psychic processes and is thus subjected indirectly again to the causal nexus.

In both cases there is set up a monism of causal determination. And it is this which excludes freedom. From the Kantian theory one can learn that freedom is never possible where a single type of determination reigns throughout the world in all its strata. Freedom is only possible where, in one world, at least two types of determination are superimposed one upon the other: only in such a world can a higher determination adjust its determinants to a lower, so that, viewed from the lower, an actual Plus of determination comes into existence. Hence the mistake in ethical naturalism and psychologism is by no means determinism, nor even the causal type of law, but solely determinational monism. Over and above natural causality there remains nothing which can determine the will.

It is to Kant's lasting credit that in the human will he recognized, besides the causal interweaving, a second type of determination, and in moral conduct generally secured a positive position for it within the all-pervading causal nexus. That he left it categorially indefinite is of course a defect. But the deficiency can be made good. Thus causal determinism is rendered innocuous. It is restricted by a second, a non-causal factor. The metaphysical exaggeration of causal domination in the world—its exclusive reign—is abandoned.

### (c) THE ERROR OF INDETERMINISM

Before Kant, the thorough-going determinism of the cosmic process was universally regarded as an absolute obstacle to freedom. The result was that efforts were made at any price to break through this determinism. And accordingly indeterminism was postulated, at least within certain limits. It was striven for; an attempt was made to wrench it from the uniformity of nature. Fichte in his youth was typical of this stage of the problem; before he became acquainted with Kant's teaching, he was inwardly engrossed with it. He felt determinism to be slavery, indeed an outrage upon man; yet he was unable to defend himself against it. This is why he came to look upon Kant's doctrine as a deliverance.

Now if from Kant's point of view we survey the whole alternative of determinism and indeterminism, we can criticize the two theories at the same time.

We have seen that the error in determinism is not thorough-going determination itself, but simply the monistic and exclusive supremacy of one single type of it. If we once more restrict natural uniformity to Nature and assign to the mental realm another kind of uniformity, peculiar to itself, the latter without further ado is free as regards the former. But how does the matter stand with indeterminism? Wherein does its mistake consist? Or in positive freedom do we perhaps retain something of indeterminism?

Indeterminism finds scope for chance. In this metaphysical sense, "chance" does not mean indeterminedness, but only a determinedness which is not conditioned by anything else. Hence the "accidental" is not properly what is undetermined, it is only detached from the nexus which binds all existence in a unified and thorough determination. This is neither a meaningless conception of chance nor one which can be empirically controverted. Unconvincing is the objection to it, that the unsophisticated man is always prone to regard as accidental everything of which he does not comprehend the causes. Although most of what is called "accidental" may be so designated merely because of human ignorance, there might very well be something which had determinedness purely in itself.

But the relation of the ontological modalities speaks to the contrary.[1] The "accidental" is something actual. Actuality, however, is constituted of possibility and necessity. The actual must be at least ontologically possible. But ontological possibility—unlike the purely logical—does not consist in mere freedom from contradiction, but in the real series of conditions. In the strict sense a thing is "really possible," only when the whole series is at hand, down to the last member. On the other side, however, it is then not only possible, but also necessary, that is, it can no longer fail to appear. It could fail to appear, so long as at least one condition in the series was lacking. If that also were added, nothing more could prevent the real actuality. But exactly this inevitability is ontological necessity. The consequence is this: all that is ontologically possible is precisely thereby ontologically necessary also. Hence, in so far as only the possible can be actual, everything actual must at the same time be ontologically necessary.

Now possibility and necessity are relational modi. They connect one existent with another. Accordingly, if in everything really possible there is concealed a covering relation of ontological possibility and necessity, everything actual is bound to the all-pervading relations of existence and to its order, and there is nothing ontologically "accidental."

In this modal order lies a radical refutation of indeterminism, a proof of the existence of a pervading determination throughout the world. Now if moral freedom were negative freedom of choice, the problem of freedom in the negative sense would

[1] Cf. Chapter XXIII (*b*), Vol. I.

therewith be decided. And because the pre-Kantian philosophy understood freedom as freedom of choice, it laid the whole weight of the question upon the alternative of determinism and indeterminism. The fact that for everyone who was intellectually honest the scale of determinism held the heavier weight can arouse no wonder. In this way is to be explained the scepticism which had become widespread in ethics. For without freedom moral Being is something purely illusory.

For the first time the magnitude of Kant's achievement in his solution of the "third antinomy" can at this point be rightly estimated. As soon as one replaces negative freedom by "freedom in the positive sense," the situation is reversed at one stroke. Not only is indeterminism false ontologically; it is also shown to be a false ethical requirement. There is no need of it at all. There is a πρῶτον ψεῦδος involved in thinking that moral freedom should signify indeterminedness, and could exist only in a world at least partially undetermined. It exists unhindered only in a totally determined world. In such a world its one condition is that the cosmic determination be not monistic, that is, not confined to a single, all-dominating type of determination which reduces everything to one level.

But the ontological law of complete determination by no means contradicts this condition. It does not at all affirm that every existential determinedness must needs be of one kind, the causal kind, for instance. In the one world there may be unlimited scope for many types of determination, one superimposed upon another, the higher of which as compared with the lower always has the character of a Plus of determination, and hence is free "in the positive sense."

### (d) THE TELEOLOGICAL CONCEPTION OF THE WORLD, ITS CLAIM IN THE QUESTION OF FREEDOM

In the Kantian theory of freedom there is an omission, and indeed an omission in its presuppositions. It proceeds entirely from the causal antinomy; accordingly it presupposes that the determinedness of the cosmic process is wholly causal. Of course a kind of proof for this is found in the "analogies of experience." But the proof shows only that the causal law is a valid law of Nature; it does not show that causality is the only kind of natural nexus. For this a second proof ought by rights to have been forthcoming, if the causal antinomy is to embrace the whole of the problem.

The modal proof of a universal law of determination is of no help here. This law only affirms that in general everything existent is determined, but not that all determination is causal. It only posits the thesis of complete determinism as such, but leaves quite open the type of determinism. Hence, so far as this law is concerned, Nature might be determined altogether differently, for instance, finalistically. And it is a fact of history that immediately after Kant the teleological conception of Nature emerged once more (in its most pronounced form with Schelling) and continued to prevail in the idealistic systems. But if one glances backwards from Kant, one ultimately finds almost everywhere the teleological conception of the process of Nature. It emanates from Aristotle, who is pre-eminently the classic representative of this view, and survives throughout later antiquity and the middle ages and far into modern times. Almost the only exceptions are the materialistic theories and those akin to them, which in respect to philosophic questions proper are not to be taken at all seriously. Even Spinoza can scarcely be accepted as a causalist; precisely in categorial structure his conception of *causa sive ratio* is ambiguous.

The pure causal concept, which modern natural science has elaborated, forced its way but gradually into philosophy. Even Leibniz himself, for all his ercognition of it, allowed it validity only as a phenomenal externality of existential connections and propped it up metaphysically with a unitary teleological nexus. In the historical line Kant stands practically alone, however much he seems to be a model on this point for present-day scientific thinking.

Accordingly we cannot avoid turning our attention also to

the teleological conception of the universe. The question at issue does not concern the general metaphysical appraisement of teleology, but this alone: What becomes of freedom, if the course of nature be determined not causally but finalistically? Does the same scope remain for positive freedom, or does positive freedom become an impossibility?

### (e) THE ERROR OF FINALISTIC DETERMINISM

The answer must be sought in the categorial structure of the finalistic nexus itself. Is that nexus in a position to take on a Plus of determination over and above its own inherent determinedness, and indeed without destroying the latter? This is the question at issue.

What exactly gave to the causal nexus the capacity to take up heterogeneous determinants into its texture? This, of course: that with it at every stage a totality of determinative details is assembled, which allows of no kind of indeterminedness, and yet is not on that account a closed totality; it always stands open to factors from other quarters—if such there be. The proof of this is the dirigibility of the causal series. It is not pledged to any definite final stage; it moves on in complete indifference as to the result. In its whole dependence it is controlled from the earlier stage to the later in the same direction as the flow of time and moves with it—never in the opposite direction. What is contained in the earlier stage necessarily works itself out in the later. Hence the later stage is only in so far determined beforehand by the earlier as no new factors are added. But if such are added, they modify the determinational complex and thereby all the ensuing stages. Herein consists the diversion of the process from its direction. Nothing opposes such a diversion. In the causal nexus there is no power which would turn the process back again into its original direction. There are no "goals" to the process, which as such were beforehand laid down and worked determinatively towards the later stages.

In the finalistic process all this is changed. It sets out with the fixation of the final goal. The means are determined backward from the end. Let us recall on this point the categorial analysis given in Volume I.[1]

The connection between the beginning and the final stage is threefold: first, by an overleaping of the time process the end is set up; secondly, from the end backwards against the course of time the series of means is determined; and, thirdly, starting with the first means, through the same series the end is actualized. One must not think of the first stage as a case of natural teleology. How it comes about that ends of a process are in general determined beforehand is here a matter of indifference (metaphysically, of course, it is by no means an indifferent matter; but it is so, for the question of categorial structure). The third kind of connection between beginning and goal, the actualization, also comes into question here only in a subordinate way; it is in a forward direction, a causal course, in which the series of means functions as a series of causes. Thus only the second kind of connection is of prime importance, the backward-running determination of the means, starting with the end. This constitutes the distinctive categorial novelty in the finalistic nexus.

Now the question is: Does this backward determination in the stages of the process allow scope for the introduction of determinants from other quarters, that is, for positive freedom?

One may reflect as follows. A newly arriving determinant within a complex of determinants already at hand means that the process is diverted. It thereby changes its direction, it moves forward to something different. But in a teleological process what does a change of direction mean? It can only mean that the end is missed. But this signifies that the teleology of the process is itself suspended, destroyed, violated. Hence the finalistic process is differently related to a factor introduced from other quarters; it cannot incorporate the latter. At every stage its system of determinants is a closed totality which resists any addition. If one thinks of an introduction of hetero-

[1] Cf. Chapter XX (*b–e*), Vol. I.

geneous determinants, two cases are possible. Either the new determinant is stronger than the finalistic nexus; then the process is diverted and the nexus is broken. Or the finalistic nexus is the stronger; then it overcomes the disturbance, cancels the diversion that has occurred and leads the process back again to the end. In neither case does that occur which alone can fulfil the meaning of positive freedom: the incorporation of another kind of determinant into an undamaged nexus. In the former case the nexus is injured; in the latter the determinants are again extruded—they are, as it were, paralysed in their efficacy (in other words, in their determinative power).

One can easily visualize this relationship. In the causal nexus the moving power of the process is behind and inheres in what has preceded. It works like a mechanical propulsion (which of course is only its simplest case), like a blind necessity, indifferent to what the process brings forth. That is why an incoming Plus of determination in it is every time simply one component more, which according to its direction and force determines the result. Let us transfer this spacial picture to the finalistic nexus: in its third stage the moving power is in front (in the direction of the process). But this third stage is efficacious quite differently, not like a push, but like a pull, like a power of attraction. The end is at the same time the magnet of the *nexus finalis*. From it also there issues a necessity, but not a blind one that is indifferent to the result; it is a necessity which is bound to the content of the pre-established result. The finalistic nexus at the same time sees in anticipation. This is why it cannot allow an intervention "from outside" to occur; it offers resistance to such an occurrence at any price; it cancels every diversion. A power of attraction continues to be bound to the attractive point, when it is once present to the mind. In it the goal stands fixed beforehand. In spite of every diversion it always leads the process back again to itself, as the point in view.

In a world determined finalistically throughout, such as

the later metaphysics under the spell of a time-honoured prejudice accepted almost unanimously, moral freedom is an impossibility. The categorial structure of the finalistic nexus bars it out. If a teleology of the existential process was onto-logically fixed, there would be no place in the world for the existence of morality, and all ethical phenomena would be phantom-appearances. Man would already be pre-ordained in his will, in his spiritual attitude, indeed in all his behaviour; and all accountability, every feeling of responsibility would be an illusion—perhaps a gracious one, but just the same an illusion. There would be no room for a moral being. "Man" is possible only in a world not teleologically determined.

This is why the ethical problem in its full significance could not make itself felt until the teleological conception of the world was overthrown. This is also why Fichte and Hegel must needs miss the ethical problem, just as the pre-Kantian philosophy had missed it. Kant continued to be misunderstood in the essential point of his ethics. For it was he who in this matter, from a right instinct for the problem, although not with complete clearness of insight, took the only possible line of procedure. What looks like an omission in his theory—that the antinomy is only a causal, not a finalistic antinomy—, is proof of his profound understanding of the real problem. Not only would a finalistic conception of the world have utterly missed the greatest achievement of modern thought—deliver-ance from the nightmare of teleology—, but it would also, being the antithesis of the achievement, have rendered impossible the solution of the antinomy of freedom.

A finalistic antinomy cannot be solved. What Kant's con-temporaries felt as a deliverance in his theory of freedom was indeed a deliverance from determinism, not, however, from causal determinism, as is generally supposed, but from finalistic determinism. It was precisely causal determinism which re-mained unaffected.

In finalistic determinism inheres the great πρῶτον ψεῦδος, from which in fact Kant's *Critique* freed ethics.

# DETERMINISM, CAUSAL AND FINALISTIC

## (a) METAPHYSICAL PARADOXES

THE problem which now confronts us has something extremely paradoxical about it. The indeterminism to which men have been in the habit of taking flight, in order to be able to rescue moral freedom, has proved itself to be not only false metaphysically but superfluous. The causal determinism which has been most feared has been shown to be perfectly innocuous; but finalistic determinism, which has been supreme for so long in philosophic theories and has been held to be harmless, has turned out to be the real evil, the destroyer of human freedom.

Here everything must be learned all over again. This can be done only by tracing back to their bedrock the categorial connections which in this matter are the decisive factors.

Why have men expected the reverse relation of the two types of determinism to the freedom of the will? The answer is easy. From of old the causal nexus has found a congenial home in those metaphysical theories in which the freedom of the will fared worst, pre-eminently in the materialistic theories. Conversely, where a stricter concept of freedom has emerged in the history of philosophy, it has somehow been most closely attached to universal cosmic teleology.

But behind this historical association of motives is undoubtedly hidden also a kinship of system. That sort of determination which—at least in tendency—issues from values, namely, the pure Ought-to-Be, is evidently akin in its structure to the finalistic nexus. In the Ought inheres just that pressure towards a goal; values are the points at which idealistic tendencies aim. And where the tendency becomes actual, for example, where a person's disposition or will alters, there the tendency becomes a positive finalistic relation. In volition proper there are always valuational materials which constitute the contents of ends. In its categorial form, Will is already a finalistic nexus; it is the teleology of man; it is what makes him superior to other entities and enables him to actualize values in the real world. What stands in the way of such actualization is only the fact that everything real brings with it its own causal determinateness, which vastly restricts from the very beginning any desire of control over it. But now if one thinks of the causal nexus as penetrating into the innermost Will, the will seems to be cramped and the teleology of its aims is from the start subjected to a mechanically efficacious selection of contents. This, however, means that the more one mechanizes the world, so much the more does one restrict the teleology of man—and with it his freedom of will—; and the more one teleologizes the world, so much the more does man as a teleologically effective being fit homogeneously into it.

This is a view which, whether unconsciously or consciously, floats before teleological thinkers, in so far as they are interested in the freedom of the will. To the unsophisticated mind it appears self-evident; and yet it is the grossest metaphysical blunder which can possibly be made in the ethical field. The misleading element in it inheres in the undeniable homogeneity between the finalistic nexus and the Will (at least as the carrier of the Ought), and the equally undeniable heterogeneity between the mechanism of the causal series and the teleology of every tendency that is directed towards a value. But it is exactly this homogeneity and this heterogeneity, which upon closer categorial analysis give the lie to the misleading presupposition, a presupposition which is always accepted as if it were self-evident.

This, of course, would not be the case if the essence of freedom inhered in teleology as such. Then, in a universe determined throughout teleologically, not only man but every natural entity would be "free." But such is not the essence of freedom, not even of "freedom in the positive sense." Teleology is only a kind of ontological determination—along with causality and other possible kinds. Freedom, however, is by no means simply a kind of determination, but is a specific relation between at least two kinds of determination, namely, the relation of a higher to a lower, in so far as both co-exist in one and the same real world and apply to one and the same occurrence. Among the beings which are subject to the lower type of determination, that one is then free "in the positive sense," which in addition to this subjection also comes under the law of a higher determination.

### (b) A Reference back to the Law of Categorial Dependence

Both causal and finalistic determination, when taken in the absolute sense, that is, when monistically applied to the whole cosmic structure, commit exactly the same blunder, although in the opposite direction. Both reduce the world to uniformity; they give it a type of relational simplicity, which excludes freedom. A universalized causal determinism converts man into a mere natural entity, it degrades him; a universalized finalistic determinism transforms Nature into a being that is directed to ends, into such a being as man is; it raises Nature up to his level. Both theories reduce everything to a common denominator. They thereby nullify the uniqueness of Moral Being in the world. And again they thereby extinguish man's freedom; but with it at the same time morality itself. The positive significance of a free being in a determined world can be due to nothing else than to his superior position, to that heterogeneous Plus of determination which he has over and above other actual entities.

Hence in both cases the mistake lies not in the determinateness itself, but in the monism of determination. Nevertheless the kind of error in causal determinism is different from that inherent in finalistic determinism.

We can best see this if we return to the laws of categorial

dependence, which have already been cited in another connection.[1] As the types of determination have unmistakably the
character of categorial structures, the three laws of dependence
—the law of strength, the law of material and that of freedom—
must necessarily reappear in them, as soon as two or more of
the types are superimposed one upon another in the same
world, and thereby set up a stratification. In relation to the
problem before us the three laws must be specified:

1. The law of strength: the higher type of determination
is dependent upon the lower, but the reverse is not true.
Hence the higher is at the same time the more conditioned and
in this sense the weaker. The lower, on the other hand, is
the more elemental, the more fundamental, and in this sense
the stronger. The inversion of this relation is indeed conceivable in the abstract, but can never be demonstrated from
the nature of determinational types.

2. The law of material: every lower type is for the higher one
which is raised upon it, merely material. Now as the lower is
the stronger, the dependence of the weaker upon the stronger
type of determination extends only so far as the scope of the
higher form is limited by the determinateness and peculiarity
of the material.

3. The law of freedom: every higher type, as compared with
a lower, is entirely a new structure, which (as a categorial
novelty) is raised upon the lower. As such it has unlimited
scope over and above the lower (the material and stronger)
determinateness. That is, despite its dependence upon the
lower type of determination, the higher is free, as over against
the lower.

Now evidently the causal nexus is a lower, the finalistic
a higher type of determination. This is already seen in the
simplicity of the former and the complexity (the three stages)
of the latter. Besides, the finalistic nexus is an incomparably
richer, more intensive, more self-contained kind of dependence.
The categorial analysis proves this through the impossibility

[1] Cf. Chapter XXXVIII (c), Vol. II.

of diverting the finalistic nexus without destroying it. In it the system of determinants at every stage of its advance is a closed system and cannot be enlarged. In regard to the causal nexus there is no question as to such an exclusive bearing. In that it admits at every stage any kind of determinants, it proves itself to be a far laxer, a merely minimal determination, which, indeed, holds absolutely fast to what it actually determines, but in so doing is not bound to any predetermined result.

So much for the new problem. It now remains for us to draw the inferences.

### (c) The Ontological Dependence of the Finalistic upon the Causal Nexus

The first inference is that in the relation between the causal and the finalistic nexus—as it is actually at hand in the whole world of ethical reality—, the causal process (being the more elementary) is also the stronger and more fundamental, but the finalistic process holds free sway above it, as above its own material.

The superior strength of the causal process is quite evident. The finalistic nexus itself in its third stage takes on the causal form; in the actualization of the end the means function as causes and the end takes the form of an effect. Herein is clearly reflected the categorial law: the finalistic process is dependent upon the causal, the former can appear only where the latter is present. Active volition and action, the categorial structure of which is finalistic, are impossible except in a world which is already causally determined throughout. Impotent yearning of course and a purely inward attitude are possible even in a non-causal world. But the volition includes the determination of the means from the point of view of the end (the choice of means is "for" the end). Now, if the causal complex of the means did not entail a definite effect, how could a given means be found for a given effect—namely the effect which in the end is aimed at and for the sake of which alone the means is chosen?

The backward-running determination (the second stage in the finalistic nexus) has as its presupposition the forward-running causal determination; in anticipation this is foreseen. From the beginning the selection of means is a selection of causes—namely, of the causes of an effect aimed at.

Lastly, in the third stage of the finalistic process, the only point of interest is that the chosen causes actually produce the desired effect. Whence it clearly follows that the foreseeing nexus—and with it the will, conduct and actual constitution of the teleological entity—advances so much the more powerfully, the more the causal determinedness of all the real processes is fixed and absolute. A finalistic nexus floating in the air without a causal basis is an empty abstraction, a categorial impossibility. It is ontologically possible only in a world causally determined throughout, as a second, a higher, process based upon a causal nexus.

For the problem of freedom this one side of the relation is extremely instructive. In categorial structure the will, whose freedom is under discussion, is teleological. In the causal antinomy the question is concerning the co-existence of the freedom of the will with the world's all-pervading causal nexus. The Kantian solution showed that this co-existence is possible. But now it is further shown that precisely for the freedom of the will, that is, for the introduction of a higher, a finalistic determinant, this co-existence is indispensable and necessary. To state the point more exactly, a free will with its finalistic mode of efficacy is altogether possible only in a world entirely determined causally. Such a world—ontologically considered—does not stand in an antithetic relation to freedom of the will. The causal nexus is not an obstacle, but a positive prior condition. It is the lower type of determination upon which alone the higher can be raised. In a world which is not so determined not only is the teleology of a free will an utter impossibility, but equally so is all teleology—whether that of a divinely absolute providence or of a human limited foresight.

## (d) Categorial Freedom of Teleology above the Causal Nexus

The second consequence of the stratification between the causal and the finalistic nexus was that the latter is superimposed upon the former and, entering as something new, is categorially "free."

Even this, in its ontological relation, is easy to understand. As the superior strength of the causal nexus depends upon the basic law of the categories, so the scope of the finalistic nexus depends upon the law of freedom. The causal nexus, although indeed its necessary condition, is only its material condition. A purposive relation as such can never be brought forth from it. The causal trend knows no connection with goals which are given from another quarter; their attractive power acts as a new determinant along with the causal determinants. This means that the causal nexus always stands open to the introduction of a purpose and attaches itself to that purpose unresistingly, so far as the purpose knows how to make use of the given causal complex as a means.

From the point of view of the finalistic complex, everything in the causal connection is "accidental." Causally it is not accidental; rather is everything step by step, as an effect, profoundly necessary and by no means able to occur otherwise than it does occur, if no other factors are added. But this merely causal necessity is a finalistic contingency; whether aims, somehow embodied in it (that is, introduced from other quarters), are being actualized or not, is in fact perfectly external to the causal texture, and is in this sense "accidental." The outcome of the causal process is blind, without predetermination. What is not seen and determined beforehand is not an end, and is teleologically contingent.

In this teleological contingency of what is causally necessitated inheres the categorial freedom of the finalistic determination within a world throughout determined causally. One might express the matter thus: a causally determined world is in itself still teleologically undetermined; hence a merely causal determinism, so long as it is not made monistically absolute and is not extended in an irrational way to altogether non-causal relations, is at the same time teleological indeterminism. Hence in this respect indeterminism regains a conditional justification. Its legitimate meaning is simply the scope of a higher determination resting upon a lower one which is at hand. And this simply means that a world under laws of nature that are merely formed causally stands open to the setting up of ends and to the purposive activity of any being capable of foresight and predetermination.

Here man's freedom shows itself to be an ontological function of his unique place in the stratification of two types of determination. His is a dual position; he stands under a twofold determination. As a natural being, even to his inmost desires and repulsions, he is determined causally, a plaything of the eternal powers of Nature, of powers overwhelmingly superior and operating both through him and altogether irrespectively of him. But as a "person" he is the carrier of another sort of determination, which emanates from the ideal realm of values. In his sensing of them he finds himself in part determined by the claim which values make upon him in the form of the Ought. And it is this kind of determinateness which manifests itself in his purposive activity. He can only transform into ends what he feels to be of value. But in converting values into ends, he transforms them into realities. He positively creates what causal necessity never could bring forth, a world of ethical actuality in the midst of an actual Nature. Through his purposive activity, that is, his categorially higher form of determination, which originates with him, he proves himself to be an entity superior to the powers of Nature, a Being in whose hands forces blind and aimless in themselves become means to ends discerned and posited beforehand. And indirectly, in the commitment of his personality to objectively discerned values (those that are situational) as well as in his guidance of purposeless events towards values, he attains the higher values, the distinctively moral qualities.

## (e) Causal Monism, its Inversion of the Categorial Law of Freedom

Now for the first time it is possible to present in distinct outline what was vaguely suggested above: namely, that the error in both kinds of deterministic monism does not inhere in the determinism but in the monism, and that nevertheless the kind of error in the one is the opposite of that in the other. It is now clear that each of the two theories violates one of the categorial laws of dependence, while the other fulfils it. Hence the mistakes are complementary to each other.

In causal monism—that is, in the universal mechanistic view of the world—the basic law of the categories is preserved, but the law of freedom is violated. This becomes clear, as soon as we have understood what these laws assert. For here, in a realm which contains the finalistic nexus, in the realm of ethical actuality, the superiority of the causal nexus as regards "strength" is carried to the extreme and is assigned absolute dominion. Hence the superior strength of the lower determination is, to say the least, preserved intact. But it is not only the strength of the elementary, of the condition, of the material, but an absolute superiority, which completely swallows up the self-subsistence of the higher determination. The law of freedom is violated. This law affirms that the causal nexus only in so far conditions the final nexus as the quality of the material conditions the form but cannot determine the goals themselves. These remain free. In causal monism causality is by no means regarded merely as the material of purposive actualization, but also as the concrete determinant, or at least as that which in the fluctuations of human fancy selects the possible ends.

This at least is the meaning of the theories on the subject. In accordance with its entire attitude the mechanistic view of the universe cannot see that in the sensing of values there is a unique and wholly autonomous law of selection—the law of the order of rank. Indeed, it also cannot see the autonomy of the values themselves and of the teleological determination which emanates from them. Hence, whenever it reflects upon value and the Ought, it is infected with valuational relativism: according to it value depends upon "evaluation," but this is regarded by it as a function of natural inclination, of craving, of pleasure; and these, again, are presented as subject to physical causality.

In this way the categorial law of freedom is turned completely upside down. The finalistic indifference (the contingency) of the causal nexus fails to be recognized; the lower determination, which according to its nature is only the stronger, is made the ruling authority over the higher and is set up, contrary to its own nature, as the higher. And the actually higher is thereby made categorially unfree.

### (f) FINALISTIC MONISM, ITS INVERSION OF THE BASIC LAW OF THE CATEGORIES

In finalistic monism, in the view that the universe is teleological throughout, the opposite mistake is made. Here the law of freedom is retained, but the basic categorial law is violated. Here domination by the finalistic nexus, which in one realm (that of ethical actuality) undoubtedly still has the causal nexus within it, is expanded to the extreme. Accordingly the categorial freedom of the higher determination is, to say the least, preserved. It is not only the freedom of that which as a higher formation is raised over a more general and lower formation (as over its own material), hence not only a freedom which is bound within the limits of a given determination, but also a boundless freedom, an absolute superiority of the higher determination, as one which already prevails over the lower from beginning to end and throughout the whole field. One cannot say that thereby the lower determination is suspended; it is indeed contained everywhere in the third stage of the finalistic nexus. Hence categorial dependence also subsists here. But only immanently in the finalistic nexus. There exists then

no causal occurrence in the world, behind which there does
not already stand a teleological backward-moving determination, and which, therefore, is not at bottom a finalistic occurrence. All the causal processes are then bound to ends; there is
no causal necessity which would be at the same time a finalistic
contingency. The causal process is not itself suspended; but
it has ceased to be a process that runs on in blind indifference.

In this absolute categorial domination of the teleological
determination (freedom) the narrower meaning of moral
freedom is utterly obliterated. This narrow significance consisted in a pre-eminence of the moral being, in a Plus of determination which distinguishes it from other entities. But if
natural processes (even those within man as a natural being)
have already within them a teleological connection with ends,
there is nothing left over for human teleology to perform
except to let the natural processes run their own course; man
cannot divert them to other goals; nature in and outside of
him, with its macrocosmic powers, is absolutely master over
him. Every attempted diversion of the predestined courses
unfailingly leads back to their "natural" goals.

Evidently the inversion of the basic law of the categories
is the crux of the matter. This law affirms that the higher
determination as compared with the lower is never in absolute
domination, while the lower is always the presupposition of
the higher. Hence it affirms precisely this, that the causal
nexus also exists for itself without finalistic bondage, and that
the finalistic union with ends is rather added to it in a particular case, if in an entity capable of it such a union is introduced as a heterogeneous determinant within the given system
of determinations. But then, for the manifestation of a finalistic
bond in the course of the world, there is need at once of a being
which has the categorial potentiality to achieve the end. Only a
foreseeing, value-sensing entity, capable of intention and of
purposive energy, is of this kind. Hence it is the categorial
law, which provides scope for "freedom in the positive sense,"
as the freedom of a teleological being within a non-teleological

world which is determined causally but is finalistically "contingent."

In teleological monism this law is turned upside down. Finalistic neutrality, "contingency" and an ever-open teleological divertibility of the causal process are fundamentally overlooked by it. A world throughout finalistically determined, even down to the smallest detail of its particular processes, is undivertible. The higher determination, the nature of which is to be the weaker and to be valid only within a narrow circle of higher phenomena, is endowed with the concretely dominant power of the stronger, and hence transformed, against its nature, into the stronger and more universally valid determination. But thereby the really stronger and more elementary determination is made dependent and weaker.

### (g) METAPHYSICAL MECHANISM AND PANTHEISM

The ontological possibility of moral "freedom in the positive sense" rests upon the stratification of types of determination in one and the same world, as well as upon the complementary relationship prevailing in it, between the basic categorial law and the categorial law of freedom. Man, if he is to be "positively" free, must be determined on two sides; and each of two kinds of determination must be self-sufficient, even if self-sufficient in different senses.

The peculiar position of a free being in a determined world has its categorial meaning in this, that in it two heterogeneous orders conflict with each other, each with a claim to dominate the world. Existential uniformity and the order of the Ought, causal determination and teleological, must each at the same time have in such a being the seat of its cosmic struggle for the world. And only so long as the struggle is active does there exist a free being. With the victory of the one or the other, man becomes determined by one side (monistically), and thereby positively unfree. If the causal nexus in him controls the end posited, mechanism rules completely, and man, as

Lamettrie would have it, is converted into a "machine." But if the finalistic nexus dominates the natural processes, then the cosmic ends, ruling with almighty power, stand over against the weak, finite purposive efforts of man, who can make no headway against them. He is lamed, fettered, predestined even in the most secret aspirations of his heart, even in his sensing of values. This crippling of man is quite distinctively his moral undoing. It becomes evident wherever the metaphysic of the telos lets fall the harmless mask of mere naturalistic theory and shows itself as a tyrannical autocracy. This appears most fully in the pantheistic systems, the sense of which is that the all-dominating teleology of an absolute Being has entered into the world, indeed even into Nature itself, and is identical with the universal cosmic order.

Pantheism is the most radical inversion of the basic law of the categories, the most perverted perversion of the fundamental metaphysical relation which runs through all the specific relations of the universe. In it every teleology of man is summarily handed over to God, the course of the world is entirely the actualization of His ends; and to man there remains nothing over but the rôle of the puppet on the stage of the cosmic comedy.

The cause of this comedy (which is of course extremely congenial to the craving for formal metaphysical unity) is the crudest of blunders in regard to categorial principles. The highest, most complex and concrete principle, the one which according to the basic law must be most conditioned and the "weakest," is made the strongest and the least conditioned. The world is no longer a profoundly puzzling and highly complicated structure, but as simple as a crystal. This theory, however, pays for its transparency by the complete ejection of the human ethos and its manifold significance.

# ONTOLOGICAL REGULARITY AS THE BASIS OF FREEDOM

## (a) THE APPEARANCE OF DETERMINATIVE DUALISM

IT is now in place for us to close with a metaphysical survey our whole discussion of the categories which appertain to the problem of freedom. This of course reaches far beyond the ethical problem, but exactly on that account we can most strikingly show how the ethical question is rooted in the elementary problems of ontology.

If positive freedom is possible only where heterogeneous (but not antinomic) types of determination are placed one upon the other, if this freedom converts man into the centre of contest between causal and finalistic, between ontological and axiological determination, the inference seems unavoidable that at the basis of it all there exists a metaphysical dualism of determinations which runs throughout the cosmic structure and becomes visible in the ethos of man. If this should be verified, the traditional misgiving on the part of all systematic philosophy in regard to dualism would be immediately aroused. Can we acquiesce in a primal separateness? After all, is not the domination of teleology to be preferred (as Leibniz, Schelling, Hegel and so many others, because of this predicament, have stated it), without shrinking from the *sacrificium intellectus*, which in the problem of freedom cannot then be avoided?

On the other hand the question must first be raised: What exactly is the objection to a justification of dualism? The traditional aversion to a primal cleavage can bring forward nothing in defence of itself except this, that the aversion is a fact. A pictured unity is more satisfying to our craving for system, because it offers greater comprehensibility. That is all. And it is just the same with the dualisms in other departments of thought. But the demand for systematization is only a postulate, and indeed a rationalistic postulate; and perhaps it is only at first glance even that—for it is highly questionable whether unity itself can be any better grasped than disunion. The world can be better understood under the presupposition of unity, but better only in the sense of unification. Yet what is the good of a forced unification, if it be itself neither comprehensible nor verifiable! Moreover, dualisms, upon which in certain directions thought strikes as upon something ultimately conceivable, need not on that account be the ontological ultimate. Behind the dualisms there may in fact exist quite other fundamental relations, pluralisms or monisms of Being. And although such possibilities can be reckoned with only hypothetically, it is nevertheless evident that merely to leave the question open takes away all ambiguity from the dualism which has presented itself. We do not know the "ultimate"; and we must never regard the farthest conceivable as the ontologically final.

But a further question runs in this fashion: Is the dualism of causal and finalistic determination in the ethical problem really the ultimate of conceivability? This question can be confidently answered in the negative. The ontological perspective which categorial analysis opens out before us is in reality quite different and much wider. We must not detach the ethical problem from the wider metaphysical background. This in fact certainly gives a very different picture. It no longer belongs to ethics in the narrower sense and can be developed only in a universal doctrine of the categories. But at least as a perspective it can be presented here without restriction and with no other confirmation than its own import. Its justification must be reserved for another and more radical analysis.

The perspective itself can be developed from the point of view of categorial stratification as follows:

## (b) Types of Determination, their Ontological Relation to Stratification

Behind determinational dualism there is a pluralism which, viewed as a whole, is more unitary than the dualism. Causality and finalism for instance are ontologically far removed from being the only types of determination. There are many; every department of being has its own; more correctly stated, every stratum of being that is categorially higher has a type of determination which is higher, every lower stratum one that is lower. But we are not acquainted with them all, especially not with the higher. Of the lower, however, some may be cited.

There is a special type of mathematical determination which penetrates all relations of quantity, size and measure. It is given in the necessity of mathematical inference, as it is present and conceived in every calculation. It is far removed from being merely an ideal law or merely a law of thought. It is at the same time a law of actual existence, and indeed is more elemental than the law of causality. It is not as such a law of the temporal process; but, being more elemental (stronger) and more universal, it accompanies the temporal processes; it is in the causal nexus which controls the process, being contained there as a categorial element and presupposed. And upon it rests the mathematical calculability of natural events.

But even mathematical determination is not the most fundamental. Beyond it there exists a still more general kind, which has nothing to do with relations of quantity and size, but with the relations of Being in general. In the ideal sphere of Being it is known as logical determination, and is ordinarily formulated as the "law of sufficient reason." This has nothing to do with causal sequence in time nor with mathematical inferences concerning quantity; but it reappears transformed in both. And in the domain of real existence there is a quite similar mode of determination, which is approximately conceivable in the relations of dependence among the most general categorial elements. For instance, it can be understood most definitely in the interdependence of the modalities, in which the determinational law at the basis of all the special types of nexus can as such be brought into view.[1] This "ontologically primary" determination undergoes many transformations through all the higher realms of being and their specific determinational types. So far as can be seen, it is the most universal foundation.

From these few examples one may see that the question concerns a thorough-going relationship of strata. Every existent stratum has its peculiar categorial complex, and to each of these a particular type of determination belongs. And as according to the laws of stratification[2] the categories of every lower stratum are transformed in the higher one and reappear strengthened in something specifically new, so naturally the lower determinational types also reappear in the higher. But it has been proved that wherever the laws of stratification hold, the basic categorial law and also its corollaries, the law of material and that of freedom, are valid. We can there see in advance that in the superposition of different determinational types there is a connection, ontological and throughout unitary, between different kinds of determination, and that in this connection the lower kind is always the stronger and more fundamental, while the higher is the weaker and materially the more conditioned, but nevertheless in its higher distinctiveness is "free."

This changes the situation, in so far as the moral freedom of man, thus viewed, is only a special case of the categorial freedom which appears from stratum to stratum. But at the same time the picture is changed in another particular. In the causal antinomy, the causal nexus and that which is axiologically directed are diametrically opposed to each other. At first glance the opposition strikes one as more glaring than it is in fact. The reason is that several strata have been overleaped, strata

[1] Cf. Chapter V (c), Vol. III.     [2] Cf. Chapter XXXV (c), Vol. II.

the determinational types of which we of course do not
know but whose presence we cannot on that account doubt.

The causal nexus is the determinational type connecting
physical bodies and processes. Upon it is raised, as next in
height, an evidently different determination, the biological,
which together with the more general causal connection contains besides an unknown novelty. Men have often enough in
vitalistic theories regarded this novelty as equivalent to the
finalistic nexus. But this is of course a premature identification—in our ignorance of any matter we involuntarily snatch
at the next higher type that is known—, yet the tendency which
here comes to expression is not without justification. For it
must be a higher type. The type is manifested in the peculiar
systematic functioning of the organism, in its self-preservation
and self-development, its reproduction, in the merging of the
individual with the life of the species and in the descent of the
species, which is in truth an ascent. It is as perverse to wish
to explain these phenomena by mechanistic causation, as it is
unjustifiable to interpret them teleologically without further
grounds for doing so. We know only the determinational type
of the mechanical world and then, several strata higher, that
of man's purposive activity. And on that account we are disposed in naïve fashion to start with the presupposition that
the organic world which undoubtedly as regards its stratum
lies between the two, must be determined either causally or
teleologically. But this is nothing but the $\pi\rho\hat{\omega}\tau o\nu$ $\psi\epsilon\hat{\upsilon}\delta o\varsigma$. And
it cannot be avoided, so long as we cling to the narrow outlook
upon a special problem—upon a single stratum of existence.
But the error is evident the moment we extend the view to the
determinational relationship between strata.

To assert that we cannot scientifically understand the biological type of determination is to say little. Whether we shall
ever understand it is a matter of indifference as regards the
fact of its existence; it is only a question of biological investigation; and that the investigation must pursue the path
from below upward (from the causal nexus), must not deceive

us in regard to the non-causal weft (the categorial *novum*) of organic determination. At all events ontologically there is no doubt concerning the fact of the intermediate member.

But it is not the only intermediate member. In the midst of the biological realm consciousness emerges, as a new, and once more a higher, mode of being. We find it always bound to an organism, originating and vanishing with it; and nevertheless it is something essentially different. We can follow the transition here still less than between mechanism and organism; yet it is given in this linking of consciousness to the organism and through its inclusion in the evolving temporal character of the natural process. There can be no doubt, on the other hand, as to the uniqueness of the law of consciousness. But the distinctive note of its inner determinational mode, in so far as it rises independently above that of the organism, is not on that account comprehensible. Hence we stand here face to face with a further, an unknown and perhaps in principle an irrational mode of determination, the psychological mode. Here also— from the side of naturalistic psychology—attempts have been repeatedly made to understand the order of consciousness according to the analogy of mechanical uniformity. Naturally such attempts could not but fail. They all rest upon the same πρῶτον ψεῦδος as the analogous attempts in biological theory. But the scheme of the finalistic nexus is just as little suitable here, although the domain of consciousness stands very near to the realm where finalism is valid.

Above consciousness as a temporal real psychic Being and, once more, exempted from its psychological law, although resting upon it as a basis, rises for the first time the world of spirit. It also has more than one stratum; and one of its strata is the ethos with its relation to values. Here it is no longer consciousness, the subject, but the person, which is the central fact. The categorial relationship in which subjectivity and personality stand to each other has been ontologically treated in another part of this book;[1] all that is now needed is to

---

[1] Cf. Chapter XXIV (*d*), Vol. I.

bring the result of that presentation into the total perspective. Subjectivity exists without personality, but personality does not exist without subjectivity. Consciousness is the categorial basis, the "material" upon which the higher formation of the person is built. Hence there is also here a stratification, where the categorial laws of dependence hold good. Personality is the higher category, consciousness the stronger and more general. And precisely on this account the distinctive novelty of personality as such is categorially "free" as regards the order of consciousness, free in everything which appears as really distinctive of it. This is why the teleology of man, his valuational consciousness and his moral freedom cannot be wholly explained by psychological factors. In it a determination of a unique and higher kind reigns, anchored not in the subject— just as little as in the organism or in the causal mechanism—, but in the ideal realm of values.

### (c) The General Twofold Law of Strength and Freedom

The series of the existential strata and of the determinational types corresponding to them is by no means exhausted by what has been said above. Neither in the upward nor in the downward direction can one lay one's finger upon anything as really the "last." But there is also no need of doing so. Any discernible section is sufficient to enable us to know the law of the whole concatenation. The latter is the categorial order of dependence, or the twofold law of strength and freedom.

Each of the determinations involved in the total stratification is dependent upon the whole series of the lower ones; it is "weaker" than these, is conditioned by them and narrower in the extent of its validity. But it is never dependent upon the higher determinations; it is stronger, more fundamental than these, and wider in extent of validity. Herein the basic categorial law is fulfilled in the stratification of the determinational types. There is accordingly no personality, no teleology, without consciousness; no consciousness without organic life; no organic life without a causal structure of nature (mechanism in the wide sense); no causal mechanism without mathematical order; no mathematical entity without the ontologically primal and basic relations. This is also why there is never a really complete personality of a higher order than the single human person (inasmuch as only he is linked to a consciousness); this is also why there is no finalistic nexus without a causal nexus, why freedom can exist only "in the positive sense"—never in the negative—and only where the lower determination prevails. Hence is manifested here the ontological law which forbids indeterminism (even of a partial kind) as well as teleological determinism on a cosmic scale. Indeterminism would make a chasm in the structure, and thereby shatter the higher formation, the distinctive existence of which is in question; but cosmic teleology would be an inversion of the basic categorial law, and would thereby destroy completely the significance of the finite being.

On the other hand, however, this dependence is only that of a one-sided conditionality. The higher determination in its distinctive character is never determined by the lower. Hence the lower is only a structural element, only "material" for the higher, and the latter has scope above it; that is, the lower does not interfere with its individuality, allowing it to be built above, to be super-determined. In this respect the relation of the higher to the lower is seen to be that of form to matter. Matter is passive, indifferent, non-resisting as regards form. But form as against matter is "free." It is indeed bound by what is determined in the matter and can have free play only within the area which matter grants to it. But this determinacy does not refer to the individuality of the higher (of the form). Its scope has limits only "in the downward direction"—only as regards the lower determination—; "in the upward direction" it extends to infinity.

This spatial metaphor, applied to the relative altitude of the strata, helps us to visualize the comprehensive validity of the law of freedom. It is a mistake to suppose that the complete determinism of a lower nexus could invalidate the autonomy of a higher stratum of structures and their determination. It is an utter misconception of the matter to imagine that the mathematical order could determine Nature, the mechanical order the organic world, the organic order psychic life, or the psychological order spiritual being. When once we have seen this truth, we understand that anyone completely misses the mark, if for the sake of the autonomy of a higher determination he thinks himself obliged to accept indeterminism as regards the lower existential strata. He fails to understand the autonomy of the higher. Rather is every higher determination *eo ipso* autonomous and "free," despite its inferior strength and its material dependence. It can of course achieve nothing contrary to the lower, but it can achieve everything with it and through it—but this only means that the lower is the stronger.

For this reason indeterminism of every kind—as an interruption of a determination within its own area—is not only a theory which is false but is one which fails to understand the problem to be solved. For every lower nexus leaves the existential stratum of a higher one undetermined. From its point of view all that is more complex and categorially higher is only so far "contingent." Only from the point of view of the higher and specialized determination is it necessary. Hence the mathematical order is not to be explained by the merely logical or the ontologically primal (the modal) order, nor the causal nexus by mathematical principles. For the latter, the causal nexus is "contingent." But organic life is equally contingent from the point of view of the bare causal nexus; psychic life, from the organic point of view; the ethos of personality with its active teleology of values, from that of psychological connections. At every stage the higher form exhibits a new autonomy.

How strong the indeterministic prejudice still is in our times we can infer from the various new attempts to defend it. Among them that of Boutroux deserves special consideration on account of its metaphysical outlook.[1] Boutroux also starts from a kind of stratification of uniformities. But with him no law is uninterrupted or valid without exceptions. They all determine only in part the structure of the existential stratum to which they belong; they leave them in part undetermined and open for other kinds of determination. Hence all laws have a certain contingency as to their validity; they are under no strict necessity. Also in this interpretation the higher order always is free as regards the lower—but only in so far as the latter has gaps in it. Naturally then freedom of the will is a special case; it is indeterminateness, negative freedom.

This theory is profoundly instructive on account of its two weaknesses. In the first place there is nothing to prove the "contingency" of laws of Nature. In the whole circle of natural laws, so far as they can be known, we are acquainted with no gaps in their validity. Time and again, science has had the experience that laws which do not hold good throughout prove upon closer investigation to have been falsely observed or falsely conceived; that is, they are not the real laws of nature. As soon as one has penetrated to the essence of the matter, forthwith complete necessity and universality are restored. And in the second place, granted that contingency really existed, it would contribute nothing to positive freedom—of course also nothing to the contrary—, much rather would it stand in complete neutrality. However paradoxical it sounds, there can be no doubt that a perfectly determined existence provides as much scope for new determinations from other quarters as does imperfectly determined existence. In general, there is ontologically no limit at all to the possibilities of further complexity in the determining factors; the determination can always go on indefinitely further, namely, "in the upward direction." There is no absolutely last and definitive determination. To express the matter bluntly: in its own way one determinant determines just as completely as ten raised to the tenth power; the only difference is that the existential

[1] Emile Boutroux, *De la contingence des lois de la nature*, Paris, 1913.

height of the determined structure and its complexity are different. To every $n$ elements that make up a closed complex, a 1-plus-$n$th-element can always be added without any destroying of the $n$ elements. But thereby the total resultant must be different. Thus at any time an axiological component can be joined to the given natural categories (physical or psychical), without encroachment upon them. They will be contained undisturbed in the direction of the Will, but this itself will be a different direction. With causality there is no conflict at all; hence there is no conflict to be avoided by any contingency-hypothesis.

The only question is concerning the proof as to the non-causal origin of the new determinant. But this proof cannot be established by any relaxation of the laws of Nature. Never within a lower determination can scope for a higher one be sought—so long as we seek it there, we arrive at most astonishing hypotheses—; only above the lower can such scope exist. But there it is always unlimited.

### (d) THE GENERAL GRADES OF CATEGORIAL FREEDOM AND THE SPECIAL CASE OF FREEDOM OF WILL

Ontologically freedom in the positive sense is not an exceptional phenomenon. It inheres not only in man; it is common to all strata of Being, and is variously graded. It exists in every stratum in relation to all lower ones. Hence it attains its highest grade in the highest stratum. In its own way an animal is free as compared with inanimate nature, which is clearly manifested in its self-movement, its sensitivity, and so on; consciousness is free as compared with the organism to which it is bound. At all events the freedom which inheres in man's volitional determination is a very different one, and is by no means to be placed on a level with that of consciousness or that of an animal. But just such a difference runs through the whole series of the strata. In each one the freedom is entirely different, and not only in degree but also qualitatively. It is each time conditioned by the peculiarity of the determinational types which are erected upon the lower one. But the categorial principle, upon which their manifestation depends, always remains the same.

For in the one principle running through all is to be found the reason why the Will also, notwithstanding its causal determinedness, can nevertheless be free in its axiological relation, and why the finalistic nexus, notwithstanding the fact that it is conditioned by the causal nexus, nevertheless in comparison with it is self-subsistent in a world already determined causally throughout.

If we consider the freedom of the will in this wide connection, it does not constitute a unique problem. It is one of many grades of the categorial freedom which reappears from stratum to stratum. This derogates in no way from its significance. But it adds to the significance of the other phenomena of freedom which are parallel to it. Fundamentally these have no less import. It is simply that for man and his outlook upon life they are not of equal urgency and on that account are easily disregarded. For freedom of the will is the only basis of man's ethical Being. But in itself the fact is no less significant, that the autonomy of organic life rests upon the mechanism of systems of energy which are bound together only causally, that the autonomy of consciousness is based upon organic matter and that the strata of spiritual life in their turn rest in their autonomy upon a psychic basis.

What so particularly intensifies the causal antinomy is precisely the failure to recognize the intermediate members. If we knew how the categorial structure of organic and psychic determination is constituted—and perhaps still more how the intervening grades—, the causal antinomy would undoubtedly assume a very different character. Then the question would be concerning the contrast between organic and axiological determination, or even between merely psychological and axiological. The two are entirely different antinomies. But the fundamental categorial relation—strength and height, material and freedom—even here is the same. Hence the way in which the antinomy would need to be solved would not be different. Whether stages are overleaped or not, is a matter of no significance to it. For however small or great the categorial separation in height may be, the lower determination always is the stronger; but the higher, being above it, is "free."

*Section III*

THE ANTINOMY OF THE OUGHT

# CHAPTER VIII (LXXII)

## CRITICISM OF THE KANTIAN DOCTRINE OF FREEDOM

### (a) THE CAUSAL ANTINOMY: ITS LIMIT

AN antinomy which can be solved is not a genuine antinomy. The self-contradiction involved in it is not native to it, not being inherent in the essence of the matter. It exists only for a certain kind of human presentation, for a particular way of viewing the subject. When we have mastered this, we see the opposition to be merely a false appearance. It is to Kant's credit that he solved the causal antinomy, that is, that he showed it to be a false appearance, even if he did not give clear expression to this fact. The illusion, however, becomes perfectly clear, when we remove the idealistic drapery from his doctrine of freedom and trace back its metaphysical meaning to the simple categorial law which is distinctly recognizable behind it.

In the foregoing chapters this task was of course not so much accomplished as hinted at. But the larger ontological background in which moral freedom is set needed to be clearly outlined. It has revealed the fact that behind the seeming antithesis lies a simple determinational relationship of stratification and dependence. Thereby a swarm of crude errors is swept away.

The positive result may be summed up thus: neither the causal nexus nor any other kind of lower determination offers any obstacle to "freedom in the positive sense," that is, to an autonomy of ethico-teleological determination of the will by valuational principles, which outside the will can determine no real structure. In the sphere of ethically actual life the autonomy of moral principles may herewith be accepted as ontologically certified.

But it is another question whether the problem of freedom is hereby already solved, indeed whether it is on the whole fathomed to its depth and in detail. Here the greatest surprise awaits the investigator. Kant was the first to note the incrustation of embarrassing difficulties, but he failed to penetrate far into them. And, moreover, it was his idealistic rationalism which set a limit to his insight. The relation to the causal nexus—and, if one takes a wider view, to every lower determination—is not the only relation which is involved in the question of freedom.

Kant was right in maintaining that the will is not in need of being less determined, but of being more determined than a merely natural entity. In place of the phrase "not determined from without," the positive phrase must be introduced "so much the more determined from within." But since inner determination wholly attaches to the ethical principle, a transformation of the problem is here tacitly assumed. Freedom of the will refers, according to Kant, exclusively to the autonomy of the principle. He had a certain right to be satisfied with this point of view; for him the principle is anchored in the practical reason. His moral law is valid as a legislative act of reason. And it is, moreover, this same reason which demonstrates its freedom in following the moral law. But, subordinating itself to its own law, it is actually determined by itself. Hence the autonomy of the principle is its own autonomy.

(b) The πρῶτον ψεῦδος of "Transcendental Freedom"

Yet herein is contained a whole nest of arbitrary assumptions. Especially has it been shown to be false, that moral principles emanate from reason. But even granted that this were so, we should thereby have only a "transcendental freedom" of reason, not the freedom of the person as an individual entity; hence not a freedom of the will. In the Kantian sense, "reason" is not individual, but is the universal reason in which individuals participate. The "moral law" is the principle of a "transcendental subject," a practical "consciousness in general," not otherwise than the twelve categories are principles of a theoretical "consciousness in general." Hence transcendental freedom is not at all freedom of the moral person. For he is merely the empirical individual.

Now consider what this means exactly. By moral freedom we mean that self-dependence of the human being which enables him to impute something to himself as a value or disvalue, to assume responsibility, to be guilty of something. If, however, the freedom—that is, the positive decisive authority for his own commitments, resolution and so on—does not inhere in him as an individual person but in some universal "practical reason," then what he does cannot be imputed to him, but only to the "free" entity which stands behind him, hence to universal practical reason. It, not the man himself, bears the responsibility and the guilt.

Accordingly a new πρῶτον ψεῦδος is here exposed to view, and indeed this time it is one which emerges into view only on the farther side of the causal antinomy (when this has been solved),—a mistake to which Kant was prone on account of his predisposition to regard the problem of freedom as concerned only with the causal antinomy. As a matter of fact, the meaning of the problem is thereby altogether missed. Kant means to prove the freedom of the will; yet he does not notice that he is actually proving something altogether different— something, to be sure, which is essential as a presupposition of freedom of the will but is nevertheless not that freedom itself: what he proves is merely that the principle is autonomous.

Now if we also grant that the principle is a principle of reason, still man's view of the significance of his capacity to bear responsibility and to be the carrier of moral values and disvalues is not in any way affected thereby. In the problem of freedom man does not want to know in how far a "transcendental subject" is responsible and accountable for him, but in how far he himself is so. The meaning of all approval and disapproval, all reproach, of every accusation or punishment would with one stroke fall away, if his individual responsibility and guilt should prove to be illusory.

## (c) THE OUGHT AND THE WILL: THE SECOND ANTINOMY OF FREEDOM

Further reflection brings us still nearer to the root of Kant's error. The universal fact in regard to ethical consciousness is this: it possesses autonomous principles, but it is not coerced into following them. Whether they consist in an imperative or in a diversity of values is a matter of indifference. In any case it is only an Ought, a demand upon consciousness which issues from the principles. Pre-eminently with Kant a conspicuous part is played by the fact that the moral law does not determine the will in the same way in which natural laws determine things—hence not at all as a law but as a command. But it inheres in the essence of a command, that it can be transgressed. In the categorial analysis of value and the Ought, it was this general circumstance upon which all nearer specifications depended.

But for the person this means that he is not bound to the moral claim of the principle. He may grasp the trend of the commandment and surrender himself to it, but he may also not seize upon it, indeed he may expressly reject it. Naturally in the latter case he is determined by other powers—whether these be only natural forces in him, inclinations, impulses, instincts, or moral tendencies from other sources, which prove to be stronger. Were his will coerced by the Ought, it would not be a moral will and his decision could not be imputed to him. He is responsible only in so far as he is not constrained, that is, only so far as he has in face of the principle a freedom for or against. Hence it follows that freedom subsists not only as against natural law, but also as against the Ought as a principle. The Ought and the Will do not coincide. Also they are not necessarily in opposition. Nevertheless there is a disparity between them. And to this is due the fact that they can be opposed to each other.

Herein is the crux of the antinomy which is new and which is an addition to that of causality, the antinomy between the Ought and the Will. Even here, before the term can be shown to be justifiable, it may be shortly designated as "the Ought-antinomy."

With it a new stage in the problem of freedom begins. The causal antinomy with its whole complex of problems is only preliminary. It is concerned with the freedom of the will only as against the general uniformity of existence. Now it is seen that this uniformity, however much it may be the pre-supposition of moral freedom, is not enough. It is only half of the problem. Still a second freedom of the same will must be added, freedom over against the moral principle itself.

Naturally this freedom also must be "freedom in the positive sense." It cannot consist in indeterminedness, but only in a determination *sui generis*. For even in this connection the moral will is not an undetermined will. But it must not be the determinedness of the tendency inherent in the Ought, hence not determination issuing from the principle. It must be a determination which accompanies the principle and yet is independent of it. What then determines the moral consciousness to decide for or against the principle? That it cannot be the principle is evident. But this is only the negative side of the matter. Thus far one only sees that with the autonomy of the principle and the reality of its scope above the causal nexus nothing has been gained in regard to the positive essence of freedom, or even in regard to its ontological possibility as a self-subsistent counter-authority residing in the individual person, set over against not only the causal context of actuality, but also against the ideal Ought-to-Be of values.

The mistake on this point, into which theories of freedom usually fall, lies in the presupposition that a will is so much the more a moral will in proportion as it is directed to moral values and is determined by them. But this is true only upon the presupposition of an individually free decision for the principle. Without such a decision there is no morality in the fulfilment of values. Even if the person were unconditionally determined by moral principles, still he would not on that account be "morally good," for he would not be free. Then his consciousness would simply be subjected to an authority which would be outside of him, in some cases over him. He could not be identified with the authority, hence could not be responsible for what he did, willed or even merely consented to under its determination. Such a will would be neither good nor bad. It would be subject to the moral law (respectively to values) just as a process of nature is subject to natural laws. In it morality, equally with immorality, would be nullified. Much rather, therefore, would a Will morally perfect in this sense be morally indifferent, that is, it would no longer be a moral will at all.

It is a radical mistake to regard a person's mere fulfilment of value as morality. From this mistake spring a host of fundamental errors. The greatest conformity to values would be precisely where there was the least freedom, namely where there was complete determination by the principle. And precisely in that case there would be least morality. Only on the part of a free being, a being who, when confronted by the value could do otherwise, is conformity to value morality.

Here is shown the radical nature of the difficulty which apparently inheres in the simple fact that moral values are founded upon freedom. They are founded not only upon man's freedom as regards the causal nexus and the cosmic process, but also upon a freedom which he must have as regards the values themselves. This is something profoundly puzzling, an antinomy which inheres in the essence of the ethical Ought-to-Be itself. The Ought-to-Be of values, in so far as it bears upon man, means on the one hand that he absolutely ought to be precisely as the moral values require of him, and on the other hand that his being thus should not be absolute and inevitable. There must at least always be the capability of being otherwise; there must be no necessity of being as he ought to be, at least none issuing from the values themselves. They put in the unconditional claim to rule the life of whoever is their carrier; and nevertheless they demand that their sway shall not be unconditional. Only if he be not unconditionally determined by them do they assert the right to determine completely the human being who is capable of manifesting them.

Hence the freedom upon which moral values are based is not freedom from the causal antinomy, not freedom in the sense of unlimited scope for determination issuing from values over and above the universal ontological determination of cosmic events. This is only its *conditio sine qua non*. The service rendered by the Kantian theory is limited to the establishment of this *conditio*. Beyond that it does not reach. Kant was not acquainted with the higher stratum of the problem of freedom. He indeed tacitly presupposed it and dealt with it; but he did not draw it into the solution of the problem. On the other hand, one finds in Fichte a significant contribution to the solution of this stage of the problem. He recognized the bearing of the antinomy, which exists between the Ought and the Will, upon the question of freedom.[1] But we do not find even in him an adequate appreciation of this achievement for the metaphysical investigation of the problem. He gives only a passing

[1] Fichte, *Sittenlehre*, 1812, Vol. XI, p. 49: "The life of the ego is freedom, that is, indifference to the life of the understanding." (With Fichte the understanding is here equivalent to moral principle.) "In the actuality of appearance the ego is a unique life, which can and also cannot, a Will over against an Ought. A life which confronts the life of the understanding, which carries only an ideal form, and the energy of which attains only to the status of a law or an Ought." The view of the problem here presented scarcely leaves anything to be desired as regards precision. But instead of following up the problem, Fichte immediately passes over into his favourite notion of the "nullification of freedom."

glance into the depth of the problem. His over-hasty desire for positive results prevented quiet concentration. The idealism of the "absolute ego" provided no means of grappling with this problem. Here is seen the first open breach in the idealistic theory of freedom which recognized only a single stratum of reality.

### (d) THE KANTIAN PROBLEM OF FREEDOM AND THAT OF THE RELIGIOUS SCHOLASTICS

For Kant the problem was still simpler. He did not have the individual subject in mind, but only the ethico-transcendental "subject in general." And this coincided with the practical reason, of which the moral law was the autonomous principle. At least with him the distinction between the moral person as a "rational being" and the universal practical reason did not enter into the question of freedom, that is, into the question as to who exactly is free and carries responsibility. For him, accordingly, the freedom of the will was proved by proving the autonomy of the principle and the whole difficulty was directly disposed of with the causal antinomy. Kant does not meet the point that, when faced by the law, Reason which promulgates the law ought to have freedom of decision, that therefore, when face to face with itself, the practical reason ought to be free. Conceivably he did not meet it because the question did not arise. And if it had arisen, it must have destroyed forthwith the identity which had been set up between legislative reason and the free moral being.

Hence with Kant the problem of freedom suffers from a one-sidedness which is the more striking, when we consider that in the traditional presentation of the problem, as it prevailed among the Scholastics, there was no trace of one-sidedness. The ethics of the middle ages, which was embedded in religion, committed a different error. It conceived of man's freedom in relation to the divine purpose (to providence and predestination). Thereby it twisted the ethical meaning of freedom into an extra-ethical significance which was metaphysically much more heavily weighted and, as a problem, was itself far more difficult to understand.[1] In detaching the ethical problem from this metaphysics, Kant gained a new point of attack. But he met only half of the ethical problem.

The other half which, with his transcendental-idealistic predisposition, he did not and could not meet, was contained in the old religious conception. "Man's freedom as against God" necessarily embraced the whole meaning of ethical freedom. For even as against God the point under discussion is man's accountability, responsibility and guilt (sin). The religious interpretation is precisely this, that God not only rules providentially in natural law, but also speaks directly in the moral commandments. He is legislator, but it is to man that the commandment applies. Now if man is free only as against the course of nature, but not as against the commandments of God, then it is altogether beyond man's power to transgress the commandments, hence also to decide in accordance with them (and thereby with God).

Now just this is the characteristically religious attitude of man to God, that he can act against God, that is, can "sin" and actually does sin. One accordingly sees that in the religious problem of freedom more was contained than merely "transcendental Freedom." According to the latter, if one connects it with God, in all human transgression the guilt would need to be assigned to God. But the meaning of divine judgment is that God imputes the guilt to man. Hence man's capacity of sinning against the divine commandment is the exact religious analogue of moral freedom, not only as regards the causal nexus but also as regards moral principle (correspondingly as regards values).

The Kantian doctrine of freedom overwhelmed this side of the problem, as it had been handed down. Ethics must now dig it out again. Ethics must restore the full twofold meaning of the old idea of freedom, yet without injuring the Kantian

[1] Chapter II (a, b), Vol. III.

achievement of detaching moral freedom from the religious problem. Only by a synthesis of the Scholastic and Kantian problems can we reach the full content of the idea of freedom and, with it, the second and higher aspect of the question.

# CHAPTER IX (LXXIII)

## FALSE WAYS OF PROVING THE FREEDOM OF THE WILL

### (a) THE SO-CALLED "PROOFS" OF THE FREEDOM OF THE WILL IN GENERAL

NOTHING has been so much and so stubbornly "proved" as the freedom of the will. For man's understanding of himself —for his ethical consciousness as well as for his real ability to assume responsibility—nothing is of such decisive significance. Only he who believes that he is responsible can carry responsibility. On this account the question of the freedom of the will is the most practical and important of all questions. But to give the answer to it is perhaps the most metaphysical of all tasks. One does not exaggerate, when one says that all the proofs for the freedom of the will which have been laid down are fallacious. They are so simply for the reason that they do not clearly detach the practical question (the postulate) from the ontological question as to possibility. Either they consider the former by itself, without taking the latter into account, or they distort the latter in the interest of practical requirements. Philosophically both of these procedures are equally untenable.

Of the three kinds of error which ordinarily obscure the problem,[1] we have already discussed two in treating of the causal antinomy. The third still remains to be considered. One meets with it at the very entrance to the higher problem. It concerns the theories themselves, the methods of proof, not only the concept of freedom. As regards these methods of proof, one must not of course scrutinize them too pedantically in detail; there would then remain very little, even little of a negative nature, to learn from them. One must attend to the

[1] Cf. Chapter III (a), Vol. III.

spirit of the theories, to their way of looking at the problem. We shall then find that they are not lacking in thoughtful views which contain something attractive, so long as one does not examine them too closely. It is a subject on which the speculative skill of great thinkers has shown astonishing fertility. In the following pages we can naturally discuss only those particular theories which are typical and instructive.

Kant's error which we have just examined may be classed among the metaphysical theories which have distorted and overloaded the concept of freedom itself. It retains the form of a $\pi\rho\hat{\omega}\tau o\nu\ \psi\epsilon\hat{\upsilon}\delta o\varsigma$. With Fichte the case is different; in his elaboration of the problem he penetrated to the second and higher antinomy. But in his theory he remained far behind his own conception of the problem.

It is extraordinarily difficult to approach freedom from the right point of view. While the problem is one that concerns action, freedom itself is not on that account a kind of act to be classed with a person's other acts; it is rather something specific, which is common to all moral acts. That thinkers prefer to connect it with the will is because they choose the will as representative of all action. What then is that actional factor in all moral acts which constitutes freedom? Kant had sought for it in reason. If this was not individual reason, still it was consciousness. Hence with Kant the question under discussion was a freedom of consciousness. But the problem changes when a new level of investigation is reached.

## (b) FICHTE'S FREEDOM BEHIND CONSCIOUSNESS

We must bear three things in mind: first, that causal determination "from without," notwithstanding its cosmic universality, does not exclude inner self-determination in its own sphere; secondly, that freedom is not a negative state of being free "from something" but implies a unique determination "towards something"; and, thirdly, that this unique determination is not identical with determinedness emanating from the principle. When we bear these three points in mind, we easily find ourselves forced in the exactly opposite direction, that of seeking to discover the positive determinant at as great a depth as possible within the nature of the person, and accordingly within the subject. This tendency seeks its justification in the view that the more inward we conceive freedom to be, so much the likelier are we to find the character of positive self-determination realized in it.

In this direction the youthful Fichte took a decisive step, when (in 1794) he elaborated his theory of freedom from the point of view of his doctrine of science. The "ego" is the carrier of freedom, it is the determinant; not, however, the ego which appears empirically, but a deeper, a metaphysical ego. In the conscious ego the will already manifests itself as completely determined. Accordingly it must bring this characteristic with it from somewhere. The determinedness cannot come from this side of consciousness, from the natural world; hence it must come from beyond, from something which lies behind consciousness, from something which consequently cannot itself be conscious. The whole ego is not in consciousness. Its own proper depths are hidden. There must exist a volition prior to volition; there must be one that is metaphysical before the one that is conscious. And the prior one is the free volition, because it gives determinateness to the conscious volition. Fichte goes still farther: he sets up the "absolute ego" as identical for all consciousness and thereby falls back into the Kantian error. This is the climax of the matter. But here we may disregard it; even for Fichte it is not a theoretical necessity. Schelling, for example, following in the footsteps of Fichte, left wider scope for individuality.

But what is the consequence of this placing of freedom behind consciousness—even if one does not transcendentally universalize the background of the ego? Consciousness then is at all events not free; not the conscious will, but something else behind it which directs it is free. Now as regards this something else we do not know what it is; we do not know whether it is of the nature of a will, consequently whether its determinative power is in any sense a freedom of will. At least it is not the freedom of that Will which alone we know and to which in our sensing of morality we attribute responsibility. No benefit accrues from calling that background of the subject an ego; it is not the conscious ego which alone is known to us. Hence on the basis of such freedom it is not possible to ascribe to oneself responsibility for its volition and action. The responsibility does not fall upon that volition which I can answer for because its decision took place in the light of my consciousness, but upon the constitution of the metaphysical ego which is quite independent of my consciousness. The moral consciousness cannot be accountable for what it does not itself decide.

It is certainly a fact that we have a consciousness of freedom. But the question in regard to it is that of seeking for the explanation of it. Fichte looked for this in the depth of the ego. Now granting that he was metaphysically right in presupposing this deeper stratum, nevertheless we do not come by such a route to a freedom of consciousness—at least not when starting from the consciousness of freedom—but rather to a still vaster unfreedom of consciousness. Empirical unfreedom has become a metaphysical unfreedom. The conscious will is crippled by a determination imposed by the absolute ego.

The Fichtean freedom behind consciousness is a radically erroneous speculation. It misses exactly what it is striving for, the freedom of the moral consciousness. Hence determination through an absolute ego not only is untenable ontologically, but would be ethically wrong, even if ontologically it were correct. It would involve a radical extirpation of freedom. Unquestionably it surrenders one of Kant's essential achievements; Kant kept strictly to freedom of consciousness (although consciousness of a transcendental order). Fichte may have been quite right in holding that consciousness is something which metaphysically is secondary. But that point is not in question here. To hold that only the primary can be free is a prejudice which rests upon ignorance of categorial laws. Although consciousness be secondary, the question is, whether in the onto-logically secondary there exists something unique (a novum), which the structures that are ontologically primary do not possess. Consciousness might very well, as the higher, more complex and conditioned structure, which it ontologically is, have a determination peculiar to itself, despite its dependence and its categorial inferiority in "strength." And this would be fully adequate to allow of its moral freedom. But this question is raised neither by Fichte nor by any one of the many who refer freedom back to the depths of the irrational, which for human penetration always stands directly behind consciousness.

### (c) The "Nullification of Freedom" by Fichte in his Later Years

In its earlier phase the ethics of Fichte practically identified freedom and activity. That identification explains his failure. Naturally an activity of consciousness can have its root in a primal unconscious activity, but a freedom of conscious-ness cannot be rooted in the freedom of the unconscious. Here there is a lack of orientation to concrete phenomena, to responsibility and accountability. Not every activity is linked to responsibility, not to mention the fact that also not every responsibility depends upon an action. Indeed, freedom is radically different from activity. There exists an unfree activity as well as a free inactivity, passivity or inertia.

Fichte was well aware that here there was something not in order. And in his second period he drew the inference. But his conclusion was not in favour of freedom—also of course not in favour of activity—for he discarded both. In his "Advice concerning the Life of Blessedness" he places above ordinary morality, in which the will stands on this side of good and evil and is capable of either, a "higher morality" to which man can soar. In this higher state the will has finally committed itself to the good; hence it no longer possesses the freedom to be good or bad. It also is no longer in need of such freedom;

it has chosen once for all. Only the imperfect will needs to be free. But only until it has committed itself. The transition to the perfect will, which no longer has an Ought over it, takes place in freedom. But in this unique and final act of freedom the will "exhausts" its capacity, it "uses up" the substance of its freedom; and then for it there is "at the root of its Being no freedom left over."[1] According to this view, man's true act of freedom is the self-annihilation of freedom, and at the same time the annihilation of the ego and of the Ought.

Fichte should have added that this is also the extirpation of morality, inasmuch as the "higher morality" is in truth not morality at all. As a matter of fact the whole conception belongs to the sphere of religion, and not to ethics. In it ethics is abandoned. The demand which religion makes is different from that which morality makes. The will which can no longer choose anything but the good, is no longer a moral will; and personal values, which are not based on freedom, are no longer moral values. This does not imply that such values which are no longer moral, are altogether lower values, inasmuch as a perfect will can scarcely be of less worth than an imperfect will. The manifestation of a higher order of values in man—we may without offence call them religious values—has nothing at all repugnant to common sense in it, also nothing in contradiction to the ethos. But one must be clear on this point, that they have altogether ceased to be ethical values. For the latter are necessarily grounded on freedom—at least in principle—and can no longer be manifested in a being who has "consumed" his own freedom.

"Higher morality" is a misleading term. It implies the preservation of morality beyond morality. And this is the error in Fichte's concept of a freedom that can be exhausted: it holds up before us the picture of freedom beyond freedom; it allows the perfect will which has ceased to be free to pass as a moral will and its values as moral values, as if they were still the values of a free will.

[1] Fichte, *Anweisung zum seligen Leben*, W.W.V., p. 514.

Here the second antinomy of freedom, the inner one of the Ought—which Fichte himself discovered—is totally misunderstood. For by its very essence the moral Ought exacts perfection from the imperfect will and not from the perfect,— that is, from a will which can also do otherwise, but not from one which cannot do otherwise.

### (d) SCHELLING: FREEDOM, APPARENT AND ABSOLUTE

Another view, more closely allied to Fichte's earlier teaching, was advocated by Schelling in the *System of Transcendental Idealism*. A consciousness of freedom is involved in all moral consciousness. In all its decisions the will "appears" to itself to be free. On this basis it imputes responsibility and guilt to itself. This "apparent freedom" haunts consciousness as arbitrariness. In fact, however, it is quite consistent with being determined from without. The case might be with it as with "unconscious production," whereby Schelling's idealism explained the origin of the outer world. As here the subject in beholding is not aware of his own productive activity and therefore regards as given the objects which he has produced, so in "apparent freedom" the subject could be ignorant of the powers determining his will and on that account regard himself as free. This illusion is confronted by the fact that the mere consciousness of volition is the consciousness of an activity, a spontaneity, hence also a consciousness of a self-determination.

If now we compare with this appearance an absolute will, which should really be determined only in itself, we see that the reverse difficulty meets us here. Such an absolute will is not a conscious will; its freedom is not an object of its own apprehension; hence it provides no consciousness of freedom, no apparent freedom; the will accordingly cannot be experienced by the volitional subject as its freedom. Yet in moral freedom precisely this is demanded. For in the first place the consciousness of freedom is given in the will, and in the second place the meaning of responsibility consists in the knowledge of freedom. Hence neither the freedom which merely appears but does not exist, nor that which merely exists (is absolute) but does not appear suffices for the concept of moral freedom.

Schelling escapes from this embarrassment by a synthesis of the two: "it is only the appearance of the absolute will which is freedom proper."[1] Freedom then consists in this, that to the subject the Innermost, the absolutely subjective, "becomes an object." At bottom it is an identical proposition which is to untie the knot: the essence of the freedom which appears is to be the appearance of the absolute freedom which in itself does not appear. This is easy play for the idealist. For him the meaning of whatever is in the subject—even in its primal unreflective metaphysical origins—consists in this: that the subject turns in upon itself, is reflected and thus comes to appear.

In truth the single given point of contact, after as before, is the apparent freedom. It is precisely the "absolute will" which is not given but inferred. And not until its appearance would there be real freedom of consciousness. If, after its idealistic drapery has been torn away, one understands this theory as an argument for the existence of the freedom of the will, the outline of the argument is this: there is a consciousness of freedom, therefore there must also be a freedom of consciousness. The latter is tacitly inferred, and indeed the inference is from the mere phenomenon of the thing to the existence of the thing. This unpleasantly reminds one of the old *conclusio ab essentia ad existentiam*, as it is contained in the well-known ontological proof for the existence of God: because there is a concept of a most perfect being, there must also be a most perfect being. Of course there is a difference between a phenomenon and a concept. But between an ontological inference from a phenomenon and an inference from a concept there is in principle no difference. Phenomena, like concepts, do not involve real existence. Freedom and God are not given, but both are thought of as real. And consequently there is nothing

[1] Schelling, *System des transcendentalen Idealismus*, Vol. III, p. 577.

behind the concept of God but a phenomenon, the phenomenon of the consciousness of God. Against the latter nothing more can be said than against the consciousness of freedom. But both are only facts of consciousness; from them the reality of their alleged contents cannot in the least be inferred. The analogy is most striking when the argument for the existence of God is cast into the Cartesian form: I could not have so perfect a concept, if there were not a perfect being from which I could have derived it, for it could not have emanated from me as a finite being. The same shape may be given to the argument for freedom: I could not at all have a consciousness of freedom if I were not really free, for an unfree being would not be in a position to feel himself to be free.

The error is plain. In neither case is the possibility of illusion taken into account. In the same way one could also prove the reality of the *mundus fabulosus*. Here then the specific problem of freedom is not solved; it is not even seriously stated. The problem consists in the question whether there corresponds to the consciousness of freedom a freedom of consciousness or not. If we knew beforehand of such a correspondence, no further problem would be at hand, and there would be nothing more to discuss or to prove. That there is indisputably a problem of freedom is the result of our not knowing. And the consciousness of our lack of knowledge is far removed from being an arbitrary or a merely contentious scepticism. Much rather is there something profoundly incomprehensible in the essence of freedom, something which makes the conception of it seem to be full of contradictions. In this respect also the concept of freedom is not unlike the concept of God.

From the consciousness of the actuality of a thing the actuality itself of the thing never follows necessarily, although this may be established from other quarters. Of course some actuality or other is always concealed behind a consciousness of actuality; but it may be something entirely different from what the phenomenon presents. Accordingly, just as the existence of God does not follow from the conception or from the consciousness of God, however clear, so real freedom of consciousness (that of the conscious will) never follows from the given consciousness of freedom, however unescapable and imperturbable this may be. The imperturbability might be the consequence of a necessary illusion.

This fact is in itself perfectly clear. It shows that by analysing phenomena no headway can be made with the problem of freedom—as is the case with all metaphysical problems. The fact is a demonstrable phenomenon and as such is not to be controverted.

But from this circumstance it by no means follows that there is no freedom of the will, just as little as the non-existence of God follows from it. Neither does it follow that the phenomenon does not prove something or other. But it does not prove the reality of freedom. And upon this point the question now turns. What the phenomenon of freedom really proves is still to be investigated. Like our consciousness of God, the consciousness of freedom is under the special suspicion of being bribed by partisan bias. In both cases the most vital interest of man depends upon the matter for which the phenomenon is cited as a witness. However commonplace may be the saying that the wish is father to the thought, there is in metaphysical questions of such urgency no human thought which can boast that it is above such suspicion. Step by step there is need here of critical and most sober deliberation, in order to escape from this ancient and always open pitfall of philosophy.

### (e) Leibniz' Theory of the Absolute Self-Development of the Monad

There was still another error in the line of approach taken by the older rationalistic philosophy. For it there was relatively little difficulty in proving the reality of freedom. According to Leibniz every soul is an absolute substance which receives no influence from without. It brings its state of determinacy with it into the world; hence it is the carrier of a primal determination. Every human life is then at the same time an attempt to achieve such a primal determination. For this latter has the character of a previously given end in itself, with the power of an inner principle. Although of course in this connection "soul" must not be taken as identical with consciousness, still there is a tendency to understand consciousness also in this sense. With such a primal originality on the part of every single individual we arrive at an ethical monadology, an absolute pluralism of principles, in that every single soul has its own ethical law, the fulfilment of which is laid upon it as a task, a law which it can finally know and impose upon itself as a norm.

Naturally in this theory nothing is proved or can be proved. But still it has the merit of having directed the question of freedom towards its true goal, towards a strictly individual freedom of the will. It was on this side especially that Leibniz built his theory. Of course in his doctrine of monads the individualism is metaphysically exaggerated. He admits no influence at all upon the soul from without. All determination comes from within. A monad can develop no characteristics whatever, save those inherent in its original predisposition; and these it develops inevitably. Its whole life, mental as well as physical, is self-development. Leibniz' occasional statement that the soul is a "spiritual automaton" is of course not very appropriate; for he does not mean a mechanical effect of circumstances, but a teleological sequence. It is a point in view, a determination towards something, a specific kind of unfulfilled perfection, which is hidden in the predisposition of the monad. And only for this reason is the life-process in it a development. In this sense the statement is to be understood, that everything which takes place in the soul depends upon the soul, "and as the on-coming condition is determined only by it and its present condition, no greater independence can be given to it than in this world-picture."[1] Freedom consists in this greatest

[1] Leibniz, *Théodicée*, 64.

possible independence—for in the "present condition" is concealed the primal predisposition, the teleological determination—, hence this freedom is from beginning to end a real, a metaphysical, not an "apparent" freedom.

If this theory, after its exaggerations have been removed, could be verified, one might think that here freedom of the will in the genuine and distinctive sense must necessarily be proved. Behind the individual will, directing it, there stands no general law, no transcendental subject, no absolute ego. Even in its metaphysical foundation it is individual. Hence what a man does, wills or even only bears within himself as an inner commitment, is to be attributed to himself alone. He is an absolutely accountable and responsible being.

And still this is not the case. Here another mistake is committed: the freedom of the monad is not the freedom of consciousness, but that of a deeply unconscious metaphysical entity. Already in his predisposition man is here actually predestined. He cannot will or act otherwise than he must, with his given predisposition. From the beginning he has indelibly a character which he did not himself create nor choose, and he remains bound to it. This is shown in the circumstance that not alone do the will and the ethos, but also all the inclinations, feelings, affections, in short the whole structure of his mental being, possess this greatest possible independence. Indeed, ultimately the same holds good concerning all entities, even the lowest, which have no consciousness, and the totality of which constitute nature so-called. "To draw the question of freedom to a close, it must be recognized that, strictly taken, the soul contains in itself the principle of all its actions, and even of all its passions, and that the same holds good concerning all the simple substances which are spread throughout nature, while freedom exists only in intelligent substances."[1] The last clause is characteristic. In it is a recognition that a consciousness of inner determination is inherent in freedom proper. Nevertheless, with all monads the principle is the

_____
[1] *Op. cit.*, 65.

same: and a stone accordingly would be just as independent, just as much inwardly determined as a man.

In this one sees clearly that the self-unfoldment of the monad is anything but moral freedom; and all the illustrations which Leibniz cites to the contrary are either inconsistent with his theory or incompatible with freedom of the will. There lies at the very basis of his theory a thorough-going teleological determinism; and we have shown above how this allows no room for freedom.[1] With Leibniz also freedom is traced back to the unconscious depth of the human being, and thereby its moral character is lost. The whole import of the question here lies in the "greatest possible independence" of outward influence. But moral freedom by no means consists in such independence. Far more characteristic of it is inner self-dependence. Leibniz indeed was mindful of this, but it is not the self-dependence of the conscious moral will, but that of an inner fate, which rules over the will and in it. Yet under all circumstances, however individual it may be, fate is the absolute opposite of freedom.

### (f) SCHOPENHAUER'S DOCTRINE CONCERNING INTELLIGIBLE CHARACTER

Many successors have fallen into the Leibnizian error. Most notorious is the vulgarization of the theory by Schopenhauer. Here the substantial character of the soul is surrendered and with it absolute independence from without. The universal domination of natural causality, even in the life of the soul, is recognized, as it was by Kant. Empirically man is unfree. But appeal is made to the primal self-determination of man. Schopenhauer rightly saw that such an appeal is not prevented by causal determinism in so far as he bases himself upon Kant's solution of the causal antinomy. And he goes still a step further than Kant. Kant had referred freedom to the "intelligible character." But it remained unsettled whether this was

[1] Cf. Chapter V (e), Vol. III.

an individual character or a general one. With Kant the evidence for its existence was the unity of the practical reason, but it was applied to the individual person and his moral self-determination.

Schopenhauer passes beyond this ambiguity, in that by him in Leibnizian fashion the intelligible character is individualized. According to him every man has his own intelligible character. At the beginning this is once for all given to him, it is unalterable; it is a genuinely indelible character. The amusing metaphysical adornments which Schopenhauer knew how to bestow upon this notion are not pertinent here. There is ultimately a primal unitary power, the world-will, which stands behind the intelligible character, and this is indeed a teleological power, even if values are not its goal (one might rather infer from Schopenhauer that it aimed at disvalues). The construction of a super-temporal act of choice is of no use here; it is altogether an impossibility, because it already presupposes the very same freedom of choice which the intelligible character was to explain. At all events man, the secondary product as he exists, the empirical, conscious, and (as he thinks) morally responsible being, already has his indestructible character in himself, and can never go counter to it. He is enmeshed in his metaphysical determination.

It is most astonishing how Schopenhauer could believe that with this theory he had proved the freedom of the will. Even if one concedes to him all his unproved premises, still his thesis as to intelligible character would be the extreme opposite of that autonomy of the person, which alone would be ethical freedom of the will. His proposition affirms the direct antithesis to genuine freedom of the will. If it were proved, freedom of the will would thereby be finally disproved. Theoretical confusion in argument could not go further.

But the ground of the error is the same, not only as in Leibniz and Schelling, but also as in Fichte. An argument which proves the autonomy of something different from the conscious will itself, hence the freedom of some power which stands behind it, proves in fact something altogether different from freedom of will. Indeed, thereby it surrenders this completely. Such was precisely Fichte's mistake: a freedom behind consciousness nullifies the freedom of the conscious will and of the moral personality.

# THE PRESENT STATE OF THE PROBLEM

## (a) CONCLUSIONS CONCERNING THE NATURE OF FREEDOM

ALL these confusions in the theory are instructive in this, that through them the state of the problem (since the solution of the causal antinomy) is clear in its details. Approximately we can now say what properly inheres in the nature of the freedom of the will and what is theoretically required by it.

1. The causal antinomy showed that there must be positive freedom, not indeterminateness but determination of a peculiar kind.

2. The determining factor must not lie outside of the subject (or person), hence not even in the values or any other autonomous principles.

3. The determining factor must also not be set indefinitely deep in the subject, but only in the conscious stratum; otherwise there is no moral freedom (Fichte's mistake). Hence freedom must lie neither on the hither nor on the further side of consciousness, but solely in it itself.

4. Yet the determining factor must also not be assumed to inhere in a consciousness that is super-individual, for instance, in the "practical reason" (Kant's error); otherwise it is not freedom of the person. Hence the Kantian interpretation of freedom of consciousness must be reconciled with the Leibnizian theory of individual self-determination. There must be a freedom of the individual conscious will.

5. There must be freedom in two senses: not only freedom over against the regularity of nature (the causal nexus and any other ontological determinations), but equally there must be freedom over against moral principles and the demands of the Ought—whether over against an imperative or against the values (the antinomy of the Ought). The will must have scope

precisely as regards those principles by which as a moral will
it ought to allow itself to be determined.

### (b) THE APORIÆ INHERENT IN MORAL FREEDOM

In these main features, which are required by the nature
of freedom itself, there lies a whole series of questions which
may be summed up in the following list of difficulties. That
these could not have been brought together before was a
consequence of the metaphysical obscurity of the subject-
matter. One cannot simply pick them out from among the
naïvely given constituents of the ethical phenomenon, seeing
that they do not manifest themselves until a higher stage of
the problem has been reached. Whatever permits of being
seen on the level that has been attained has also of course
the character of a phenomenon—all genuine aporiæ depend
upon demonstrable phenomena—but here the phenomenon
has been already transferred from its original place, as given
in the naïve consciousness of freedom. The preliminary investigation which we have now made exposes to view for the
first time the new and deeper phenomenon. It was necessary
first to remove from the subject-matter the prejudices which had
become current.

The five features which have been given above present the
phenomenon of the freedom of the will, not as it is naïvely
discerned but as it must be seen after it has been criticized
philosophically, if it is to correspond in other respects to the
meaning of "moral freedom," to which moral values according
to their nature are essentially related.

First Aporia. How can freedom of the will exist in the
midst of a world completely determined? This question has
been answered above, in so far as ontological determination
(the causal nexus, the regularity of nature) is concerned. But
the difficulty is not solved, in so far as axiological determination
is also involved in cosmic determination. In accord with the
antinomy of the Ought, independence of moral principles

(of values) inheres universally in the meaning of moral freedom.

Second Aporia. How can the will be free as against the principle to which as a moral will it ought to be subject? Must it then not be at the same time determined and not determined by the principle? Here how evident is the contradiction! Is not the meaning of freedom here abandoned as well as that of the moral Ought? For precisely this Ought, which in its tendency to determine the will suspends freedom, presupposes at the same time in its own nature the relation to freedom. Hence in its tendency it suspends the very thing which is a condition of its existence.

Third Aporia. But granted that the second difficulty has been wholly solved, there would still remain another problem in connection with the first. The causal antinomy showed that, in a world already fully determined, only positive (not negative) freedom is possible, that is, only the addition of a new determinant. In so far as there is to be moral freedom, this determinant must inhere in the ethical principle (the moral law, the value). But if in the new phase of the problem (in the antinomy of the Ought) a freedom is also demanded for the will over against the ethical principle, the principle is thereby suspended as the determinant which is to be added. If the will is to be able to decide for or against the principle, evidently it cannot at the same time be determined by the principle. Accordingly that factor is here suspended, whereby the causal antinomy was soluble. Accordingly either the solution of the causal antinomy vanishes or the meaning of freedom as against the principle. In other words, the significance of the Ought-antinomy contradicts the solution of the causal antinomy: if the will is determined by the ethical principle, it is unfree as regards that principle; but if it is not determined by the principle, it is unfree in relation to natural law. In both cases, therefore, it is not a free will.

Fourth Aporia. Viewed from another side, the question presents itself in this form: How can freedom as against the principle be positive? It means simply that the will can act one way or another! But this open alternative is the form of "freedom in the negative sense," of negative freedom of choice, concerning which it was shown that it is not freedom of the will.[1] The free will is certainly not an undetermined will; but prior to the choice the will is an undetermined will. Does then the antinomy of the Ought require that freedom shall again be "indeterminateness" and thereby fall back into all the old contradictions, from which the solution of the causal antinomy delivered it?

Fifth Aporia. But granted that the third and fourth difficulties are fully met, the question still remains: How can positive freedom be individual? According to the causal antinomy, it consists in determinateness of will through the principle. But the principle is universal—whether it be a value or a moral law. Yet freedom must be freedom of the individual person. Otherwise responsibility and guilt would fall upon the principle and not upon the person. Now the principle has autonomy. But the person, so far as he is morally free, must not merely be subject to its autonomy, but must in face of it be able to decide either for or against. What then is the determinant in the person? It also must be something positive, and indeed autonomously positive, without being the autonomy of the principle. Hence the person must have his own individual autonomy in the presence of that of the moral principle. But then in the freedom of the will we have to do with an antinomy of the two autonomies, with that of the principle and that of the person. Yet as the freedom of the will is concerned with one and the same determination of one and the same will, the question arises: How can the two autonomies co-exist in this freedom?

Sixth Aporia. In face of this antithetic, which is so acute on every side, the basic question finally becomes a matter of prime importance: What exactly forces us to assume the individual freedom of the person as against the principle? Before any discussion the answer can be given: the ethical phenomena

[1] Cf. Chapter III (f), Vol. III.

solely and alone. There is absolutely nothing else which could speak for it. Yet phenomena as such prove nothing; appearance (even in the objective sense) is not existence, the consciousness of freedom is not actual freedom but merely apparent freedom.[1] Ontologically considered, phenomena can also be illusory. Nevertheless it is not to be gainsaid, that purely as phenomena they possess their own validity and that every theory, even though it be concerned with the existence of the thing itself, must at least be in harmony with the phenomena. Where then is the way out of this circle? If we start with the phenomena of the moral consciousness, how can a firm foothold be won for the existence of moral freedom?

### (c) The Third Antinomy of Freedom behind the Second

Of these six difficulties the last stands apart. The other five are closely connected with one another; they embrace the Ought-antinomy. One and the same antithetic is at the basis of them all; it simply is seen again and again from different sides.

The new element in the problem appears most clearly in the fifth difficulty. Previous to this it seemed that in the freedom of the will only one single antinomy was contained, hence also only one kind of ethical determination proper, and that for the proof of freedom the only question was concerning the possibility of including this kind of determination in the general structure of the world as ontologically determined. In that case the scheme of the causal antinomy would remain determinant for the higher problem. This is now shown to be an error. Together with the first there appears a second antinomy, a unique determination of the person in relation to that of the principle. And the question arises: Of what kind is this new determinant? Has it also the quality of an Ought, like the principle? Or is it an orderliness which determines, like a law of nature, by compulsion? In the former case, the

[1] Cf. Chapter IX (d), Vol. III.

opposition between the two autonomies would be an incurable conflict; for a dual Ought posits a dual goal and annihilates itself, where one and the same tendency receives direction from it. In the latter case, the determination of the person would fall back into the ontological sequence, and the antinomy would again become a further extended causal antinomy.

How then is the autonomy of the person to be understood in its twofold opposition: its opposition to the ontological determination of the world and to the autonomy of the moral principle?

It is this question which all the theories that were discussed in the preceding chapter pass by—and they are typical also of more recent theories. Only occasionally is there any allusion in them to the Ought-antinomy, which they do not clearly detach from the causal antinomy. Hence their radical failure to understand freedom of the will. Freedom of the "practical" reason, freedom of primal activity or of a volition anterior to conscious volition, the existential correlate of "apparent freedom," the metaphysical *character indelebilis*—not one of these is moral freedom. But what really is moral freedom? In a word, we may now say: it is the autonomy of the person in contrast to the autonomy of values—while, in the latter, self-dependence as against the sequence of nature was already presupposed.

If we examine the third, fourth and the fifth aporiæ, we find that in them also the new phase of the problem is not exhausted. It is shown that in the exposition of the second antinomy of freedom (that of the Ought), a third puts in an appearance, the second enters into opposition to the first. This new antinomy (corresponding to aporiæ three, four and five) can be analysed in the three stages of the problem.

1. According to the causal antinomy the determination of the will must proceed from the ethical principle; but, according to the Ought-antinomy, this must not be so. The second antinomy suspends what the solution of the first had established. If now the second be solved, it establishes its own

meaning; but the solution of the first thereby again comes to naught. That is, if the will is free as against the moral law, it falls again into subjection to the law of nature. Hence it appears that the first two antinomies are so related that they cannot be solved together but only in alternation; it is always either the one or the other only that can be solved. Their solutions stand in contradiction. Yet the full significance of moral freedom can be gained, only if the two are solved together. The conflict constitutes the third antinomy of freedom.

2. According to the causal antinomy moral freedom can only be "freedom in the positive sense." But according to the Ought-antinomy it must be "freedom in the negative sense." Here also the same game is played: what made the solution of the first possible is attacked by the meaning of the second. If now the existence of freedom in the second and higher sense is justified, its existence in the elementary sense is overthrown—which is an impossibility; for the higher rests upon the lower. Hence freedom as against the principle must fall away at the same time as freedom in relation to the law of nature; and then there would be no sort of freedom left. This simply follows from the basic categorial law: here as everywhere else the lower structure supports the higher. If the higher nullifies the lower, it nullifies itself. This inner conflict in the dual significance of freedom constitutes the third antinomy of freedom.

3. According to the causal antinomy, freedom of the will cannot be individual; but according to the Ought-antinomy, it can only be the freedom of the individual person. Hence the autonomy of the person enters into opposition with the autonomy of the principle, and thereby the meaning of the second antinomy into opposition with the solution of the first. If it were here a question as to two sorts of freedom, no conflict would arise; at least no inner conflict. But the question concerns one and the same freedom of the will. Its meaning is split by a twofold meaning of autonomy: the higher autonomy of the person can never mean the autonomy of the principle.

If this were so, either the principle would at all events be stripped of its universality, or the person would lose his responsibility. And nevertheless the meaning of moral freedom requires precisely the synthesis of both autonomies. Accordingly the conflict between the individual and the universal is wholly an inner one. This again is the contradiction of the second as against the first antinomy. Precisely in it consists the third.

# ETHICAL PHENOMENA,
# THEIR EFFICACY AS PROOFS

# "PROOFS" OF METAPHYSICAL OBJECTS

## (a) THE IMPOSSIBILITY OF PROVING THE FREEDOM OF THE WILL

WHEN we have once cleared up for ourselves the metaphysical significance of the complicated difficulties, we cannot wonder at the fact that all the so-called "proofs" of the freedom of the will are to no purpose. Their analysis of the difficulties shows a lack of insight into the nature of the problem. Naturally, no one who fails to see the difficulties can extricate himself from them. Such a one is like a man who, walking in his sleep, does not see the precipice.

But how do matters stand with one who has waked up and whose eyes behold the difficulties? Is he sure to be able to solve them, merely because he sees them? Just in regard to this matter no one would say so. On the contrary it is clear from the start that at the present stage the problem is more profoundly metaphysical and is far harder to solve than it was, for instance, in the case of the causal antinomy, and that we dare not promise ourselves a lucid and "satisfying" solution, such as was possible there.

Yet what cannot immediately be seen and only in the course of the investigation can become clear, is the extent of the progress which we can make. As it commonly happens that the lay mind expects far more of a metaphysical exposition than it can render, let it be said at the outset, that we cannot solve to our full satisfaction the difficulties in regard to freedom; we cannot properly settle the conflict in the mass of antinomies. Hence we cannot attain the goal which always floats before the ethico-philosophical consciousness, we cannot properly "prove" the freedom of the will. Now, whether to do this is beyond human power and whether inherently irrational remainders will forever block the way, or whether it be only that at the present stage of the investigation certain obstacles cannot be surmounted, we must at least, as matters stand, abandon the proud pretence that we have found a proof.

But the inability to prove not only is no disproof of freedom —as untrained minds are always predisposed to think—but does not even weaken the claim to freedom. Let us never forget that the thing we are trying to prove exists or does not exist, quite independently of whether it can be proved. Hence even false proofs never prove anything against the fact which they attempt to substantiate; their defects are always only defects in the proof itself. Thus it was with rational theology in regard to the "existence of God"; the proofs have been proved to be false, but it would be absurd on that account to maintain that the existence of God had been refuted. It is the same in regard to freedom.

The freedom of the will is a metaphysical question. In regard to all metaphysical truths the proposition holds good that in the strict sense they can be neither proved nor disproved. Nevertheless they can be discussed as problems. Although one must expect no ready "solutions," the results of a purely objective treatment may be highly illuminating. Metaphysical problems are in general such that an insoluble, an irrational remainder is left over. This persists despite every advance in insight. And the nearer our understanding approaches to it, so much the more are we convinced of its irrationality. A critical examination of such an irrational element is under all circumstances an important philosophical task, and often the only one which it is possible to perform.

No philosophy "solves" metaphysical problems, it can only deal with them; and how far it can succeed in so doing must always remain doubtful. But every step in advance, however small, is here of the greatest significance—precisely because the problems are insoluble. Occasionally a very slight progress in insight is capable of changing the entire perspective. The advance beyond Kant's causal antinomy, which has been

made in connection with the Ought-antinomy, may be taken
as a convincing instance. That thereby only a new group of
difficulties has been opened up does not signify that the problem
has been made more obscure but signifies that it has been
made fundamentally clearer.

Now in this sense it holds good that one can move forward
from the embarrassments which have been overcome.

### (b) PHENOMENA AND METAPHYSICAL OBJECTS

Metaphysical objects are never given directly. In the world of
appearance they come into evidence only indirectly. Hence
there are no phenomena in which without further ado their
existence would be manifest. For example, whether "apparent
freedom" is an appearance of real freedom is exactly the point
in question. Nevertheless, those indications from which conclusions can be drawn are essentially phenomena. Thus also
in the problem of Being, certain existential and cognitive
phenomena are indices which point to real self-existence.
Not otherwise do certain phenomena of the moral consciousness indicate the existence of moral freedom. The phenomenal
premisses do not yield complete conclusiveness. Yet from
many a phenomenon an astonishing amount follows—with a
high degree of probability even if not with absolute certainty.
The degree varies according to the kind of phenomenon. If one
remembers that generally in metaphysical problems one does
not attain to more than hypothetical certainty, it is easy to
calculate what weight should be given to the specific discussion
of the phenomena.

The eternal disparity between knowledge and metaphysical
objects brings it about that the treatment of the problem is
limited essentially to two points: first, the clear presentation
of the facts which speak positively in its favour, as well as the
consideration of their import as metaphysical indices; and,
secondly, the investigation of the ontological possibility of the
fact itself on the basis of the existing relationships. If in both

these directions we survey the field sufficiently widely, if a certain harmony is shown, an articulation of facts and possibilities which have been examined independently of one another, a third task arises: the hypothetical formulation itself.

The third of these tasks is a dependent last link, and it may still appear questionable whether in the problem of freedom we can reach so far. The second is the metaphysical task proper. It deals with the widest categorial connections. It has to do with the Ought-antinomy, hence with the first five difficulties, and still beyond them with the third antinomy of freedom. The first task, on the other hand, must take up the sixth difficulty. In it the embarrassment concerns the relation of phenomena to Being. In other words, it must test the extent and the constitution of the given facts. And as these lie scattered over the whole field of the previously analysed acts and values, it is the natural connecting link in retrospection. Just on this account it is the first question.

### (c) Possible Methods of Proof, the Different Types

Now in the following analysis, if in spite of everything we speak of "arguments" for the freedom of the will, even of a "proof," this must be understood with all the limitations which have been made. The inclination to "prove" a thing is of course justifiable, even if the chances are against the theory. We stand not at the end but at the beginning of a strictly scientific discussion of the problem. We must therefore suspend judgment as to a future advancement of metaphysical knowledge. And, in the end, even a hypothetical proof is still a proof.

If for the moment we disregard the tasks which have just been mentioned, three types of argumentation are possible: an empirico-descriptive type, one that is purely aprioristic, and an analytical type.

The first of these at once drops out. There can be no empirical arguments for metaphysical objects. There are none even for ethical principles themselves; for there are no moral

facts which strictly conform to the principles—at least in the
way that existential facts conform to the principles of Being.
It inheres in the essence of the Ought, that the Actual need
not correspond to it. It is the same with freedom, although
for other reasons. In the moral life there are no direct facts of
freedom, that is, none that would not require explanation,
and could not be understood otherwise. Exactly herein lies
the difficulty of the problem. The relation of phenomena to
Being, of the actual consciousness of freedom to the freedom
of the moral consciousness, which is the point in question, is a
profoundly questionable relation.

Accordingly one is right in expecting a purely a priori
discussion. The cognisibility of moral principles is aprioristic.
But one notes here the difference between the position of
principles and that of freedom. Values have an ideal self-
existence, which is given along with its a priori intelligibility.
But freedom is of quite another kind; it does not appear in
ideal, but in actual structures, in living persons in their full
concrete existence. Hence the existence, which is to be assigned
to it, is real self-existence. If freedom is anything at all, it
must be an actual power, a potency of the actual man, not
merely of a human ideal. Only thus can it enter as a "determinant" into the real concatenation of cosmic events. But this
signifies that in the question of freedom is concealed a question
as to existence. Herewith the limit also is set to the purely
a priori argument. Existential problems are never soluble a
priori. They depend upon a mass of existential data. They are
ontological questions of actuality and without empirical
foundations they cannot be discussed.

This can be expressed in another way. An a priori proof
must rest upon either direct or indirect evidence. The former
fails us, because it clearly indicates the opposite of what was
to be proved: that the will could also very well be unfree is
exactly what is directly evident a priori. But indirectly only
two things at best are clear: first, the postulate of freedom,
derived from the nature of moral principles, and secondly,

the ontological possibility of freedom. But both these taken together still provide no proof of the existence of freedom. Hence the whole burden of proof, so far as it can be assumed by philosophical thought, rests upon the third type of argument, the analytical procedure. Indeed, even this has only a limited decisiveness, it attains only a hypothetical certainty; yet it goes furthest. It alone fits the subject-matter. Here one sets out from the given ethical situation, from the real as from the ideal—from the former in the consciousness of freedom, from the latter in the nature of moral principles—; and from the principles at all events a return can be made to the real ontal Being of freedom. The return has the form of an inference from the conditioned to the condition.

In this kind of reasoning aprioristic and empirical elements are fused. The points of departure have the character of demonstrable phenomena; as such, they have the value of facts. But the connections between these and the conclusion are of an aprioristic nature.

# CHAPTER XII (LXXVI)

## MORAL JUDGMENT AND THE CONSCIOUSNESS OF SELF-DETERMINATION

### (a) THE ARGUMENT FROM MORAL JUDGMENT

IN the analytical argument for the freedom of the will, three complex facts of the moral life come into consideration as points of departure: the consciousness of self-determination, the fact of responsibility and accountability, and the consciousness of guilt. These are supplemented by two further factors: the dependence of moral values upon freedom and the oppositional relation of the Ought to the will, or the nature of moral conflict. Each one of these phenomena must be considered separately as regards its actual consequences.

To be sure, it might seem that even the simple fact of moral judgment, that is, of approval and disapproval, would come into consideration here as a point of departure. That, however, is a mistake. From it follow only the autonomy of the principle and, in so far as a person makes the judgment, the subjection of the person to the principle, the autonomy of which is not the person's autonomy.

If the principle involved in the person's point of view is demonstrated, the moral judgment is explained. Even a being personally unfree—that is, unfree as against the principle—can approve and disapprove morally, in so far as he follows only the principle. It is of course another question, whether the judgment be right. For it is objectively significant only in so far as the Being who is judged is a free being. To him indeed moral value and disvalue are attributed. Hence, if the person who is judged is shown to be unfree, the moral judgment is at least invalid. But whether approval and disapproval are subject to this fundamental delusion or not is by no means discoverable from the nature of the judgment.

Its actuality could very well be the actuality of a radical error.

But this is precisely what is changed in the above-mentioned complex facts. With these accordingly our consideration must begin. What exactly is changed here, it is difficult to state in a word. We might call it the strength, or the metaphysical import, of the phenomenon. All factual complexes which have names are, in their mode of objectivity, phenomena. But metaphysically they are not of equal import; their ability to furnish evidence for the real existence of freedom varies greatly. Hence the embarrassment which came to light in the last aporia[1] is very different in different phenomena. The perplexity due to the fact that phenomena as such, strictly taken, provide no proof of existence at all, that the phenomena of freedom accordingly do not prove its actuality—because the phenomena may always rest ultimately upon an illusion—, this universal "aporia of the phenomenon" is of various degrees. It is greatest where the conditions of ordinary illusion fall most heavily into the balance, where there prevails a predisposition of consciousness to allow a definite conception to pass current, in naïve fashion. Now undoubtedly this predisposition is present in our moral judgments in regard to other persons. As evidence of this may be cited our blind and unsympathetic condemnations, that savour of our own superiority which accompanies the judgment we pass upon the deeds of others. It is easy to judge in this way, it does not go counter to our natural disposition; indeed, it generally joins in with a very elementary tendency to depreciate others. In this way we are inclined to hold another person accountable and hence to regard him as free. This circumstance naturally arouses suspicion against the metaphysical significance of the whole phenomenon of approval and disapproval.

The case is somewhat different when the moral judgment is favourable to another. Then at least the natural tendency to illusion is not so great. Yet it exists even here, for instance,

[1] Cf. Chapter X (b), Vol. III

wherever sympathies are dominant and foster the inclination to attribute positive values to another. This tendency is not always of the same intensity.

## (b) THE CONSCIOUSNESS OF SELF-DETERMINATION AS A GENERAL ACCOMPANIMENT OF ACTION

In moral "self-determination" the case is always just the same, although the metaphysical weight of the phenomenon is much greater. Not self-determination itself but only the consciousness of it is a phenomenon. Yet this latter is a pervasive phenomenon which accompanies all human action and indeed every disposition and self-commitment.

By this is not meant that with every human deed is given an explicit knowledge of self-determination. Commonly actions and dispositions are not reflective; and where reflection upon the act actually sets in—perhaps spontaneously or because of the choice involved—there the conduct proper, directed beyond itself, is easily modified, even falsified. The doer of the deed is not in this sense acquainted with his own self-determination. His awareness of it cannot at all be called knowledge. Rather is it a conviction; but it is not even that, in the sense of those convictions which we consciously stand up for and defend. Commonly it is much rather an entirely latent conviction, hidden from the consciousness of objects; it only obtrudes itself upon consciousness, when through the given situation it becomes insistent, when some kind or other of felt appeal to self-determination has arisen, or when in the presence of an alternative the moral For-or-Against becomes directly palpable. At all events in such cases a man consciously receives the inevitable impression: I can do so but I can also do otherwise; it depends upon me. This is the consciousness of self-determination.

But its distinctive mark is that it is always present in a concealed form, as a tacitly assumed, vague conviction which is not understood. In this form the phenomenon is universal.

It shows itself in this, that one can at any time become conscious of this conviction, as soon as one reflects upon it. And always, where and when one directs one's inner gaze upon this point, self-determination appears simply as a fact, as a certainty, concerning which in naïve fashion—that is, before any philosophical reflection as to the difficulties involved in the possibility of it—one entertains no manner of doubt. Indeed, this certainty goes so far that it is precisely the naïve man who experiences as something remarkable, as something apart, in extreme instances as a violation of his will, those cases in which he feels himself to be determined by influences from without. Such cases haunt him like disorders of his self-determination. Afterwards, moreover, he is accustomed to impute not to himself but to other persons or to "circumstances" the guilt of what he does at such times.

### (c) The Consciousness of Self-Determination and the Self-Determination of Consciousness

The consciousness of self-determination persists as a phenomenon which accompanies consciousness throughout. The question now is: Does it justify the assumption that the self-determination of consciousness is a reality? Only the latter would be freedom of the will proper. It is the same question[1] which confronted us earlier in the form: Does the consciousness of freedom necessarily correspond to a freedom of consciousness? In Chapter IX, Volume III, we saw that it does not. No compelling argument for the freedom of the will can be drawn from the phenomenon of the consciousness of freedom. Accordingly none also from the narrower but equally valid consciousness of self-determination. An argument of this kind would immediately assume the form of the "ontological argument" and would have all the same weaknesses. It would be necessary to infer from the appearance of a thing the real existence of that same thing.

[1] Cf. Chapter IX (d), Vol. III, in connection with Schelling.

In so far as the consciousness of self-determination is a firmly rooted conviction, it has the character of a subjective certainty; in it the personal subject is aware that in his volitional determination there is at least a factor which inheres in the conscious will itself. If to the same degree the subjective certainty were an objective certainty, no more argument would be necessary; freedom of the will would then be immediately certain and proved. But we saw how at this point far-reaching liability to illusion can be shown to exist. It is a fact, for instance, that no one sees through all his own real motives; the great mass of positively determining factors remains unknown, unnoticed, or at least unacknowledged. And whenever later reflection reveals fragments of them, a part of the illusion vanishes—that is, a part of the subjective certainty as to one's self-determination.

But if there is any liability here to illusion, the possibility also is not far removed that every determinedness may consist in equally undiscerned "motives," and no scope remain over for self-determination. In this case, despite the irremovable consciousness of self-determination and its subjective certainty, we should have complete unfreedom of the will.

On the other hand it might be argued as follows. The fact in consciousness of the certainty of self-determination cannot be without any basis whatever. For everything actual there are reasons why it is so and not different from what it is; that is, ontologically it is necessary. It must conform to the laws of modality and to the law of universal determination.[1] The consciousness of self-determination is a fact of ethical actuality; hence there must be an actual reason for it. Still this is not a proof that the actual self-determination of consciousness, that is, the existence of moral freedom, would be the reason which would best fit here and would most completely explain the phenomenon. In contrast to such a reason, every other, which from sceptical considerations perhaps one might prefer, has the appearance of being forced.

[1] Cf. Chapter V (c), Vol. III.

But it is equally clear that in this way one cannot attain an objective certainty. There are innumerable examples of quite analogous cases, in which the simplest and most obvious explanation proves to be unsatisfactory. One may recall the *horror vacui* or the *lex parsimoniæ naturæ* of ancient physics. But even where no proper falsity can be detected, still for all that the argument may be false. This is the case in the ontological proof for the existence of God. The existence of divinity need not be the reason for the fact that we have a concept of God and a consciousness of him. Were that necessarily the cause of our concept, the argument would be correct and the existence of God demonstrable. True, the theory of knowledge developed subsequently to the false inference. But the case may be taken as an example: what does not apply here, does not apply at all. From the consciousness of a thing we cannot infer the existence of just that thing. One may very well with certainty infer some ground and in specific cases a realistic ground. But the ground need not be the actual presence of that of which the consciousness is given as a fact. It may be something else.

Applied to the case before us, this means that the consciousness of self-determination must of course have its ground, but that the ground need not be the real existence of self-determination. It may be something else. At least one must not on principle reject this possibility, even if one does not succeed in discovering any specific thing which could play the rôle of a ground. Whether definite theories offer themselves makes no difference. There is indeed no lack of such theories. To mention only an extreme one: the ground of the consciousness of self-determination might very well inhere in the causal sequence, to the necessary effects of which the illusion as to the distinctive determination of the subject belonged. Such a theory especially gains weight, when one interprets it from the evolutionary point of view; a consciousness of self-determination is of use to man in his communal life (perhaps because it induces a sense of responsibility). This utility exists independently of whether it rests upon illusion or upon truth. A human tribe, therefore, in which the subjective consciousness of self-determination was dominant, would inevitably prove itself superior in the struggle for existence. Here then the entire texture of historical and evolutionary circumstances would be the "ground."

## (d) THE REVERSE SIDE OF THE ALTERNATIVE AND THE BURDEN OF PROOF FOR SCEPTICISM

The existence of self-determination then does not directly follow from the consciousness of self-determination. But naturally neither does the opposite follow, the non-existence of self-determination. The alternative, existence or non-existence, remains open.

Now how is it with this alternative itself? What is the theoretical chance of the opposing member? What could one say in favour of the assumption that the consciousness of self-determination is an illusion? It would imply on the part of man a radical misunderstanding of himself, an over-valuation at the centre of his being, a kind of metaphysical megalomania. In naïve fashion and by necessity he would be ascribing to himself an autonomy which he did not possess, he would feel that he had a power which was not his, but which, to the contrary, was on its side making sport of him. We should accordingly find ourselves in the grasp of ethical scepticism. For with the disappearance of freedom the meaning of moral values would vanish. Theory would be much less able to support this conclusion than its opposite. It would necessarily involve consequences; a new state of the problem would arise, which would impose new and insoluble tasks.

For instance, as regards its contents, the sceptical proposition is by no means negative. It affirms something altogether positive, and indeed something of great metaphysical significance. It asserts that the consciousness of self-determination is a semblance only. In so doing it makes a statement which is not substantiated by any given phenomenon. There is no consciousness of such a semblance as a universal phenomenon accompanying moral acts. Hence scepticism would need to prove its thesis, and the situation would be reversed. The sceptic believes that he affirms nothing, hence the burden of proof does not fall upon him. Without looking he shuffles this burden off on to the counter-member, which to him seems to be the only positive one. That is a mistake. Upon him also falls a burden of proof, and indeed the heavier one. Even if for no other reason, it is heavier because he deserts the phenomenon. He must show how the phenomenon is possible, how the illusion arises.

This predicament of scepticism is not peculiar to the ethical problem alone. It is the same as that in the problem of knowledge. There scepticism denies that knowledge is an apprehension of self-existent objects; it accordingly asserts that the consciousness of such an apprehension is a mere semblance. By this assertion it places itself in opposition to the phenomenon of the natural consciousness of facts; and by doing so it incurs itself the burden of proof. It must explain the semblance which it avouches. In this the sceptical thesis is seen to be far removed from the state of irresponsibility which it arrogates to itself. The error is in the assumption that it is easier to explain a mere semblance than an actual existence (namely, in this case, the actuality of the apprehension of self-existent objects). Involved in the appearance of apprehending objects is the appearance of the self-existence of objects. No scepticism can do away with this semblance; it is simply given. But scepticism, if it attempts to explain the semblance, must posit a long series of metaphysical presuppositions, in order to account for its origin. Consciousness must somehow produce the contents which it itself afterwards accepts as actually given; and it must be unaware of its own production of them. The consequence is a whole system of unconscious functions of consciousness. The metaphysic of Being transforms itself into a metaphysic of consciousness, which from start to finish has the evidence of the phenomena against it. Scepticism cannot carry this tremendous burden of proof. It ceases thereby to be a mere ἐποχή and becomes a solidified metaphysic of the dogmatic idealistic order. Here every plausibility is at an end.

In the ethical field, scepticism encounters the same issue. If the consciousness of self-determination be an illusion, scepticism must explain the illusion. Here also it has exchanged Being for appearance. Here also the presupposition that it is easier to affirm appearance than Being, is an error. In no respect is the appearance more demonstrable than the Being of self-determination. Indeed it is at a disadvantage in so far as it runs counter to the phenomenon. Here also the explanation requires a whole complex of assumptions. It would need, for instance, a series of outer determinants which did not inhere in the person, determinants which throughout would work in him and through him and which, in order to do this, must be so constituted that they would produce in consciousness the semblance of their own non-existence. Hence through them, wherever consciousness did not discern the reasons (the motives, causes, conditions), something would need to be called forth in it which would give to it the tendency to attribute to itself the primal origination of them. Such a thing is of course very well conceivable. But it is on that account neither explained nor established. Hence here also scepticism passes over into clotted metaphysics. Yet it cannot carry the burden of proof which it assumes. Of course it is not on that account refuted—one can never refute purely sceptical theses—but its alleged theoretical superiority has been shown to be an illusion.

## (e) The Phenomenon, its Metaphysical Import

The argument from the consciousness of self-determination remains suspended in a remarkable state of indefiniteness. If one looks critically into the proposition that the will is free, one sees that with this phenomenon as the starting point it can by no means be "proved." But if one looks just as critically into the sceptical side of the alternative, this will appear to be much weaker still. The reason is that it is not possible to infer the existence of freedom from the consciousness of self-determination; but nevertheless, there is in this consciousness something that presses peremptorily towards freedom. Only one must not call it a proof. Here the inherent difficulty of the phenomenon sets up its insurmountable barrier. Beyond that barrier scepticism in its weakness and the metaphysical inexplicability of the illusion cannot pass.

As an argument, however, the consciousness of self-determination is of an altogether different kind from the moral judgment. The latter has against it the suspicion of partisanship—and, indeed, of a partisanship which is due to a natural tendency. On the other hand there is in it no direct sense of self; one who passes moral judgment is concerned with the freedom of another person. In both these respects the consciousness of self-determination is altogether different. Here no natural tendency is present which could have a falsifying effect. Even if it were true that there were in man a will to freedom, which would so influence his conception of himself that he would be inclined to regard himself as free, still on the other side there is the reverse tendency, the tendency to throw off from his shoulders the burden of guilt and responsibility, to relieve his own personality of its load. This tendency is common to humanity and altogether natural; and, as compared with its opposite, it is easily the stronger. It goes counter to the consciousness of self-determination and is that which lends to the latter a certain objectivity.

As a phenomenon, the consciousness of self-determination possesses a far greater metaphysical weight than does the moral judgment. Here the conditions which favour habitual illusion do not press so close as there. On the contrary, rather is the prevailing tendency away from illusion. Hence if the consciousness of self-determination nevertheless exists universally, there must lie concealed behind it in the constitution of man an absolutely fixed and unequivocal power which keeps the balance among all these tendencies. The existence of freedom of the will would be just such a power.

One sees that, however much reasoning may fall short of establishing freedom, there is contained in the consciousness of self-determination something which brings us very near to such a conclusion. At the same time one detects throughout that behind this phenomenon other and differently constituted things are hidden, which in it do not come to expression, but which, once they are grasped, must indirectly invest it with quite another decisive power.

# CHAPTER XIII (LXXVII)

## RESPONSIBILITY AND ACCOUNTABILITY

### (a) RESPONSIBILITY AS A FACT OF ETHICAL REALITY

RESPONSIBILITY and accountability as factual complexes are closely akin to the consciousness of self-determination and nevertheless constitute different complexes. These phenomena consist not only of a subjective conviction of the person, but of a real moral attitude, wherefrom he draws the consequences which follow from his conviction. This attitude is of course a purely inward one, but in spite of that it has a decisive import in the moral life.

Here the person himself, with his moral Being, takes the place of his own mode of action; he assumes the moral quality of its value or disvalue. He answers for what he has done or willed, thereby imputing to himself the value of his deeds. He takes upon himself a load, the carrying of which is not in the line of any natural inclination or interest but is contrary to every natural tendency. On this account the suspicion of any self-deception, in so far as it could spring from the customary interpretation of oneself, ceases to have any foundation at all. Accordingly the metaphysical weight of responsibility and accountability as an argument for freedom is not only far greater in objectivity and cogency than that of the consciousness of self-determination, but is also of a totally different kind. What is still latent in self-determination—the positive moral attitude of the person toward himself (and on occasion against himself)—here becomes overtly evident. For this commitment is no longer the form of a mere consciousness of something; it is not simply an "apparent" attitude behind which something else is hidden, but is itself an immediate actuality, a real fact of the moral life. Whoever imputes something to himself, whoever assumes responsibility, does so, just as unmistakably as he afterwards unavoidably bears the burden and often feels it very acutely.

This is the radical difference between the factual complex of responsibility and that of self-determination. There is no direct phenomenon of self-determination, but only a phenomenon of the "consciousness" of it. But there is a direct phenomenon of responsibility and accountability, and by no means merely a phenomenon of consciousness or, as it were, a feeling of responsibility. The assumption of responsibility is a positive act, which can in no way be disputed; it is ethically actual, like any other deed, volition, commitment or disposition. And, strictly taken, something of it is contained as a positive actional factor in all moral conduct.

In a word, we are here face to face with an actual ethical fact, which is universal and accompanies all properly ethical actions. It is this fact which we must now try to understand in its metaphysical bearings. A being who takes responsibility upon himself and carries it, must somehow be capable of doing so. But a rigid conception of just this capacity is none other than the conception of moral freedom. Consequently—so one would think—a person's moral freedom is necessarily involved in his being capable of responsibility.

### (b) Bearing of Responsibility as a Sign of Personal Freedom

It cannot be denied that this is a real argument for freedom. Its validity is still to be discussed in detail. But thus much may now be affirmed, that here there is a distinct logical connection—an affirmation which cannot be made in regard to the consciousness of self-determination.

Yet at the same time it is clear that the freedom to which this argument points, is the genuine individual freedom of the person, not mere autonomy of the principle or of a universal practical reason. The central point at which this becomes evident is where a man assumes with his whole personality the responsibility for his conduct. This act does not mean a mere acceptance of the consequences, so far as they actually affect the person himself, but a drawing upon himself of all the inner, the ideal, the axiological consequences, together with those that are real, even those that affect other persons only. The originator finds himself involved in whatever occurs through his initiative, indeed even in what only might have occurred; he is aware that it is he himself upon whom rebounds everything, not merely what has actually been brought about. In so far as he enters with full consciousness upon his undertaking, he already, before any action has taken place, draws down upon himself as the originator every possible consequence. This back-reference to himself is aprioristic, it does not first wait for the occurrence. Indeed it is present even where the man's foresight is incapable of surveying the consequences. The very venture inherent in the inadequate anticipation is what the person takes upon himself in his initiative.

The freedom which is manifested in the assuming and carrying of responsibility is not a principle which is behind consciousness; it is not a freedom which is prior thereto, not a metaphysical background. It is in the strictest sense freedom of the individual moral consciousness. Here are fulfilled the two basic requirements of Kant and Leibniz: on the one side it is an autonomy of consciousness and on the other an autonomy of the individual. These taken together exactly furnish what is needed in the second and higher plane of the problem: a freedom of the conscious individual person when he is faced with the moral principle, that is, a freedom in regard to the claim of the Ought, wherein the For-and-Against stands open. It is a second autonomy together with that of the moral principle—in the sense of the second antinomy of freedom. For this is precisely an antinomy of the two autonomies.

Two authoritative factors always inhere in any responsibility: one which is responsible, and one before which it is responsible. The latter is the moral principle—every value is such an authoritative factor; the former is the person in his ability to fulfil or not to fulfil the requirement of the principle. If the person were simply subject to the principle as to a law of nature, he would succumb to it and would have no autonomy in relation to it. But if he entirely lacked apprehension of it, if he were without a valuational sense and impervious to the claim, he would be altogether heteronomous; there would be nothing in regard to which a decision would devolve upon him. For in regard to no other law is he called upon to decide; in regard to every other he simply conforms. In both these cases he would be without responsibility. But responsibility is constantly upon him; he takes it upon himself at every step in life and carries it as something that beyond all question falls to his share—often with only a vague foreboding of its pressure, often with a distinct consciousness that he is carrying it and with the will to do so, even when the load oppresses him. This is evidence within him of personal autonomy, the visible sign of his freedom.

### (c) ACCOUNTABILITY AND THE CAPACITY AND CLAIM THERETO

Near to the fact of responsibility and closely akin to it stands the fact of accountability. It is not identical with moral judgment. The act of imputing exists independently of the alternative between approval and disapproval; indeed it exists even where there is complete abstention from judgment—as is the habit of the morally modest man. This independent existence is most evident before an act has taken place, where one is witness to the moral risk which someone assumes in initiating an enterprise. One does not perhaps see as yet whether it be for good or for evil, but one already knows that it is the person of the one who acts, upon whom the credit or the guilt must fall. One discovers aprioristically in him—and indeed without reflection, but in a simple-minded way—the primal originator; and one senses the responsibility which he takes upon himself. Moral judgment of course presupposes such imputation but is not involved in it.

Accordingly in imputation the factual character is not the same as in moral judgment. For instance in judgment one may err, but imputation may be right. In judging (even in approving) one may encounter the opposition of the person who is judged and at the same time respond to his feeling as regards the imputation. The converse is also possible. In imputation as such there is no taking of sides, but simply an adjudicating of authorship.

In the fact of adjudication there are three stages which can be distinguished.

In the first place, the act of imputation itself. It is essentially a matter of indifference whether this act be one's own or that of another person. Imputation is not inherently an individual act which would have for itself a particular subject. It is a communal, inter-subjective fact, exactly like the universality of theoretical views. For instance, as with these latter it holds good that each one who grasps the situation must necessarily form the same judgment as everyone else, so here: whoever simply sees that a person is acting must necessarily attribute to him the value or disvalue of the deed. This "must" is in no sense an Ought, it is a rigid necessity; no one can avoid it.

This means that here is encountered a fundamental aprioristic relationship. Hence the universal inter-subjective validity. From the outset everyone sees any person's act—his own or another's—from the point of view of freedom. He does not "experience" the freedom, but prior to all experience he presupposes it. This is why in general any person's deed appears to us as an "act," his striving as a volition, his behaviour as morally relevant. This conception is involved in the mere consciousness that it is a person we are dealing with. But this is what binds one person to another, uniting him who imputes with him to whom something is imputed. For of his own accord the latter has the same conception. It is the communal attribute of all personality as such, that its conduct is ascribed to it.

Secondly, there is the accountability of a person. In the person to whom something is imputed, this is what answers to the act of imputation. Without it an imputation would be an error. There may be such an error, for there is such a thing as unaccountability. In such cases there is naturally no question of freedom. But in the problem of freedom the point under discussion is not at all whether every human being at all times and in every relation is free, but only whether there is generally such a thing as personal freedom or not. If in general it exists, the question is answered in the affirmative. Side by side with it there may be unfreedom; that would make no difference as to the existence of freedom.

It is just the same with accountability; it is not a universal dignity accompanying all human conditions. And it is in accord with this circumstance that our moral consciousness can very well distinguish unaccountability—at least in principle, for it is in regard to the individual case that error arises. But the point at issue is the distinction as a principle. Genuine accountability, however, just as one who imputes it presupposes it—and no less in the case of self-imputation—is nothing else than moral freedom. Hence exactly the distinction which even the unsophisticated mind makes here provides the evidence for the existence of moral freedom. And here also, exactly as with the bearing of responsibility, it is not an autonomy of the principle, nor that of a metaphysical background to personality, but the autonomy of the person himself in his individual, conscious will—freedom of the will in the strict sense of the word.

But the third and decisive stage in the fact of imputation is the claim which the person makes to imputation. One might at all events suspect accountability of being spurious, if the person to whom it was ascribed repudiated it as an unjust charge. It might rest upon an illusion, if the person did not acknowledge it. It would be said that upon this point there is an illusion; and perhaps one might add that all accountability which is not acknowledged by the person himself is fundamentally open to question. But this is a casuistical problem which we need not discuss. How freedom and unfreedom are distributed in real life and wherein one recognizes them, those who know human nature may decide. In principle the only question is this, whether there be any genuine freedom of the person at all. And upon this question an unexpected light is thrown by the fact that on the part of the person who is concerned there is a clear and fully deliberate acceptance of imputation.

This acknowledgment may assume a very definite form. A man of high moral development confirms the imputation which others make, not only by imputing to himself whatever he does but by asserting his right to such imputation; indeed he feels his human dignity to be violated, if his accountability for his deeds is denied. Such a denial he regards as an avowal that he is not accountable, as an attempt to deprive him of his moral Being as a person, and on that account as a degradation and a kind of attack upon him in his capacity of self-directing agent. Indeed the morally mature man rightly repels the well-meant exculpation—whether on the ground of "circumstances" or of mental "condition." He insists upon being responsible, if he feels himself to be so. He keeps watch upon his reputation for accountability. For him there is here far more at stake than what he experiences in the depreciatory moral judgment: the value which is at the basis of his personality is at stake—his freedom.[1]

This valuational phenomenon was set forth in our table of values. Now the reverse side of the matter is presented. In the claim to imputation is contained one of the strongest positive indications of the ethically real existence of freedom. For this claim runs counter to every natural interest, to all indolence, to the all-too-human weakness of shifting blame from off one's own shoulders. Here is evidence of a real power in the constitution of personality, which introduces into life a totally different point of view, whenever the person has reached a high moral level. This point of view is that of a strictly personal autonomy.

[1] Cf. Chapter XI (*f*), Vol. II.

It is no theory which furnishes this point of view. On the contrary the theory is based upon it and must reckon with it. It lands the theory in the most difficult embarrassments, but the theory can dispose neither of the point of view, nor of the embarrassments. The only thing that can be done is carefully to analyse the situation.

### (d) THE BASIC ETHICAL CAPACITY OF THE PERSON

In the factual complex of responsibility and imputation the embarrassing difficulty of the phenomenon begins to be lightened. These facts also have a phenomenal character, as does everything that is intuited. But they are not phenomena of interpretation as is the consciousness of self-determination; they are phenomena of living tendencies, powers, claims, in short, of real actional factors. They are of significance only if they are rooted in real personal freedom. In every other case they are not only a diversified system of illusions, but even in themselves are meaningless; indeed as illusions they are senseless, because they must inevitably not only falsify the moral consciousness, but also the ethico-actual conduct of man.

The claim to accountability and the assumption of responsibility are in this connection especially characteristic. If I do not impute to another what lies within the domain of his responsibility, I fail thereby to recognize not only a principle which determines him but the man himself as a moral person. If anyone deprives me of the responsibility which I take upon myself, he sins against my essential nature as a person. He does not, as it were, deny my specific valuational qualities—on the contrary, he might deny them if he conceded to me my responsibility—but he denies something more fundamental: my capacity to manifest any moral qualities whatsoever, a capacity which is the fundamental condition of my moral existence.

It is as little possible to state what this fundamental condition is, as to state what is the categorial structure of freedom itself.

Each is deeply hidden, the inmost metaphysical essence of personality. Perhaps one comes a step nearer to this distinctive characteristic, if one tries to interpret it as the basic ethical capacity of a person. Of course nothing is gained by the name. But the matter can always be more nearly outlined, if one considers it in its extreme special case.

As an example, we find such a case in a man's capacity to make promises, to commit himself to obligations, to enter into contracts and—what in these acts is the *punctum saliens*—to go security for himself, with his own person to commit himself to something. Here we have the elementary, the simplest instance of the taking upon oneself of responsibility and of the tacit claim to the right to have one's actions attributed to oneself. Now the greater a person's capacity to assume responsibility, to pledge and commit himself, so much the greater evidently is his moral power, the import of his humanity. What here increases with responsibility is the person's basic moral capacity.

If we extend this capacity from the special case which we have chosen to the general situation in all moral conduct, the moral power of man is widened into a universal potency of personality as such, upon the degree or stage of development of which his whole moral being depends. For his "moral" values are precisely those alone which are related to such a basic capacity. That this universalization of the power in question is not arbitrary but, in fact, underlies the quality of all moral values, we have already noted in another connection, where we were treating of the valuational expansion of reliability.[1] As a man's fidelity is the pledge of his intention, so the pledge of his whole moral conduct is the fundamental moral capacity of man.

Once more, this factual complex is objective, not a mere matter of interpretation. It is a constituent in the sphere of ethical acts. It is a certainty not for a single person as such. It is inter-subjectively valid, valid for the guilty man as well

[1] Cf. Chapter XXVI (c), Vol. II.

as for him who imputes the guilt. In the factual complex of responsibility and accountability is contained an unmistakable element of ethical actuality—and no minor one; for the whole actuality of human ethical relationships depends upon it. It would deprive this of its meaning, if nothing real, if no fundamental fact of ethical actuality, corresponded to the general actional fact of the basic moral capacity.

But such a fundamental fact could only be the real moral freedom of the person. It would constitute a complete solution of the radical difficulty inherent in the phenomenon. The reality would be in harmony with the phenomenon.

### (e) THE CATEGORIAL SELF-SUPPRESSION OF ETHICAL SCEPTICISM

Even at this point one must not omit to discuss the counter-question of scepticism, no matter how much or how little foothold still remains for it.

One may direct the discussion against any point of the argument one may choose, for instance, against the one we have just been considering. It would be "absurd," if no fact of ethical reality corresponded to the universal actional fact of a person's fundamental moral capacity. This admitted, what guarantee have we that the "moral" life, the Being of a person and of his actional world, is something which it is reasonable to believe in? Perhaps it is something altogether senseless, and perhaps over this meaningless thing is spread only an appearance of meaning? Here also we should then be confronted with a radical delusion which would dominate the whole moral life and would falsify it. Then the moral life would itself be only an appearance. The persistent delusion would here be more radical than in the case of self-determination, in so far as it would depend not upon the consciousness of an act, but upon the act itself.

This may be conceived in another way. Granted that a basic fact of ethical actuality really corresponds to the actional fact,

still its content need not be the same. Hence, if the actional
fact has the character of a fundamental capacity—in which the
categorial structure of a positive individual freedom is clearly
discernible—yet no real fundamental capacity need correspond
to it. It might be some other reality. What appears in the sphere
of actional consciousness as a fundamental capacity, might be
shown to be something quite different in the sphere of reality
upon which it rested. It might be such a construction of
ontological conditions that it constrained consciousness to
believe in a fundamental capacity. Then once again freedom
would be only a general and necessary illusion.

Let us disregard the circumstance that this sceptical thesis
is far weaker and more forced than the other, which was
directed against the existence of self-determination. Let us
further ignore the circumstance that in the same way the burden
of proof falls upon it, although it is naturally far less able to
bear the weight. Nevertheless it is in itself conceivable; it
cannot be denied a priori. We cannot bar out the possibility
that responsibility, accountability, indeed even the right to
have one's actions imputed to oneself, is a radical illusion
inherent in the constitution of the alleged moral life. These
arguments are not so absolutely cogent that the possibility is
unworthy of consideration. "Freedom" would then be a category which completely dominated consciousness, but was
purely subjective—just as, for instance, anthropomorphism in
the cosmic consciousness of mythological man; but in reality
there would be as little freedom in a person as there is an
essence in the forces of nature like that of man. The hypothesis which it would require, bears of course a far more
complicated stamp: the illusion would be in principle socially
useful—otherwise no one would of "his own free will" submit
to existing standards,—and it would accordingly be assumed
that a primeval process of historical selection had raised the
illusion to its present-day perfection. If we once assent to such
a daring hypothesis, what will be the consequence?

If it were conceded that the discipline of the great self-deception were the shortest way for the human race to attain communal life, would that be a proof that the result, man's consciousness of freedom, was nothing but a function of a biological necessity, hence the exact opposite of genuine freedom? Would it not rather be a proof that the subtle mechanism of such deception had a categorial form of a far higher order than that of the communal life-process—even if one added the higher functions of the racial life and its macrocosmic development? What can never be ontologically denied is that, where higher structures begin to manifest themselves, there also a higher law prevails. No genetic process can change this matter. On the contrary, such a process itself is always subject to this categorial law. The same is the case with the lower processes of selection: at best they explain the genesis as such, but not the categorial peculiarity of that which has come into existence. The latter, in so far as it is a "higher" form than that from which it arose, has necessarily also a higher structure, law and categorial pattern. But necessarily with the higher form a higher principle enters in.

But what is the result, if we apply here the categorial law of dependence? The higher category is the weaker, the more conditioned, the dependent category. But it is not on that account provided by the series of lower categories. Rather is it always, as compared with them, a novelty. It raises itself above them as form above the material which is indifferent to it. In short, a higher principle is always and necessarily "free" as regards a lower. Above the latter it has unlimited scope. This categorial law, the "law of freedom," reigns here;[1] and with it reappears precisely that which the whole complicated theory we have been considering attempted to eliminate: personal freedom. For the higher form, which here is under question, is none other than the person.

The outcome is extremely instructive. One does not escape freedom, even if one denies it. Of course by a merely negative scepticism one cannot detect this fact. But negative scepticism

[1] Cf. Chapter XXXVIII (c), Vol. II.

is lazy thinking, it spares itself the labour of piercing beneath the surface. It has no logical foothold in itself. As soon as one elaborates its thesis and constructs an hypothesis by which the appearance of freedom can be explained, one inevitably experiences what one least expects: one arrives again at an original unique principle, at a determinant of a higher order in the nature of the person. But such a determinant is the precise ontological meaning of positive individual freedom. The burden of proof which falls upon whoever denies freedom —for he certainly cannot deny the "phenomenon" of responsibility and imputability—not only makes his thesis illusory but turns the proof against itself in its theoretical consequences: while meaning to controvert freedom metaphysically, he who denies it proves it against his will.

His whole circuitous route was superfluous and might have been spared. Real freedom of the moral person still remains by far the most tenable hypothesis. It is not only the most direct and simple, avoiding all theoretical bye-paths; it is also the explanation which lies nearest to the facts, the one which the unsophisticated mind finds itself already accepting. It places us in no opposition to the uniform evidence of the phenomena and therefore needs no proof as against them. It is only where one comes in conflict with such evidence, that one makes statements for which one must bear the burden of proof.

### (f) THE REALITY AND THE APPEARANCE OF FREEDOM. META-PHYSICAL WEIGHT OF THE ARGUMENT

In this matter the methodological state of the case is plainly a more general one, it is not peculiar to the ethical problem. Clear evidence of this is furnished by the parallel between ethical and epistemological scepticism, as has already been pointed out.

We can see now that the parallel is complete. In ethics as in epistemology a withdrawal from the phenomenon avenges itself. An elaborate hypothesis must be built up; and if it succeeds, it proves that it presupposes exactly what it meant to refute: in the case of epistemology, the self-existence of the object; in the case of ethics, freedom.

In the problem of knowledge, if one has happily eliminated the self-existence of the object, the "functions" themselves of the subject, upon which the appearance of self-existence was said to rest, show themselves to be self-existent, as a real metaphysical back-ground of the subject. For they could not be proper functions of consciousness; otherwise the subject would necessarily be acquainted with them and see through their appearance. But he does not see through them. Hence we have only exchanged one self-existence for another. In the problem as to the knowledge of objects one cannot escape their real self-existence.[1]

Likewise with the problem of freedom. If we have happily eliminated the freedom of the person from the factual complex of responsibility and imputability, the functions of the willing and acting subject, through whom we mean to explain the appearance of freedom, show themselves on their part to be of such a grade of structure that categorial freedom again attaches to them according to the basic ontological laws themselves. The kind of determination which one is called upon to explain in the consciousness of freedom does not resolve itself into the components (as such), from which one could explain it most adequately. But if one adds the higher categorial determinant—and one cannot avoid doing so—it is just this which according to the categorial law of freedom is "free," as over against those very components by means of which, as being their unfree resultant, it was intended to be accounted for. Hence the same comedy recurs here also: one has only exchanged one freedom for another, namely the directly felt and conscious freedom of the person for an inferred freedom of the categorial principle of the person, which as such is of course not conscious. But the distinction is not a difference in the matter, but only in the way of looking at it. Metaphysically

[1] Cf. *Metaphysik der Erkenntnis*, 1925, Chapter XVI (c).

both are one and the same freedom throughout. The "principle" of a person is nothing but the essence of the person, which is also implied in the unreflective consciousness of self-determination. We cannot escape the existential reality of personal freedom. All links of thought are bound to the substance of the problem and are embraced in it; if they do not begin with it, they end with it.

Hence also we may be quite serene in assuming the evolutionary hypothesis of "origins," for it is irrelevant to the problem of freedom. In itself the way anything has originated is an interesting question, but it decides nothing as to the thing itself. Moreover it is perfectly plain that how an impersonal being may have become a personal being can never be better known than the structure of the personal being itself. Therefore, to try to understand the personal being through the process of its origination would for this reason alone be an erroneous procedure, even if the nature of the person be ontologically dependent upon the mode of its genesis, and even if its genesis do not have its categorial principle in the nature of "man."

In fact imputability and responsibility are perhaps to a high degree capable of being cultivated, as in the individual they can be acquired by education and even by suggestion. But on this point one must not forget that they have as their presupposition the distinctive and original germ of personality: its basic ethical capacity, its real self-determination. Accordingly if responsibility and imputability are in any sense real—and who would deny that in some sense they are so?—then in some sense self-determination likewise is real and at all events not purely an illusion. Of course in what sense this is so, and what it properly is in itself, can by no means be inferred therefrom. But these questions do not belong to the problem of freedom. We cannot withdraw the veil from the metaphysical nature of freedom. That is an unreasonable request, as it would be ontologically unreasonable to expect to withdraw the veil from the nature of existence. To attempt to touch the mysteries of the irrational is childish presumption. To know the limits of what can be in general comprehended is the distinguishing mark of criticism in all questions and investigations. The problem of freedom, like the problem of existence, is not as to the nature of the "ultimate." It inquires only into the existence or non-existence of freedom. In that alone is the crux of ethics, as of ontology.

But hereby we have arrived at the same self-determination, the problem of which we were obliged in the preceding chapter to leave half solved. The consciousness of self-determination was not equal to proving the existence of self-determination. It is otherwise with responsibility and imputability. As an argument their metaphysical weight is greater. What did not follow from the consciousness of self-determination—its real Being and its inherency in the nature of the person—this does in fact follow from the more cogent argument of responsibility and imputability.

In the fact of the assumption of responsibility and the claim to accountability the individual moral consciousness clearly discloses the point in the personal Being where it is self-dependent. This is disclosed as something without which not only responsibility but even the appearance of it could not exist. The phenomenon of illusion as a permanent conscious factor in the human ethos leads back to the same basic metaphysical presupposition as the real responsibility of the person. Only if one could remove from the world the whole phenomenon (including the possibility) of permanent illusion, would self-determination and personal autonomy vanish. But the phenomenon is given; and by no theoretical device can it be eliminated from the world.

Both the appearance and the real Being of responsibility presuppose the person as something unique in kind and therefore ontologically self-subsistent. In responsibility, for instance, the person is in evidence twice: once as holding himself responsible, and then as the tribunal before which he is responsible. For at bottom all ethical responsibility is self-responsibility, that is, not only for but before oneself. If one cares further to elaborate the metaphor of the tribunal, we must think of values as upon the judgment-seat; but they take their place there not by their own initiative; again it is the person who allows them to be enthroned; for it rests with him, what values he sets up as judges over his actions. His autonomy is different from that of the values and exists along with and over against their autonomy. Now if one yields a place to the thought of persistent illusion, the person of course as an agent holding himself responsible thereby vanishes. But the tribunal remains what it was. Yet one cannot explain its presence away. Else even the "phenomenon" of responsibility would vanish. But this is sufficient to restore the real being of responsibility to its full rights. For before a real tribunal apparent responsibility is in truth nothing less than real responsibility.

If accordingly one wishes to determine more closely the metaphysical weight of the argument for responsibility and accountability by the degree of its certainty—for there can be no question of an exact measure—it must be said that the argument never attains more than the general character of merely hypothetical certainty. We can in no way grasp freedom itself; one cannot be convinced directly of its reality, as one can of the reality of something which can be experienced. Responsibility and imputability are not freedom itself, but only rest upon it. The argument from them is always analytical, an inference from the conditioned to the condition, that is, a hypothetical argument.

But it is not at all on that account a weak argument. We learned this from the analogy to the parallel theoretical argument in the problem of knowledge and Being. The phenomenon of responsibility and imputability has the same metaphysical weight as that of knowledge. As the latter involves a reference to the reality of things, so the former involves a reference to the reality of freedom. The same hypothetical certainty prevails here as there; in both cases the sceptical counter-thesis (which in itself is always possible) leads back to the very thing which it is contesting, and contrary to its intention proves thereby what it wished to refute. Hence the hypothetical certainty of both conclusions is a high probability and one which is far removed from being vague. The real existence of things is rightly accepted as that which in the realm of the real is metaphysically most certain. Accordingly, if the certainty of freedom stands on the same level, its actual existence is as well established.

# CHAPTER XIV (LXXVIII)

# THE CONSCIOUSNESS OF GUILT

## (a) THE SENSE OF GUILT, CONSCIENCE, REMORSE AND THE WILL TO GUILT

THE phenomenon of the consciousness of guilt does not form the basis of a separate argument. It is closely akin to the complex phenomena of responsibility and imputability. And what follows from it can only be the same as with them. But as the question is concerned not only with the content of the sequence, but also with the degree of its certainty, there is a difference here.

The consciousness of guilt is something more specialized than responsibility. The latter accompanies every moral act; before the act it exists in the assuming of responsibility, as well as after the act in the carrying of it, and in the pledging of oneself personally to it. But guilt exists only as a consequence; it first comes into being in moral transgression. Whether we regard the transgression as an outward act or in the bent of the commitment makes no difference here.

In this narrower phenomenon we have a peculiar intensification of what also lies concealed in responsibility: the burdening of the person and the necessity of his carrying the burden. Here the burden is more keenly felt and more elementary; at the same time it is also more imperative and inevitable. One can still either assume or waive responsibility, simply because it is a part of the decision. But one cannot shift guilt from off one's own shoulders; it starts up threateningly against the person himself, it falls upon him with its weight and presses him down. Indeed it can overwhelm him with its load, so that he can no longer stand upright. It can drive a man to despair and to confession. For the person's power of endurance is limited.

The state of guilt is not a thing anticipated, but it is in the highest degree real and is felt to be real. It bursts in upon a man like a fate. He makes no mistake about the guilt. It is suddenly there, judging, contradicting, overpowering. But nevertheless he feels that this bursting-in is not from outside. A power rises within himself, which brings evidence against him. What was already latent in the responsibility, the inner court wherein the person is twice represented and at the same time divided against himself, comes for the first time in the state of guilt to drastic expression, to the most convincing inner reality. Everyone is acquainted with this phenomenon as the voice of conscience and, with its peculiar moral character, as "remorse." Ethically these are elemental manifestations, independent of all reflection. By an inner necessity they follow upon the deed, as soon as its ethical disvalue is felt. This necessity and inevitability—portrayed by the ancients in the mythological figures of the avenging Erinnyes—constitute the consciousness of guilt, a witness to self-determination with a cogency altogether quite different from that of responsibility and imputability. Here, straight from out the depth of human nature, something native, unfalsified, speaks out to the moral consciousness, something over which the man has no power.

But the metaphysical meaning of this manifestation lies in its reference to real self-determination. For guilt signifies authorship, and indeed not that of some guiding power above or behind the person, but authorship exclusively on the part of the person himself. On this account the consciousness of guilt is unequivocally connected with personal self-determination. The accusing conscience is the consciousness of that origination, fused with the concomitant consciousness of being contrary to value. From this fusion we distinctly hear strife issuing; to recognize ourself as the author of disvalue conflicts with our self-esteem—to acknowledge the deed with our own moral Being and at the same time to reprobate it, in the same moment to be witness both for and against ourself.

Here a fact of the moral life is at hand, which inverts every natural inclination of man. Here finally the possibility of any subjective falsification of the phenomenon is excluded. No one would load himself with guilt, so long as he could avoid it, so long as he could, as it were, say to himself that the matter was not so bad, or that he was not the originator of it. It is against his will that the guilty man takes the load upon himself. This is very different from the phenomenon of responsibility. There is a delight in responsibility, a truly exalted feeling accompanying the thought of being responsible! But delight and exaltation in being guilty are repugnant to common sense.

Against this view one cannot bring the fact that there is nevertheless a will to guilt. Of course there is such a will; and it is one of the most astonishing manifestations of the moral life.[1] But it speaks not against but for the reality of freedom in the Being of the person; hence it agrees exactly with what issues from it, with the phenomenon of the sense of guilt. For it is not a will to guilt for the sake of guilt, but a will to endure the guilt for the sake of one's freedom. Whoever has loaded himself with guilt, can rid himself of it only at the price of his own autonomous personality. The escape from guilt is not worth this price. It is the person himself who is the carrier of the guilt, and to relieve onself of it means to relieve oneself of one's personality. The person surrenders his autonomy for a price; he gives up his selfhood. Thus disburdened, he is no longer a complete human being, no longer a person of full value. This is the metaphysical reason for the will to guilt. Hence, if the guilty man raises himself to the exalted feeling in which he can carry his guilt, this feeling is in truth the high sense of freedom. As such, it is full of significance, because personal freedom is a fundamental value. And the person's standing by this is ultimately the same evidence for the reality of moral freedom which inheres also in the sense of guilt itself with its moral load, in the bad conscience, indeed in remorse and in the despair of the guilty one.

[1] Cf. Chapter XI (f), Vol. II.

## (b) The Strength of the Argument

Hence the strength of the argument from the factual complex of the consciousness of guilt outweighs considerably that from responsibility and imputability. The paradox in a man's oppressive witness against himself is the same as in the will to guilt, when rightly understood. In both phenomena the deeper metaphysical Being of the person rises with its claim to inviolability, as against the empirical person with his violation of values. The manifestation of that Being behind the empirically acting and erring person is nothing short of the manifestation of freedom in man.

An evolutionary interpretation of this manifestation is throughout a hopeless undertaking—although in the case of other phenomenal complexes such an interpretation might have some meaning, even if it were not ontologically tenable. Not alone the burden of proof, which it cannot carry, is against it, but its own sheer inner absurdity. As regards responsibility and accountability the discipline and survival of the fittest to live constitute a naturalistic explanation which is at least free from inner contradiction. For even as permanent illusions both these are means towards an end. But as regards the consciousness of guilt, this is no longer the case. It tends to stultify the person himself, to oppress him, and in extreme instances it is nothing short of adverse to his life. His life is not advanced but hindered, if in him the consciousness of guilt is awakened; and indeed it is so completely checked that he is stultified, if afterwards his guilt is again impugned.

Here the person comes forward as a witness against himself, accuses himself, struggles against his own most vital interest. How could he do this, if there were not another reason for it in himself, if in him as a person there were not something of greater import, something distinctive of him, which demanded this negation and violation of life, precisely in order to preserve his integrity?

But again, in its categorial nature, such a characteristic

could only be something independent, a primal determinant of the person, hence an autonomy not of the principle and not of some unconscious background, but alone of the individual moral consciousness. Only if a higher inner value, the value of the person as such, with the reality of which his moral Being stands or falls, requires this self-negation on behalf of its own integrity, is it explicable how a man conscious of guilt is in the higher sense nevertheless the more capable of ethical life. But he is the more capable only of ethical, not of biological or even of social life. In him that inner and higher strength is then developed, which one can understand as strength only from the point of view of ethical values, the strength of the basic moral capacity of the person.

But then the whole naturalistic theory, which was so artificially constructed, is converted into its opposite. It then once more proves the contrary of what it meant to prove. For instance, the consciousness of guilt is then far from being an illusion. Rather does it rest upon actual guilt, and the one who is conscious of it is also in ethical reality the guilty one. The pivot of self-determination in him is revealed as the goal at which self-imputation aims.

This also is of course not an absolute certainty; but it is a hypothetical certainty of a high degree—of the highest which is possible within the whole genus of hypothetical certainties concerning metaphysical objects, which cannot be directly brought into the realm of the given. Here the phenomenon is very closely connected with the reality. Even according to the extreme evolutionary interpretation the pivot of self-determination remains a pivot; it does not vanish. In the struggle for the moral existence of man it is precisely the factor which succeeds. But since, according to the phenomenon, it signifies in its content the consciousness of freedom, it must at the same time, as the existing germ of the personal life, signify ontologically the real freedom of the moral consciousness.

But also in this argument, as in all which proceed on similar lines, there is still the demand for a second proof along other lines, which must form the logical correlate: the proof of the ontological possibility of such freedom. For with the solution of the causal antinomy there is no such freedom proved to be possible, no autonomy of the person, but only of the principle in the person. If, however, the autonomy is not also onto-logically possible, all the hypothetical certainty, however high, falls with one stroke.

### (c) THE IDEAL AND REAL ESSENCE OF THE INDIVIDUAL PERSON

Here a warning must be given against a misunderstanding. It might seem that the innermost essence of the individual person, whose freedom is under discussion, is nothing other than the value of personality, of the individual ethos, as it appears (for instance) transparent to the loving glance in the empirical personality of the loved one.[1] The value of personality also is rightly recognized as a kind of innermost essence; and, more-over, it is individual in each separate person. Hence one might think that it is this which in the consciousness of guilt accuses the actual personality, in so far as the latter does not accord with it. It would then assert itself, in that it would deny the actual personality. This would accord very well with the nature of the ideal of personality in so far as the antinomic relation between it and the actual personality exists apart from this denial. But it would be the actual personality which into the bargain would sanction the value of personality in the accusation which it directed against the actual person, because at bottom the actual person, despite his shortcomings, feels himself to be more deeply identical with personality as a value than with his own empirical inclinations.

In any case this might be right, if personality as a value were not a mere ideal form. For moral freedom is throughout an actual power in the living person; it is by no means a mere value, a mere Idea. Of course in both the question concerns an inner essence of the separate person. But as values in general

[1] Cf. Chapter XXXII (b) and Chapter XXXIII (a, f), Vol. II.

have on their part only ideal self-existence and for their actualization must always wait to receive power from another quarter, personality as a value is altogether only an ideal essence. But since self-determination, responsibility, imputability and the consciousness of guilt are real phenomena, freedom also must be a real essence, so far as it is the basis of personality.

Still another matter needs to be mentioned. All moral values are linked to freedom. Hence they can never be identical with it. Ethical freedom is self-determination not only as against natural events, but also especially as against the valuational claim of the Ought; hence also as against that of personality as a value. Yet it inheres precisely in the nature of the latter, that it is not once for all the determining element in personal conduct, but can be just as well rejected as accepted by the person. The real empirical personality, accordingly, has precisely towards it the freedom of the For-or-Against. This freedom is something fundamentally different.

That which as conscience raises its accusing voice against the man, is therefore not his ideal ethos, but another power in him distinct from this—a power which of course directs from valuational points of view—and hence incidentally from the point of view of personality-value, but is not itself identical with ideal values. It is a real authoritative power in the man, which here puts in a claim for values. And that which sees itself to be the object of accusation is just as much a reality in him. The transgression is naturally a transgression against values; but that which commits the transgression, and that which on the other hand rises up in the name of the violated value, are both not of an axiological but of an ontological nature. In this way the fact is to be explained that neither as a doer and transgressor, nor as a bearer of guilt, is the man the ideal personality.

Nevertheless there is one point at which the ideal and the actual essence of the person, the personality as a value and the personal freedom, are very closely connected. But this matter must be discussed by itself, in a more fitting connection.

## SUPPLEMENTARY GROUPS OF FACTS

IN the problem of freedom the three groups of facts which we have already analysed are the principal ones and they have always been so regarded. But they are not the only ones from which arguments may be derived. Ethical reality is full of other phenomena which are just as definitely based upon freedom and which on that account have some weight for the argument. These phenomena are only less significant and less cogent logically. But it is not as if they could be merged into the three principal groups. They are altogether independent. For this reason typical instances of them deserve to be mentioned here.

For example, there is a moral sense of being worthy and unworthy, of enjoying good fortune, of living through something great, of experiencing love, trust, friendship, or even only of possessing some outward thing of value. In those who are morally mature, this sense of worthiness is most highly differentiated in regard to one's own person; but it extends to other persons just as profoundly, even if not so intensively. It is something wholly immediate, something anterior to all reflection. It gives evidence of a primary demand of the moral sense in the person that there should be provided a counterpoise in his own moral being to the values which have been tendered to him, that to a certain degree there should be established a valuational balance. This demand would be meaningless, if the person were not capable of such a special independent equipoise and indeed master of it. But the condition implied in being a carrier of personal values is freedom; and the state of being master of them is personal freedom in particular. In characteristic fashion this phenomenon, when reversed, is still the same. A person makes the reversed demand upon life, indeed—only too humanly—upon fate, that the worthy man should receive values in proportion to his worthiness. Man cannot of course carry out this requirement, and actual life is proverbially indifferent to it (the sun shines on the just and the unjust); nevertheless it is rooted deep in the moral sense and may perhaps be regarded as the most popular of all the manifestations of the moral consciousness. To feel no satisfaction at the good fortune of the innocent and highly deserving, no indignation at the triumph of the reprobate, is rightly looked upon as morally perverted. Here is the subjective and in this respect justifiable source of all eudæmonism. For the essential matter is not the fulfilment of a requirement but the significance of the spontaneous requirement itself. Thus the postulate of human happiness is not simply an ordinary utopia; as a vision, it also has a place in critical ethics.

Personal freedom is likewise reflected in retaliation, revenge, punishment, reward and in everything that is akin to these. The question here is not as to the right to punish, just as little as to the much disputed objectionableness of revenge, or indeed as to the moral dubiousness of the effects of reward. The question simply concerns the significance of these phenomena, independently of their moral value or disvalue. And in this connection it is again evident that they are to be traced to the real essence of personality, which is taken as the autonomous originator and to which as such recompense is assigned. If there be no such originator, if the person possesses no real freedom, then retaliation, revenge, punishment are not only morally assailable, but are simply senseless, purely imaginary phenomena. They are imaginary in the literal sense of the word: revenge is then not revenge, but a tragic mistake; punishment is not punishment but an unnecessary evil in the world.

It is the same with all domineering, all ruling over others, with lust of power and arrogance. Here is manifested a highly spontaneous relation to other persons. It is not the blind power of a compulsive energy, but the wide-awake energy of initiative, which is proved by the fact that on principle it challenges the initiative of others, overcomes it, usurps its right. The significance of arrogance and lust of power is not at bottom the valuational presumption of the person, but his presumption that he is free. Hence his violation of another's freedom. The arrogant man as such is not vain, the vain man may be obsequious. As in humility there is no suppression but only spontaneous subordination, so in arrogance and lust of power there are spontaneous expansion and the usurpation of freedom. Here we find freedom running wild, rampant, overreaching itself. This phenomenon, even in its disvalue, is ethically significant, as a manifestation of the reality of freedom.

These are illustrations. The moral life exhibits an abundance of similar phenomena. In the object it aims at, every kind of conduct between persons, every distinctive disposition, points to the same metaphysical presupposition. It is directed towards another person as if toward a being who is self-determining, accountable, responsible. Of course one cannot see this so clearly in love and hate,[1] but one can see it in respectfulness, contempt, honour, admiration, disfavour, jealousy; one can see it still more clearly in belief, trust, self-surrender, in promises, assent, advice; but also in distrust, suspicion of anyone, in deception, misguidance, and so on.

[1] Whence it follows that love and hate are by no means typical dispositions. Whoever starts only (or predominantly) from them may very easily overlook the problem of freedom. Even Scheler's depreciation of the question of freedom must have had its root in such a procedure.

# CHAPTER XVI (LXXX)

## OUGHT AND THE WILL

### (a) Gaps in the Argument

In all hypothetical reasoning there is a gap which can never be filled up from the reasoning itself, but only from some other source. In the sciences there are hypotheses which are established by facts. And there are others the certainty of which can at least become approximately complete. Metaphysico-hypothetical certainties are of neither kind, not even the certainties concerning personal freedom. Here we can see clearly the boundary beyond which the degree of certainty cannot advance. It is due to the kind of facts involved. Beyond imputability, responsibility and the consciousness of guilt there are no facts; and if as a basis of the argument for freedom those mentioned are inadequate, the remaining phenomena are of no use at all.

Now one might think that even the three fundamental phenomena are not yet exhausted, that, if one had only had a better grasp of them psychologically or phenomenologically, the hypothetical certainty of freedom might have mounted unlimitedly or even to absolute certainty. But that is not the case. It might be thought that psychologically, or even as parts of ethical actuality, these phenomena may still in many particulars contain for us something hidden and be capable of being philosophically worked out; but concerning personal freedom they can never give anything else than its appearance, its phenomenal existence, so to speak. They are indeed far more than the mere consciousness of freedom—the phenomena are facts of ethical reality—; but such facts do not transform real freedom into fact. They prove it to be only a condition of the facts. The reason for this is the radical difficulty native to phenomena.

Hence, as for the service which these groups of phenomena really render, the depth of our phenomenological understanding of them is of no use to us at all. The fact that freedom is a condition for their existence is evidently the same in every stratum of real ethical phenomena. But insight into this condition in all the stages of its effectiveness is as far as ever from being a proper understanding of the nature of freedom. Naturally at every stage illusion regarding this factual situation is possible. But it is everywhere the same confusion of phenomenon with existence—an error which, independently of our understanding of the phenomenon, is due to philosophical *naïveté*.

So, despite progress in understanding, the uncertainty necessarily continues to exist. There is a permanent and inevitable gap. And the sceptical counter-thesis—provided it does not pass over into positive affirmation and theory—is not removed from off its hinges.

## (b) The Weft of the Non-Identity of the Ought and the Will

Hence one naturally seeks for further security to one's position. One turns to the relation of the Ought to the will, upon which the second antinomy of freedom and with it almost the entire series of the elaborated difficulties depends.[1] Of course no new argument is found there, beyond those already considered. But a new light is thrown upon the facts there set forth.

As the perpetual desideratum of knowledge is to establish thorough agreement between presentation and object (between "thought and Being"), so the aim of all ethical claim upon man is to establish thorough concrete agreement between the Ought and the will. While in knowledge the presentation must adjust itself to the real fact, so here the task of the actual personal will is to adjust itself to the ideal Being of values. Here accordingly the question is concerning a self-adaptation of the real to the ideal.

[1] Cf. Chapter X (b), 1–5, Vol. III.

For the agreement required by ethics is as little achieved as that required by science. The will is not as it ought to be, at least never completely so. Were all volition determined purely by the Ought, man would be perfect, and the actualization of the moral claim would be behind him instead of in front of him. Precisely because this is not so, this actuality, the positive existence of the Ought, is a problem for him.

The non-identity of the content of the Ought and the will as an outcome of the merely required agreement—which altogether produces but a partial identity (and perhaps only a minimum)—is absolutely essential to the situation of ethical life. It is a basic ethical fact, and indeed a reality. Complete identity on the other hand exists only as a vision, as Idea— of course as an Idea which at the same time has valuational quality and thereby has the general significance of valuational actuality.

When we have once appreciated the objective nature of the non-identity, when we are confronted with the existing clash between the Ought and the will, the question arises as to what kind of a duality lies behind the clash. At best the positive will —and this is not the morally "pure" will—is determined in part by the moral value, but in part also through wholly different factors. For it is determined throughout in the sense of external and inner (psychological) unfreedom. Concerning this unfreedom we have seen that it undeniably exists and cannot be doubted, so long as we do not arbitrarily extend its meaning. The empirical will is always determined by the outer and inner situation together with all the causal elements involved in it. Now if the valuational determinant enters into this complex, an occasion for antagonism between the Ought and the will arises through the disparity between the valuational determinant and the causal complex. The value for instance determines according to the Ought—so far as it determines at all—; but the causal factors determine commonly in another direction. They do not allow the value to arrive at full domination.

What kind of an opposition is contained in this discrepancy? Clearly it is the more general oppositional relation between the Ought and Being. In the empirical Will the axiological and the ontological uniformities meet each other; the former in the shape of all natural inclinations, of all emotions and impulses, the latter in the intervention of the valuational sense. Hence we again stand before the old question which was involved in the causal antinomy and was solved. The essence of the matter accordingly cannot lie there. For, as a matter of fact, we are here confronted with the second antinomy of freedom. The whole reason, accordingly, for the opposition between the Ought and the will cannot be found in the opposition of the Ought and Being. Something else must be contained in it.

(c) The Part Played by the Purely Valuational Antinomies and by the Empirical Conflict of Values

It is quite natural that one should trace back all moral conflicts to the opposition between natural tendency and valuational tendency. This conception has become popular through Kant's contrast of "duty and inclination," which is of course narrower but is still typical. Hitherto almost every system of philosophical ethics has moved comfortably along this uneven road. But if we look to the structure of the table of values, so far as we can survey it to-day, we are immediately struck with a second and quite different reason for conflicts; values reveal among themselves a certain opposition, which can be intensified into a sharp antinomy.

Our discussion of the table of values showed how there exists in all valuational antinomies a tendency towards synthesis. At least the consciousness of values is always looking out involuntarily for syntheses. But as it cannot achieve them at pleasure, not to mention the practical execution of them in life, there remains nothing else for it to do than to take upon itself the conflict among the values and decide by its own initiative. Now inevitably every such decision is at the same time a fulfilment and a violation of them. For the decision can be in favour only of one side, never of both at the same time. Accordingly when confronted with the conflict in a concrete case, a person will necessarily be blamable on one side, and that through the very initiative whereby he seeks a way out of the conflict.

Besides this, there is another kind of conflict which is not carried into the contest through the valuational antinomies, but issues solely from the situation itself. If I dread to speak the truth, because I do not wish to tell what has been communicated to me in strictest confidence, the conflict is not between the two values—truthfulness and trustworthiness—as such, but wholly in reference to the given case. The two values themselves in no way clash with each other—rather may one say that they reinforce each other, because they are in content akin—: but the situation is of such a nature that I cannot satisfy both at once. Conflicts of this kind—empirical conflicts in regard to values—are the most frequent in our moral life.

This point of view gains in significance, when we bring into consideration that all human effort is finally directed somehow to values, and that a pursuit of disvalues as such is never to be found in the constitution of man. At most we might make an exception of the purely instinctive tendencies, like, perhaps, the passive tendency to inertia or the active one of up-rushing anger. But otherwise, so far as intelligence accompanies the tendency, it is directed by a consciousness of values.

Even the doer of moral evil forms no exception. The thief wills to possess the material goods: as such they are valuable, they have a goods-value, while the possession of them is a situational value. Otherwise no one would steal. This does not make the act good; for it violates a still higher value, the moral value. But in it one sees that the conflict is of a thoroughly empirical nature. We are no longer accustomed to regard it as such, because the difference in the grade of the values is too great; the two sides do not seem to be in the same class. Yet precisely in an extreme example one clearly sees how there is concealed behind the obscure opposition of duty and inclination a quite plain and clear opposition of value and value. One only needs so to choose an instance where the goods-value stands very high, while the moral value, which is violated in striving for the goods-value, is negligibly small and where the lack of it is felt to be trifling—which subjectively in the mind of the wrong-doer is generally the case—, and immediately the empirical character of the conflict becomes clearly evident.

### (d) THE PART PLAYED BY THE VALUES OF PERSONALITY AS THE BASIS OF FREEDOM

The inference to be drawn from this circumstance is that the opposition between Being and the Ought (or between natural and valuational determination) is only a subordinate one. Side by side with it in complete palpability and independence stands the opposition between Ought and Ought. For as every value has an Ought-to-Be peculiar to itself, so in every conflict of value with value (even when it is empirical and is conditioned by the situation)—however trivial it may be—there is contained an ineradicable Ought-conflict. This it is which first gives its significance to the opposition between the Ought and the will. The moral conflict is not one between the Is and the Ought, but is inter-ethical: what diverts the will from the Ought is the Ought itself. For of values there are many; and the situations of life are of such a kind that not all the values which are touched upon in them can come into their own at the same time.

If now it appears evident that from this point of view light is thrown upon the relation of the Ought to the will—and thereby upon the question of personal freedom—this becomes especially striking, when we remember in addition that the table of values contains not simply general values, but also those which have a positive Ought-to-Be for each individual. There are also values of personality. And although these do not permit of being spread out before human action as ends, still they have undoubtedly a selective and advisory influence upon human conduct. And much depends upon such an influence, where it is a question of decision and commitment.

This is the point where the real volition, which is always individual, receives a Plus of determination from the source of its distinctiveness as a unique principle. There is an individual Ought-to-Be which is just as purely ideal and absolute as a universal Ought-to-Be; and with the latter it enters into conflict wherever it puts in a simultaneous claim. But since all volition and conduct are individual, its claim ought never to be absent.

This again changes the situation in an essential respect. Hitherto it has appeared as if all volition, when it stands in opposition to the pure Ought, is in the wrong as compared therewith. It looks so, when one sees behind its deviation from the Ought only inclination, impulse and emotion. And it is the same, when behind it there is a conflict of values, in which the lower one leads the volition away from the higher, when for example the passion for possessions (for things in them-selves valuable) obscures the sense of justice. But it is otherwise when personality as a value plays a selective part in the volition. Personality itself then diverts the volition from the direct pursuit of something which in general ought to be (for instance, justice); but it does not necessarily divert "downwards," it may also divert "upwards." By their whole generic nature the values of personality are the higher values. Hence while the more universal values are the "stronger" and must in so far claim more unconditional assent, the higher fulfilment of humanity does not lie in their direction, but in that of the values which personality prefers. Accordingly the conflict of the Ought and the will—in so far as the former is understood only in the sense of the universal values, and it is ordinarily so understood—is distinctly in favour of the will.

Here it is a question as to the shifting of the centre of gravity in the ethical problem. In our wider perspective, it is well worth while to keep this in mind. An exclusive supremacy of the universal values leads to an absurdity. If there existed only a general Ought, then universality would needs inhere in the essence of the Ought and in values; but all ethical individuation would necessarily be something which ought not to be, or something indifferent, either something evil or something neither good nor evil. In this way one arrives inevitably at the ancient metaphysics which, since Plotinus, has dominated so many theories, according to which the individual is only a moral compromise. The individual is necessary, in order to allow the principle in general to become actual; for it can become actual only in the deeds of a particular person. But the necessity for the individual is something sinister, a curse, since that necessity drags the principle down from its height, draws "matter" into the purity of the principle and obscures the latter. Hence originates imperfection, the Descent.

This time-honoured system of metaphysics contains a profound misunderstanding of the individual, not only as a value but also as an ethical force and as the carrier of freedom. Indeed, we find in it one of the sources of the deep-rooted tendency to deprive the individual of freedom, as is the case with innumerable theories of providence and predestination.

In this way not only is the being of man, which is always individual, degraded and his elevation to purity and freedom transformed into some universal and superhuman state to which man ought to "return," but the whole ethical conflict and the opposition between the Ought and the will are externalized, reduced to an opposition between matter and principle, wherein it makes no difference whether matter be conceived as neutral "nature" or as "evil."

This conception, together with the solution ("The individual ought not to be"), which still survives in many present-day ethical theories, teaches a totally false ethics of the individual— false because it is not in harmony with self-evident valuational facts. Plainly there exist values of the individual and by no means in persons alone; it is only that in persons they acquire pre-eminent ethical significance. Depreciation of the individual is a disastrous misconception of man as a value. The truth is

the very opposite: the individual is not an instance of degradation, not a descent, a compromise, but an elevation, an ascent,
an advancement to a higher form, to a value structurally
superior. The loss to the universal values, which here occurs,
is accordingly not a loss in value; it concerns only the right
of the higher value.

The outlook of the individual is now opened out upon a
conflict among values and thereby upon the situation which
lies at the basis of freedom. Freedom is rooted in moral conflicts
within the ethical sphere; and in them empirical volition itself
in its opposition to the Ought, indeed in its failure to fulfil
the Ought, has the Ought as its background. Not as though a
volition selected by personality as a value were already free;
but the axiological opposition of determinants in it is the condition of possible freedom. Only where value stands against
value—and indeed values of similar grade—does there come
into question the actuality of a decision proper. Every misconception of this fact externalizes the Good of the ethical problems,
as these are simply given in actual situational conflicts; and the
misunderstanding must afterwards lead to arbitrary metaphysical constructions.

### (e) PERSONALITY, ITS IDEAL AND ACTUAL AUTONOMY

The distinctive value and the absolute Ought-to-Be of the
personal individual stand otherwise firm and need here no
further proof.[1] Likewise the antinomy of the universal and
the individual running through all valuational strata, as well
as the kindred antinomy of the collective unit and the individual, may be accepted as proved.[2] We need attend here
only to the consequences.

If every particular value is autonomous as compared with
every other, so also the value of the individual in the person is
autonomous as compared with universal values. This appears
as a highly important statement, when from our analysis of

[1] Cf. Chapter XXXII, Vol. II.          [2] Cf. Chapter IX, Vol. II.

value we recall wherein the content of personality as a value consists. There we saw that its content is the individual order of preference for the universal values, which is adjusted to the absolute order of rank. It is simply the selective factor which inheres in the preferential principle; and it is this which is here added to the universal (the absolute) order of rank with its individualizing tendency.

Now one would of course go completely astray, if directly from this selective factor one tried to infer personal freedom of the will. The temptation lies in this, that selection is simply "choice," and that freedom—even when positive—unmistakably contains something of the character of "choice"; on the other side, since in this there is a reserve of personality as compared with universal values and such a reserve must pertain exclusively to volition—in so far as it is autonomous over against the Ought—, the temptation to identify the value of personality and freedom of personality is a truly annoying one.

Nevertheless, we have already explained above why there is an illusion in such a point of view:[1]

1. The value of personality is only the ideal essence of the person, but free will must be the actual essence. It is precisely the empirical person who must be free, for only *his* conduct is subject to imputability and responsibility, and hence must be attributed to the person himself and not to the Idea of his personality.

2. The actual empirical person is just as little coerced by his ideal personality as he is by the universal values. He may fall short of the one as much as of the others; hence he is just as free toward the one as toward the others. The positive, the determining—and in this sense selective—principle of volitional decision, cannot accordingly be that of personality. Otherwise the absurdity would arise that the self-same principle, for or against which the person was to decide, would be at the same time the decisive factor in this decision.

3. Finally, it may now be added that that freedom of a

[1] Cf. Chapter XIV (c), Vol. III.

person which consisted in the mastery of ideal personality over him could not in any case be freedom of consciousness, hence also not of the will which is conscious and is alone accountable. For there exists no such immediate consciousness of one's own ideal personality. And where such a consciousness exists subordinately and reflectively, there is always danger of its being falsified in the reflection.

The autonomy of the person must accordingly consist in something else than the autonomy of the ideal personality. It cannot be an axiological, but only an ontological, autonomy. This is the point at which the ideal Being of values is shown to be only an element in the much more complex ethical problem. Human morality does not consist in the values as such, but in the qualitative relation of man to them. Values in general —including those of personality—are only conditions of moral being and non-being; and they are such, only in matters where human conduct is good or evil, they are only the norms under which conduct falls. But whether it accords with the norms or not, is a matter for another court to decide. And this court is the metaphysical factor proper to the human ethos, its enigmatic mode of existence which comes into consideration only in comparison with values; it is the autonomy of the actual person, personal freedom.

### (f) Freedom under Law and Freedom above Law

At the same time we have reached the point where it becomes convincingly clear that there must be an actual autonomy of personality alongside of and in opposition to the ideal, indeed that the actual is unconditionally presupposed by the ideal values—as by the moral values in general. Here autonomy stands over against autonomy, and in truth not that of personal values against that of universal values, but that of the actual person against that of values generally, including that of its own specific value. Hence, if an antinomy of the two autonomies inheres in the opposition of the antinomically placed materials, and especially in that of the universal and individual values, there is superimposed upon this in the relation of the actual person to value in general a second and now at last a truly momentous antinomy of the two autonomies. If the former is a homogeneous one between value and value, this is heterogeneous, as between value and an actual commitment to value. If in regard to the former the sense of values is in search of a synthesis, so in regard to the latter it is seeking for an entirely different harmony, for a concrete identity of Ideal and Actual, of the pure Ought and the empirical volition generally.

In the establishment of this identity which is not given— for the woof of non-identity is always in evidence—the Ideal is the fixed pole of relation, while the Actual changes and moves. Now, in the positive sense, freedom can never exist anywhere but in actual conduct. Care for the required harmony falls to the actual person, hence to him also guilt in the case of discrepancy. To him alone—if at all to anything actual—can it be given to will to be as he ought, or as he ought not, to be. Hence the antinomy of autonomous values is of course a presupposition of the freedom of the will, but does not inhere in it as such. The antinomy of the Ought and the will is not one between values, but one between the Ought and the actual ethical existence of the person.

We can only estimate how real the nature of this problem is, if we continually bear in mind that the question here is not concerning manufactured "ideal cases," but concerning any actual case that might be taken at random. Any human deed, in so far as it proceeds from any given situation with a given valuational conflict—although the conflict be not explicitly discerned—, is for its part and within its finite limits already a settlement of the conflict and tends to be an actual solution of it. The metaphysical condition under which alone this is possible, is that the actual person is autonomous not only when in harmony with the values but also and precisely when opposed to them, that is, that his autonomy as compared with theirs is the higher. Indeed, it is this autonomy which surmounts and issues from the conflict of the autonomous values, by virtue of the decision which it makes. It is this which in its variability stands over against the values; while by its initiative, and by the subordination of what is empirically given to it, there is brought about for the first time an adaptation of actual conduct to one or the other value.

In every situation three ethical elements stand related to one another: the empirical content of the situation (both outward and inward), the valuational relation which is involved in it, and the actual volition which seeks a way out of it. It is the last named which must have the initiative, as compared with the first and the second. If it has the initiative (as it were under the guidance of a value) only as regards the first, it is free merely in the sense of the causal antinomy, and accordingly is not personally free. But if it has initiative also in regard to the valuational relation, that is, if it can besides decide between the directions of the Ought under which it sees the empirical content of the situation, it is in addition free in the sense of the Ought-antinomy. Then it is personally free. Such a volition no longer possesses "freedom under the law" (as Kant's formula expresses it), but in face of the law, hence above it.

That personal freedom is concerned with an autonomy of a categorially higher and more complex type than that of the principle, even of the individual principle, is shown most strikingly in this, that the two autonomies, placed over against each other, are not only dissimilar in origin and in the carrier, but are of unequal value in the autonomic character peculiar to each. The autonomous principle, which exists also in nonactual ideality apart from the person, is an element of unfreedom in the actual person, in so far as it has power over him, and indicates heteronomy of the person. And if the person in his empirically actual determinedness of the causal kind were not determined by anything else than such "autonomous" principles, he for his part would be anything but morally free; he would be so much the more unfree. For he would be completely determined by external laws. The determining factor would not be a determinant in but over the moral consciousness, or at least outside of it.

Hence the autonomy of the principle is in itself not only no support for personal freedom—not to speak of its being identical therewith, as the idealism emanating from Kant teaches—, but as a determinant is much rather an obstacle to freedom. It inheres in the nature of all autonomy always to exist only in that wherein the law originates, but not in that which is further determined by it. The natural uniformity of things is a law within them; but in a moral being natural uniformity is a law imposed from without. Values again are not only autonomous in themselves, but also in their determination of the ethically actual, that is, over against the laws of nature. For their power of determination does not issue from these. But for a moral Being they are an external law, precisely in so far as they determine him. The origin of their determination lies not in the person but in them. Only if the person, when confronted with them, contains a source of determination of his own, with which he meets them, is he also autonomous. There is a deeply rooted error which holds that personal freedom could perfectly well exist along with complete determination of the person by a higher principle—whether it be a world-Logos, or divine providence, or an imperative of pure reason, or even a realm of values. The metaphysical trappings count for nothing; it still remains a principle which is not identical with the person. That fact alone, and not the kind of principle, constitutes a heteronomy of the person.

What holds good of the universal values must evidently hold good also of the values of personality. That these stand in a closer connection with the particular person and indicate an Ought-to-Be only for him, does not modify the relation in the least. The person does not have in himself these values and their valid Ought-to-Be; they are outside him (whether on a level with him or above him); here also he can fulfil or violate them. Also it must hold good of personality as an individual value—however paradoxical this may appear—, that as such it is for the actual person an element of unfreedom, in so far as it puts in its claim to determine him. We totally misunderstand the meaning of personal freedom, if we think that an Ought valid for one person alone would constitute freedom. The opposite is the case: nothing that has the character of an Ought, therefore, can give the distinctive mark of freedom. For freedom necessarily is what it is in contrast to the Ought. Just as a man cannot make universal values or even select them as he pleases, so also he cannot arbitrarily make or choose for himself his individual ideal ethos. He finds it as his own already at hand, not otherwise than he finds other values which are valid for him. Here as there the valuational sense receives, it does not give. Here also nothing remains for him to do except to fulfil the value or fail to do so. In face of it also the man must himself decide.

Consequently his freedom at all events does not consist in his being determined by his personality as a value. If it lay in that, it would again be freedom merely in the sense of the causal antinomy, not in that of the Ought-antinomy. It would only be "freedom under the law," not above it.

### (g) The Antinomy of the Autonomies

The statement that the autonomy of the moral principle con-stitutes for the actual person an element of heteronomy is in itself perfectly self-evident, as soon as one has understood that personal autonomy is essentially autonomy over against the principle.

This proposition is vital for the understanding of the chasm which exists between the two kinds of autonomy. It is not in the least weakened by the fact that the autonomy of the principle is a necessary prerequisite for that of the person. If we merge these two autonomies into each other, we at the same time eliminate the conditioning relationship together with the chasm. We wipe out the distance between the sphere of values and the sphere of the actual person, between ideal Being and actual

Being; we confound precisely those elements upon the separation of which personal freedom can alone rest: the Ought and the will. It was on account of this confusion that Kant could not but overlook the distinctive problem of freedom. He sought for the origin of the Ought in just the same "pure" will, the freedom of which over against the Ought stood in question. One and the same practical reason in man was to be at the same time legislator and executor of the law. In this way the power which was to carry out the law could not possibly be free as against the power which was to lay down the law.

The disastrous confusion on this issue which has disturbed philosophical ethics is not cleared away until the cleavage between the two autonomies is fully recognized. Then only does one face the authoritative form of the second and higher antinomy of freedom: the antinomy of the two autonomies.

An understanding of this matter is philosophically of more importance than seems at first sight. For it makes us certain at the same time that the two autonomies, despite their antinomic character, do not infringe upon each other. Their coexistence is secured through the conditioning relation. To see this, it is not at all necessary that one should have first solved the antinomy. It is still possible that here there is a "genuine," that is, an insoluble antinomy. What cannot be settled for finite judgment can very well be settled in "fact."

Yet a formal scheme of their coexistence may be outlined. The removal of the strife may come about in this way, that the one autonomy may be categorially of a higher order than the other, can absorb its contents, become adjusted and thereby pass beyond the other. But such a relationship comes about of itself, if we conceive the freedom of the person, as well as that of the principle, to be "freedom in the positive sense." In the negative sense personal freedom would be impossible, would not be an independent determinant, but an indeterminedness. That also would not agree with the meaning of free will; for a free will is not an undetermined will.

The holding down of a person to a series of conditions

external to him cannot make him unfree. His freedom signifies in general only that together with every determination through categories and values there is still a third kind of determination, one native to the person himself. Here also freedom means the addition of a new determinant, not the removal of one already existing. Hence, ontologically, personal freedom is related to the autonomy of the principle, as this latter is to the causal determination of the human being. It is a Plus of determination. And because it is, in type, of a higher kind, it is "free" as compared with the lower, according to the categorial laws of dependence.

We have not hereby solved the antinomy. We have only presented clearly the scheme of solution. The ontological investigation which is still before us will need to consider further the possibilities of solution proper. In anticipation it can of course be seen that an entirely definite result cannot be aimed at. Also at first it is not a question as to the ontological solubility. What the scheme shows is simply this, that in the actual ethical complex—from the consciousness of self-determination up to the sense of guilt—the situation not only presupposes and involves personal freedom, but also in the line of facts contains nothing which would make the Ought-antinomy insoluble.

We may now summarize the situation in brief. The Ought and the will are given in an indestructible texture of oppositions. If one traces this oppositionality to its origin, one finds behind it the axiological antinomies, that is, an antithetic of Ought and Ought. Now this cannot be solved, however much the sense of values searches for syntheses. At least, a person—when face to face with the conflict—cannot wait until an ideal synthesis presents itself to him. Out of his own resources, here and now, he must make a decision. As he in fact from hour to hour makes such a decision, there must be something in him which is capable of deciding in this way—independently of the correctness or incorrectness of the decision. This something remains over against the entire conflict of the Ought, carries its deciding determinant into the conflict and thereby proves itself to be autonomous as regards the conflict.

Thus, besides the antinomy of the Ought and Ought, there is a further antinomy: that between the autonomy of the Ought in general (the principle) and the autonomy of the person. Here is the antinomy of the two autonomies. The relationship now stands as follows. The antinomy of Ought and Ought has shown itself to be insoluble. But it is precisely this insolubility, which makes the antinomy of the two autonomies in the positive sense soluble. For if the former were in itself soluble, there would be no need of the autonomous decision from the other side in the case of an actual conflict, and the person would be thrown back upon the cancellation of the conflict; but if it gave another solution to the conflict than the distinctively ideal one, it would do violence to the conflict. Hence if the antinomy of Ought and Ought were soluble, that of personal autonomy and the Ought-autonomy would be insoluble. But if the former is insoluble, the coexistence of the two autonomies is the only possibility of deliverance from the conflict of Ought and Ought. Thus is found in the insolubility of the one antinomy a clear indication as to the solution of the other. This other is the Ought-antinomy. Of course its solution is not given; it is not seen through, not understood, but it is guaranteed by the factors of the problem.

If from this point we look back upon the factual complex of responsibility, imputability and the consciousness of guilt, we must ask: How does a new argument for the freedom of the will inhere in the relation of the Ought and the will? To this it may be answered: The former arguments clearly pointed back to an autonomy of the person, in whom a basic ethical capacity inheres, a potency *sui generis*; but they did not reveal this potency, they could say nothing further as to its nature. Now the opposition of the Ought and the will, by the analysis of the radical difficulties involved in it, throws the first light, although an uncertain light, upon this point. Here is established the relation of freedom to the ethical principle, to the whole sphere of values and to their ideal autonomy. It is an antinomic relation, more abrupt than the relation to natural law. And it is the new factor, the illuminating element in this vista. For an antinomic counter-member presupposes independence. But it is this which is alone of import in the nature of the person. Independence is the whole meaning of freedom in the positive sense. Seen from this point of view, the basic capacity to which responsibility and imputability refer is in fact a metaphysical Plus of determination; and it is a Plus such as a person alone among all actual entities possesses, both in face of natural law and of the moral law, both in face of ontological and axiological determination.

Precisely that which in the table of values is the despair of the conscientious searcher—the evident impossibility of solving the valuational conflicts in a manner acceptable for the life of man—is the positive and astonishingly definite solution of the no less burning problem of freedom, which endangers the meaning of human life: it is the strongest proof that personal freedom, as an actual power, stands behind the factual complexes of responsibility and imputability. The conflict cannot be solved from the table of values, hence also not on the basis of the valuational sense. But this means that it cannot be solved at all—at least not for human insight, which with difficulty grasps the highest syntheses. But nevertheless it can be solved in given cases by a *fiat*, by initiative, by the independent procedure of a being who thereby takes responsibility and guilt upon himself. And, without being solved, it is actually decided in just this way by the *fiat* of the person. To decide is not to solve. If man could solve the problem, if he could discover an axiologically adequate solution, he would not need to decide anything at all; he would only need to carry out the solution. But the given questions of life are not of this sort. Step by step in life man must decide them without being able to solve them. He can neither change nor escape them; he can only push through them, by virtue of his initiative, even if by his initiative he becomes guilty.

Thus it comes about that, wherever persons act—indeed even where their deed is only an inner commitment—, actual decisions are made. But the power which utters the *fiat* must evidently be an actual one; for it is actually determinant in the actual volition and conduct of an actual person. Hence the actual will of the actual person must be "free"—at least as regards the values involved in the conflict.

Section V

# ONTOLOGICAL POSSIBILITY OF PERSONAL FREEDOM

## CHAPTER XVII (LXXXI)

## AUTONOMY OF THE PERSON AND DETERMINA-
## TION OF VALUES

(a) THE QUESTION OF THE POSSIBILITY OF PERSONAL FREEDOM

ON the basis of ethical arguments personal freedom must be recognized as a necessary constituent of moral Being. As this necessity is that of an actuality, and hence is an ontological necessity and by no means that of something that ought to be, it must go hand in hand with ontological possibility. For, in the realm of actuality, possibility and necessity are held in equipoise.[1] Hence possibility must be present. The only question is, whether it can be demonstrated.

The question accordingly is not whether personal freedom is possible, but the more difficult one: How is it possible? Now ontological, unlike logical, possibility does not consist in mere absence of contradiction, but in the whole series of actual conditions which lie behind it, hence properly in the "conditions of possibility." It is in place, therefore, to indicate these conditions—just as the Kantian solution of the causal antinomy showed the fundamental condition of the coexistence of all-pervading causal and ethical uniformity in one and the same volition. Now, as to this requirement, it is from the start plain that it cannot be completely fulfilled. One would need besides to be able to understand to its foundation the metaphysical nature of the person. Hence there can be no question of surveying the whole chain of ontological conditions in such a way that one could really see how personal freedom is possible. With metaphysical objects, this is self-evident. What can be carried out, however, within certain limits is the selection of particular ontological difficulties, the special obstacles of which stand in the way of our conceiving the possibility of personal freedom.

[1] Cf. Chapter XXIII (b), Vol. I.

There is no lack of such points. The crucial difficulties set forth in Chapter X of this volume furnish a whole series of them. The first five wait still for their solution, although one point has been cleared up by ethical argument. But, besides these difficulties, there are still further questions which first arise in the progress of the investigation.

Hence freedom of the will on its ontological side does not permit of "proof," in the strict sense. Moreover its actual possibility can be entertained only within the limits of hypothetical certainty. What still remains to be done is in truth the most important part of the work; but to-day we are far from being able to do it. We can take only one or two steps towards clearing up the problem. The nature and the actuality of personal freedom are beyond the limits of our reasoning.

In this sense, little enough remains over, which can be done. It is limited to the treatment and solution of the difficulties in which the disposal, one behind the other, of the second and third antinomies of freedom lies in the background and renders the solution more difficult. Here, moreover, as everywhere with metaphysical aporiæ, every solution may raise up new difficulties.

### (b) THE THREEFOLD STRATIFICATION OF THE DETERMINATIONAL TYPES

The question how freedom can exist in a world thoroughly determined is only half solved in the causal antinomy. For the solution of this antinomy only shows how, together with the order of nature, a second order, that of the Ought, arises and as a categorially higher determination occupies a field above the first. But then it was shown that this field is not personal freedom, because the latter must also exist over against the Ought as a law.

This changed the situation. The determination of ethical actuality is not only determination through natural law, but at the same time through the law of the Ought. Both are rooted not in the person but in something external; hence both in the same way are for him heteronomy. The person evidently stands under both. The unsolved remainder of the question, which reappears in changed form throughout the first three basal difficulties, is therefore this: How can personal freedom exist in a world determined throughout not only by natural law but also by moral law? This question is so much the more important, since moral determination comes into actual consideration only in regard to personal beings. Hence it cannot be that the personal will here constitutes an exception. On the contrary, the personal will is the one thing in the world in which the two kinds of determination impinge upon each other.

The question, moreover, is not to be set aside because of the fact that the order of the Ought as a determinant is not ontologically universal. As a matter of fact, it determines the Actual only incompletely, only the actual will, which alone offers itself directly. It has not the inviolability of existential law; the person is capable of violating it. But precisely here is contained the question of personal freedom. For in so far as the person in his conduct is not determined by the law of the Ought, he is evidently determined by laws of nature. So at least it must be—according to the solution of the causal antinomy. This latter justifies only "freedom in the positive sense," only a Plus of determination. But the Plus inheres alone in the dominance of the Ought, as a law over men, together with that of the law of nature. How, therefore, can man be free over against the Ought as a law? As soon as he is free on this side, must he not fall under the jurisdiction of the order of nature?

This root difficulty can be solved, only if the person contains in himself a third kind of determination which, issuing from himself, throws him into the scale of ethical actuality. But if so, the determination of ethical actuality is not exhausted either in the law of nature or the law of the Ought; there is added still a personal determinant. And it must be this, upon which freedom of the will depends. The solution of the causal antinomy is wrong in one point: it cannot be that the will is only determined super-causally in so far as it is subject to the law of the Ought; the will must be determined super-causally also in so far as it is determined by its own personal determinant, together with those of causation and the Ought.

The total structure is thereby changed, in so far as there are no longer only two but three types of determination, which here lie in strata, one above the other, in one and the same ethical actuality, in the actual will, in every actual deed of a person. We know approximately—at least in their basic cate-gorial structure—only two of these types, the law of nature and the law of the Ought. The principle of the person, on the other hand, so far as it throws its own determinant into the scale, we do not know. And as there is no other access to it than through the above-mentioned aporiæ, there exists no way of coming into closer knowledge of it. We must reckon with it as an irrational factor which cannot be pursued further. But what the problem itself clearly reveals must be this, that there is a determinant of a higher type, as compared not only with the law of nature, but also with the law of the Ought. For over against the latter the person must be free.

Now if there be such a determinant, it is conceivable how a second freedom, a "freedom above the law," is super-imposed upon "freedom under the law." This follows simply from the categorial laws of dependence, according to which the lower determination is always the "stronger," but the higher is none the less "free" as compared with it; in other words, the higher finds unlimited scope above it as a material. The essential nature of personal freedom would not thereby be explained— for that we should need to understand the higher determinant—, but in principle we could conceive of it as an ontological possi-bility.

### (c) THE FINALISTIC DIFFICULTY IN FREEDOM AND ITS SOLUTION

Herewith the first difficulty may be regarded as solved, even if the solution should occasion a further embarrassment.

The determination, above which the moral person is said to have scope for a determinant of his own, is twofold: that of natural law and that of values (of the Ought). The first is determined causally, the second finalistically. Now the solution of the causal antinomy rested upon the categorial analysis of just these two types of determination. The analysis showed how the inner constitution of the finalistic nexus offered no resistance to the in-coming of extra-causal determinants from other quarters. The causal nexus takes them up and carries them along as causal links. Upon this fact rested the possibility of finalistic determination in the uninterrupted flow of the causal series. The same possibility is to the good also of the new personal determinant. The causal nexus offers no obstacle. It takes up and carries along as a causal series the novelty, which it draws into itself.

It is otherwise with the finalistic nexus. Here the results of the process are prescribed for it as its goal. The consequence is that it can take up no new determinants from other sources. At every stage it forms a closed system of determining elements which resists any outside influence. For any determinant, entering from without, shifts the goal, diverts the process from it; hence it either destroys the finalistic nexus or is destroyed by it, suspended or turned back. For the attractive power of the end has the tendency to cancel every deviation of the process from the end, and to lead the process back again in the direction prescribed.[1]

Accordingly we can understand how the finalistic determinants can be super-imposed upon the causal determination, but not how a further determinant should be able to be super-imposed upon the finalistic determination. It could find no scope there. All it could do would be either to disorganize

[1] Cf. Chapter V (e), Vol. III.

the finalistic nexus—as it might if it were "stronger"; though, if it were a "higher" principle, this would be impossible—or to be itself disorganized. In both cases there would be no freedom as against the principle of the Ought. Now, in freedom of the personal kind, a freedom is required as against the principle of the Ought; it would be a freedom as regards the existing finalistic nexus, and consequently would be required along with it. Hence it seems that here something impossible is demanded.

It is easy to see that this crucial difficulty—one might call it the finalistic difficulty involved in freedom—seriously endangers personal freedom. For, according to our previous analysis, there can be no doubt about the intolerant character of the finalistic nexus. But there can be just as little doubt about the fact that values—if they determine at all—determine finalistically.

Just here, however—, in this "if at all"—the solution is to be found. For can one properly say that values or principles of the Ought directly determine the will? Is it not equally true, that they do not determine the will? Sometimes the will pursues goals which values prescribe, but sometimes not. The law of the Ought is only a commandment, not a coercion. If here there were compulsion, inevitability, as in the case of existential law, one might very well speak of a direct determination which emanated from values. But that is just what does not happen. Hence, if one asks: How can positive autonomy of the person as a proper determinant coexist with the autonomy of values? the answer must be given: It does not at all need to exist along with the autonomy of values as an actual teleological determination. The latter simply is not, without further ado, an actual teleology of values; and only such a teleology would interfere with the incoming of a personal determinant. Whether a teleology of the will by values should take place is a matter for the decision of the will itself. The impulsion of the Ought as such is not enough to determine the will. Still another factor must always be added. And just this inheres in the actual person. It is this other factor alone which earns the title to personal freedom. It consists in the capacity of the person to transform or not to transform a value into a determinant of his own (whether as a conscious end or as a selective principle), to commit himself to it or not to commit himself.

Therefore there is no question here as to a thorough-going determinism of values or of the Ought. Such a thing would of course be a finalistic determinism and would on that account necessarily suspend the positive freedom of the person. But such a finalistic determinism of the world does not exist— not even in the ethical world of man. On this account it is a missing of the mark, to say that the processes of this world are bound to goals, that in every one of their stages there exists a "closed" system of determining factors, which excludes every further determinant; there is no nexus which either disorganizes personal human initiative or is itself disorganized; hence also there is no power which would coercively lead the diverted process back again. For there is no supremacy of values as ends, except where a person commits himself to them.

No determinism, either finalistic or of any other sort, issues from values—otherwise the person would be subject to them as to natural laws. Such a determinism would be predestination. But values as such predetermine persons no more than they constrain other actual entities. It is just here—among values— that a distinct indeterminism prevails—something which does not exist anywhere else in nature or in the whole realm of actuality. Of themselves, values have no power to move what actually exists. Such power can issue only from some other quarter, and indeed only from an actual person and in so far as he commits himself to them.[1] But this means that values determine, if at all, only with the help of just that positive authoritative power whose supremacy they would threaten, if they could directly control. This authoritative power is the autonomy of the person, in so far as he decides for a value.

[1] Cf. Chapter XIX (b, c), Vol. I.

Determination through values is accordingly in fact not only no obstacle to personal freedom but rather is conditioned by it.

This is the metaphysical meaning of the proposition that man, with his sensing of values and the trend of his capacity, is the mediator of the Ought in the realm of existence. By virtue of his freedom he is the real power which alone is in a position to transform what ought to be into what is. Wholly through him—yet not automatically, but under a summons from his freedom—ensues the finalistic determination of the actual through values.

Thus not only is the finalistic difficulty, which is inherent in freedom, solved; but an argument, which must be placed on a level with that of responsibility and imputability, is provided for the existence of personal freedom. For if the mediating power did not exist in the nature of the person, as the potency of self-commitment to values, the world would contain no determination at all through values. But such a view would contradict the vast abundance of phenomena which directly testify to the power of personal self-commitment.

## SOLUTION OF THE OUGHT-ANTINOMY

### (a) The Inner Conflict in Free Will as the Moral Will

The first of the six root difficulties presents the problem in a more external aspect. Equally external is its solution through the categorial laws, which refer to the schematism and conditionality of the determinants in their stratification. The stratification which here comes into evidence extends throughout the factual basis of all that follows, hence also of every treatment of the other root difficulties. But with the second the problem is fundamentally shifted.

The second crucial difficulty is, for instance, purely internal. It is rooted not in the relation of freedom to something coming from another quarter, (as, in the first aporia, to the finalistic nexus), but in the inner relationship of its own constituents. This is shown to be something self-contradictory. Thus conflict enters into the concept of freedom itself. The same holds good of the three later difficulties (the third to the fifth); they are the different reverse sides of the inner antinomy of freedom. But as the latter inheres in the attitude toward the Ought, these difficulties are the proper exfoliation of the Ought-antinomy.

This is seen very clearly also in the second aporia. How can the will be free as regards the very principle which ought to determine it? Yet the question concerns the freedom of the "moral" will. Now the will is only moral, in so far as it is determined by the principle and is in harmony with the demands of the Ought. But, on the other hand, precisely as "moral" Will it must possess freedom for or against the principle. Yet this means that it must not be determined by the principle. Hence the nature of the "moral" will is such that it is at the same time determined and not determined by the principle!

This is a purely inward aporia. It is neutral as regards the kind of determination peculiar to the principle. In the nature of the "moral free will" are two elements: the "moral will," that which is determined by the principle, and the "free will" which is such that it can decide either for or against the principle. In this difficulty the antinomic character is clearly manifested. We see that here either the meaning of the Ought or the meaning of freedom is suspended. In the Ought unfreedom confronts freedom, in freedom an Ought-not confronts the Ought. The antinomy of freedom appears in the Ought as an Ought-antinomy. That is, the Ought is referred to freedom; in as much as values, whose claim upon persons the Ought expresses, are in their nature values of a free being. Hence the same Ought which in its determinational tendency suspends freedom, presupposes it in its own essence. Does it then by its very trend annul its own condition—and thereby itself?

### (b) Solution of the Conflict. Exposure of Equivocations

One distinctly feels in this radical difficulty that some essential point is overlooked. What is it? In a formal way both sides of the antinomy are in harmony. Therefore the key to the enigma is not to be found in them.

It is contained in the solution of the first aporia. The person must carry within himself, besides the natural determination and that of the Ought, still a third determinant, different from both. And it must be this, through whose intervention the Ought for the first time becomes a determinant. Hence personal freedom does not encounter a determination already completed through the Ought, but one incompleted, the mere claim, the pure demand as such. And in so far as the claim is fulfilled, it is fulfilled only through the freedom. The initiative of the person is not a function of the values forcing their way through to actuality, but conversely, the actualization of the values is a function of the personal initiative. From the values themselves there issues no actualization, but only from the person, when committing himself to them. And this self-commitment occurs not under the compulsion of the values, but according to the person's own standard.

If one bears this in mind, the second difficulty is solved of itself. It is not true that the essence of the "moral" will requires it to be determined, and at the same time not determined, by the principle. Here an equivocation is involved in the concept of the "moral" will. In one instance the "morally good" will is meant, in another the will in general, in so far as it may be good or bad. For moral qualities appertain only to a special carrier, who in this sense is "moral"; but his special mark is precisely freedom. Hence in the first sense the will is determined by the principle and on that account is a "good will"; but in the second sense the will is not determined by it, but has scope to allow itself to be determined or not to be determined by it; and in this sense it is "free will." Of course even the "good will" is a free will, but not in so far as it is determined by the principle as an outward external power, but only in so far as it lends its power to the principle, which in the realm of actuality is of itself impotent, and in so far as the will brings into existence its own determination through the principle. In that case determination through the person is already a part of determination through the principle. Thus it turns out that only the free will can be moral will, and only moral will can be good and bad.

It is an illusion that in this either the meaning of the Ought or that of freedom is annulled. Behind both meanings the same double significance is concealed as behind the "moral" will. At one time by the Ought is understood determination of the will, at another time is understood what of itself can determine nothing. Each is correct, but it is taken in a different sense. The first exists where free will of itself decides for the principle of the Ought; the second, where no will of itself decides for the Ought. The principle, taken by itself, is always to be understood in the second sense. Actual determination issues from it only by means of the assistance of a free will.

In the same way by "free" will is sometimes understood that will in which the For-and-Against as regards the principle still stands open; but at other times is understood the will which of itself has chosen the principle and is now determined by it. Thus the illusion arises, as if the "free" will were both determined and not determined by the principle. Then one forgets that the will is no simple act, that the decision which it makes is only an actional factor, and that inevitably after the decision the will is richer than before by one determinant. But it is this determinant, upon which the difference depends. For the will of itself decides simply for or against the principle. Prior to the decision it is undetermined, afterwards it is determined by the principle.

But one cannot say that the will as determined is no longer "free." It is no longer so, only in the external sense that in the same case it naturally cannot a second time decide of itself, it cannot again stand prior to the decision. But it is still "free" in the sense that the decision which it made was its very own and was not dictated by the principle. In this second meaning, freedom is wholly super-temporal; for this the irrefragable continuance of responsibility, of guiltiness and of the right to imputability is a most eloquent witness.

Here arise also the final paradoxes of the second difficulty. In the Ought, freedom encounters no unfreedom but simply and solely the demand or, as it were, the challenge to free decision for the value. Just as little does an Ought-not encounter the Ought in the freedom of the person, but only the power of the person to reject the requirement of the Ought. This power of course is essential. Without it, even commitment for the value would be impossible. On this account it is also not true that the Ought by its own tendency annuls its own condition. The prerequisite of the Ought—not of course the pure Ought-to-Be, but the Ought-to-Do directed upon the person—is indeed the freedom of the person. But this is not annulled in the determinational tendency of the Ought. It holds its own even where the principle actually determines the will. For it is not the tendency of the principle which brings about the determination, but it is the decision of the will by virtue of the determinant peculiar to it. Hence the principle with its determinative tendency is so far from suspending the freedom of the person, that much rather are it and its tendency to be referred to freedom.

## (c) The Conflict of the Two Factors in Moral Freedom

According to the turn which the problem of freedom took in our treatment of the causal antinomy, only freedom of a positive, never of a negative kind is possible in a world already determined throughout, that is, only freedom that is a Plus of determination, not a Minus. The solution of the first aporia showed how nothing stands in the way of such a Plus imposed above the determination of the Ought, in so far as the latter is not a power which determines directly and actually. Now according to the causal antinomy the extra-causal determinant must inhere in the principle of the Ought. The new state of the problem, however, which is created by the Ought-antinomy, requires a freedom of the will as over against this principle. Thereby the principle as a normative determinant is again annulled; hence precisely that is eliminated, through which the causal antinomy could be solved. In that case either the solution of the causal antinomy, or freedom as against the principle, must be an error. The meaning of the Ought-antinomy comes into conflict with the solution of the causal antinomy. If the will, for instance, is determined by the moral principle, it is unfree as regards this principle; but if it is not determined by the principle, it is unfree as regards the causal nexus. Hence in either case it is unfree.

This is the problem in the third difficulty. It is not simply another form of the second; nevertheless it is easy to see that the same key must be used to unlock it. But not upon this does the import of the problem rest, but upon a new antinomical point, which no longer shows the characteristics of the Ought-antinomy, but those of a new antinomy of freedom, the third. This was analysed into three stages.[1] Of these the first is contained in the causal difficulty which has just been explained. For this led to the conflict of the two factors in the freedom of the will: freedom as regards the causal nexus and freedom as regards the Ought-principle. The meaning of the second antinomy seems to cancel the solution of the first; if one clings tenaciously to the first, one denies the second, making it insoluble. If the will is free as regards the moral law, it becomes subject again to natural law; if it escapes the latter, it becomes subject once more to the moral law.

Hence the stratification of the two antinomies—the way one after the other rules—seems to imply that they can be solved separately but not together. Their solutions stand in contradiction to each other. Yet the meaning of moral freedom requires that both be solved together. For it is one and the same will which must be free equally as regards natural law and the moral law.

### (d) THE COMPLEMENTARY RELATION BEHIND THE APPARENT CONFLICT

The question now arises: Is it then true in general that according to the solution of the causal antinomy the extra-causal determinant—in which "positive" freedom inheres—must be altogether contained in the Ought-principle? That in the treatment of the causal antinomy it should have so appeared, proves nothing. For there the question concerned only the opposition between the principle of nature and the principle of the Ought. Now the Ought-principle is found in every one of the moral values. Transcendence of the all-round compulsion exercised by the causal nexus is accordingly attained already, if scope remains above the causal nexus for an Ought-principle. But this by no means says that the person

[1] Cf. Chapter X (c), Vol. III.

in question must be determined only by an Ought-principle over and above the causal determinedness.

If now it follows from a further analysis of the relation of persons to values, that a value as such with its ideal claim is by no means an actual power for the person, but can first become such through the independent intervention of the person with his actual capacity of volition, the whole situation is changed.

The extra-causal determinant is seen to be complex. In it are an ideal Ought-constituent and also an actual and autonomous volitional constituent. And only by the help of the latter does the former become what it must be in the meaning of the causal antinomy: a determining principle in addition to natural law. Hence if the new situation created by the Ought-antinomy requires freedom of the will as regards the principle of the Ought, the new normative determinant, which must mean this principle as regards the causal nexus, is not cancelled; instead, the Ought principle comes into existence as a normative, that is, as an actual decisive determinant, only through the initiative of the will.

Thus nothing in the solution of the causal antinomy is annulled. The conflict ceases. The will, in so far as it is determined through the moral principle, need not be unfree in relation to it. For the principle does not produce the determination out of itself, but the will decides through its own self-determination. And conversely, where it is not determined by the principle (where it is morally contrary to value), there on that account it does not need simply to fall back under the law of causation. For the decision of the will, even when against the principle, is its own self-determination and as such is positive, although in respect to the principle it turns out to be negative. Hence in the one as in the other case the will is not unfree, but in both cases is free to an eminent degree. Nevertheless, in case the principle is betrayed, the will bears the responsibility and the guilt. In this relationship one sees clearly that freedom of the will does not depend upon whether the moral principle does or does not succeed in determining the will. For that depends upon the will, and not upon the principle. Whether the will decides for or against the principle, is its concern. Precisely the fact that this is its concern is its personal freedom.

The presentation of the case which the causal antinomy, taken by itself, offers, is accordingly distorted. It is first set right by the Ought-antinomy. This distortion is the occasion of all the paradoxes of the third antinomy of freedom. The opposition between the two factors of moral freedom holds good, but it is not at all an antinomic, but a positive complex relation of correlates, indeed nothing else than a complementary relationship. The solution of the causal antinomy does not depend upon whether the alien determinant which enters into the nexus is the Ought-principle (the value), but solely upon whether an extra-causal power of one kind or another participates in the determination of the will. In the morally good will it is, as a matter of fact, an Ought-principle—as to its order of rank, a higher moral value—, in the bad will it is a lower value, which ought to have yielded to the higher; but in both cases the actual determining power is not that of the value but that of the person.

This circumstance satisfies the demand for the solution of both the antinomies at once: the Ought-antinomy, in so far as the will is actually a self-determining power confronting the claim of the Ought, and the causal antinomy, in so far as the will takes over the main burden of the determinative function, which with Kant is still attributed to the universal moral law.

Here the complementary relationship of the two factors in freedom is evident. Values cannot determine except with the aid of a personal will which pledges itself to them by its self-determination; but just as little can a will determine, without having before it and directed to it the claim of autonomous values and without sensing these values as such—a claim over against which alone its self-determination has the significance of a decision. The two factors together, the objective ideal and the subjective actual—the autonomy of the principle and the confronting autonomy of the person—constitute through their peculiar supplementation the extra-causal determinant, which as "freedom in the positive sense" solves the causal antinomy.

Hence Freedom over against the Ought-principle so little contradicts freedom against the causal texture, that the latter kind first comes into being through the former kind. So little does the will, when confronting the moral law (or the values), become again a slave to the law of nature, that on the contrary, through the values, it for the first time rids itself of such slavery. But in this dual attitude towards the two heterogeneous laws is found first of all that which makes it a moral will, an individual free will, which it could never be if it stood only over against the law of nature. In a one-sided attitude of independence towards natural law it would needs succumb to the exclusive domination of the moral law and thereby would cease to be a moral will.

The relation between the autonomous principle and the autonomous person is thus no longer an antinomy, but a positive interpenetration, a reciprocal conditionality of the two autonomies. Here the possibility of genuine moral freedom finds its inner categorial condition.

### (e) THE RECURRENCE OF "NEGATIVE FREEDOM" IN THE OUGHT-ANTINOMY

The fourth aporia is more sharply accentuated than are the second and third. The causal antinomy has shown that freedom in a world determined throughout is only possible as "freedom in the positive sense." Besides, our analysis of the traditional concept of "negative freedom of choice" has shown[1] that this in any case—although it were ontologically possible—would not be freedom of will. For free will is not undetermined but

---

[1] Cf. Chapter III (f), Vol. III.

pre-eminently determined will. In all our previous exposition of personal freedom, we have assumed, as if it went without saying, that the question under discussion was positive freedom, that consequently in the nature of the person a further Plus of determination entered in, and that thereby the claim of the causal antinomy would be fulfilled.

If on the other hand we survey the Ought-antinomy, quite a different picture is presented. Freedom of will as against the principle means precisely that the will can decide either for or against the principle. But this capacity is exactly the concept of negative freedom of choice, of mere indeterminateness in regard to the principle, Kantian "freedom in the negative sense."

How then can freedom of will, if it be negative as regards the moral principle, at the same time be positive freedom in regard to the same principle? Here is the source of the conflict between what is required by its essence and what alone is actually possible under all the conditions set by the problem.

The second stage of the problem in the third antinomy of freedom has its root here. If according to the causal antinomy only "freedom in the positive sense" can exist, and according to the Ought-antinomy only "freedom in the negative sense," a clash between the two antinomies themselves is involved, together with all the constituents of the problem and their possibilities of solution. The solution of the first clashes with that of the second. If personal freedom be substantiated, the impersonal kind, which is its condition, thereby falls away. Such a thing is an impossibility. For freedom as regards principle must stand and fall together with freedom as regards natural law, simply because the latter is its condition. The lower principle carries the higher, the higher stands and falls with it. This follows from the basic categorial law. The higher by annulling the lower annuls itself. In this case freedom disappears.

[1] Cf. Chapter X (c), Vol. III.

## (f) The Scope of "Negative" Freedom and its True Relation to "Positive" Freedom

This basal difficulty is worthy of special attention, because it is different in kind from the first three. There is no question of solving it by way of the stratification of the two autonomies. Neither can we simply explain away the offensive emergence of "negative freedom," which was the presupposition. For in the relation of the will to the Ought there survives something of "freedom of choice." Rather we must investigate under what special circumstances and with what right the latter occurs. The question is the more serious, since in every naïvely ethical disposition a strain of negative freedom stubbornly recurs, to whatever extent the Kantian theory may have eliminated it. Even if this recurrence should rest upon an illusion, the illusion itself must have had its ground in the existing situation.

In the first place the possibility exists, that even the meaning of the Kantian proposition may have been misunderstood in our exposition of it. What then exactly did the nature of the causal antinomy teach concerning "freedom in the negative sense"? Certainly not that it is entirely impossible! But only that it is not possible in a world already determined throughout. And even that only in so far as it is a question of freedom as against that order of things which constitutes complete determinedness. But, in the case of the will, what constitutes complete determinedness of the world in which the will exists as an actuality? Certainly not the principle of the Ought, not values! Indeed these, as was shown, are in no position of themselves to determine anything in the realm of actuality, neither the will nor anything else. In the first instance the will itself must bestow upon them the power which they themselves do not possess.

Hence there remains only the order of nature, the causal order, as that which determines the world throughout. Over against the causal law, accordingly, the will—if it be free in another direction—must be free "in the positive sense." That it can be so only in its own peculiar correlation with values, makes no difference. For it is precisely values which do not come into the causal relation. How the will stands towards values is therefore a matter of complete indifference for its positive freedom as regards the causal law.

Hence from the causal antinomy it is not to be inferred that in relation to values the will could not be free "in the negative sense." It only follows that together with them it must form a positive total determinant, which it has in presence of the texture of causality. But how it is related to values within the total determinant depends upon "how" values determine. If they determined ethical actuality, in which the will exists, just as completely as the causal law determines natural actuality (which is the ontological foundation of ethical actuality), then the same relation as in the causal antinomy would here recur and over against the values the will could be free only "in the positive sense." But if we remember the fact that the categorial form of that determination which alone can issue from values is the finalistic nexus,[1] also the other fact that in an existential sphere which is determined throughout finalistically no freedom at all is possible, not even "in the positive sense,"[2] we see without further ado that in this case there would be no scope for freedom of will, either positive or negative.

Now it is just this case that is a wholly fictitious one. It does not exist in actuality. Ethical actuality—superimposed upon its existential foundation which is firmly concatenated and throughout determined—is not by any means completely determined finalistically in the same way. For values, from which such a determination would need to proceed, are pre-eminently incapable of it. Solely as ideals do they set up their absolute Ought-to-Be, in contrast to the ethical actuality which partly agrees with them and partly does not. Thus as regards values there is room for freedom of will. The will is

[1] Cf. Chapter XVII (c), Vol. III.
[2] Cf. Chapter V (etc.), Vol. III.

not confronted with a determinism of values—as it is confronted with a determinism of existential laws—but is confronted, at least in part, with an indeterminism of values. The causal antinomy taught us that freedom in a wholly determined sphere can exist only as "freedom in the positive sense." But it did not teach that also in a sphere not wholly determined it could exist only as positive freedom.

A sphere of the latter kind is the ethical actuality which exists above the actuality of nature—in relation to values and their trend towards finalistic determination. Hence nothing stands in the way of a freedom of the will "in the negative sense" as regards values, notwithstanding its "positive" freedom as regards the causal nexus. There is no reason at all why freedom "in the negative sense," which in naïve moral feeling is always tacitly assumed and in almost all historical theories is affirmed, should be banished entirely. It all depends upon whether it be relegated to a place within the boundaries exactly prescribed by the state of the case and be not permitted to have sway where it is an impossibility. It is impossible within the causal nexus, because this completely determines its sphere. But negative freedom is very well possible and conceivable in relation to determination of the Ought which in tendency is finalistic. For in the realm of actuality this not only does not determine throughout, but does not determine at all except by the free self-commitment of the will.

### (g) Reciprocal Conditionality of Positive and Negative Freedom with regard to Values

Yet this does not solve the difficulty. We now see clearly how the solution of the causal antinomy is not compromised, even if the will is "in the negative sense" free as regards values. We see that it is quite reconcilable, that one and the same will may have before it, as regards values, an open alternative, but as regards the causal nexus may at the same time form with these very values a positive Plus of determination. The ability to cope with an alternative has to do with another domain than that of the Plus of determination.

Nevertheless it is easy to see that the matter does not end here. Negative freedom floats unattached, so long as it is not clear how it is connected with positive freedom. For ultimately the question is not concerning two freedoms, but one and the same freedom of one and the same will. Although this has a different aspect on two sides, yet in its essence it is fundamentally one. And, again, its essence can only be positive.

Anyone must be convinced of this, who recalls the conclusion which followed from our analysis of negative freedom of choice.[1] The moral will is not that which stands undetermined before an open alternative, but that which in face of it determines itself, no matter on which side. The open alternative, therefore, is not its freedom but only its prerequisite. To be free is not the same as being undetermined. It is precisely the decided will which must be free. Otherwise it is nothing as regards responsibility and imputability. In short, the moral will is just that which is not undetermined. Hence it cannot be free "in the negative sense."

This narrowing down of the difficulty would be decisive for the whole problem of freedom as regards the negative sense, were it not that an ambiguity still lurks in negative freedom of choice. In regard to the latter it was shown that freedom of the will cannot consist in it, because such freedom must be something fundamentally different—self-determination, autonomy. But it was by no means shown that this is incompatible with negative freedom of choice as against a determined authoritative power. Rather may it very well be that the self-determining will has before it the open alternative of complying with or rejecting the principle or value, of deciding for one among several values which converge upon a given situation. Indeed, when we look more closely into such a state of things, we find that the will, wherever and however it decides for anything—

[1] Chapter III (f), Vol. III.

and especially in so far as there is overt action—must necessarily have at the least an open alternative before it. If this be entirely lacking, there is no possibility of a decision. And the converse is likewise true: where there is an open alternative, where a principle of itself sets up only a claim, without the power to secure submission of the will to it, there the alternative exists only for a will which on its side possesses the power to decide, positively for or against the principle. But from this two things immediately follow: first, that "freedom in the negative sense" must in fact exist wherever a will that is self-determining and "free in the positive sense" makes decisions; secondly that freedom in the negative sense can exist only in a will which already—and from another quarter—has "freedom in the positive sense," as its self-determination. Hence, self-determination is only possible in face of an open alternative; but the open alternative exists only for a Being capable of self-determination. Accordingly it is evident that positive is just as much conditioned by negative freedom as negative freedom is by the positive sort.

Here therefore we are confronted by a peculiar but perfectly clear relation of reciprocal conditionality. The two kinds of freedom cannot exist without each other: neither self-determination of the will without an alternative, which leaves open for it the indeterminism of values—for positive decision has meaning and is itself axiologically relevant only for or against values—, nor the actuality of an alternative in a given situation without a will, for the self-determination of which it leaves scope. As the alternative without the will has scope for nothing and therefore is no real scope at all, so the will without the alternative is a power without a sphere for the exercise of itself, a self-determination without object or content for or against which it could determine itself, and therefore a power which in reality is neither a power nor a self-determination.

## (h) Two-sided Freedom in the Self-determination of the Person

Thus much then is clear: the demand of the causal antinomy, that free will generally and under all circumstances must necessarily be "free in the positive sense," is altogether within its right—even in the Ought-antinomy, and precisely as over against values. For even as against values the will must be positive self-determination; otherwise it would be an undetermined will. But this does not prevent it from confronting essentially the same values which leave the alternative open to it. Hence it is connected with an axiologically typical situation, which we can only describe as "freedom in the negative sense."

Free will accordingly must be "positively" free under all circumstances and over against every authoritative power (every law, every principle). But in addition—and on that account—it must also be free "negatively" as regards values, while it can only be "positively" free as against natural laws. The reason for this complex double relationship is that natural laws in their own sphere of validity involve an absolute determinism, but above them values in their sphere permit at least a partial indeterminism to exist. It is in accordance with this circumstance, that the positive determinant, which the will adds to the causal texture, neither through the will alone nor through the values alone, but only through the interpenetration of the two, comes into existence, that is, through the connection of the will with the values in the decision for or against them. Hence there always exists a positive freedom behind the negative. The latter is meaningless and not actual without the former. But behind the positive a negative freedom exists only as against values, as only values are such principles as in their own sphere involve no determinism. It is otherwise over against the natural order; there no negative freedom exists behind the positive as a counter condition. For natural laws leave no scope for it.

The reciprocal conditionality of positive and negative freedom exists only in the disputed realm of the Ought-antinomy, not in that of the causal. It is simply a function of the deontological indeterminism in the realm of ethical actuality. Accordingly it is an error to carry over the problem of the causal antinomy and its consequences forthwith into the Ought-antinomy. Here the problem is radically different, because the principles, about the determination of which the question turns, are different, and different indeed precisely in their mode of determination. And in retrospect from this point of view it becomes for the first time clear, how fundamental for the exposition and treatment of the problem of freedom is a clear presentation of the metaphysical opposition between the two kinds of principle—the ontological and the axiological, as this was elaborated in the first volume. Only on the basis of this dualism in principles—whatever may be their metaphysical background—does it become philosophically clear how free will, as personal self-determination, and with it the whole series of the basic ethical phenomena, are possible.

The exposition of the Ought-antinomy of course shows quite a different front from that of the causal antinomy, but not an aspect in contradiction to it. A different situation appertains to the higher problem. The foundations which the causal antinomy discloses perdure throughout. The proposition that "freedom in the negative sense" in itself is not freedom of the will detracts nothing from its validity. Even free will over against values is not indeterminate will but thoroughly determined, except simply in so far as it is not determined immediately through them, but determined by itself when confronting them. The part played by "freedom in the negative sense" is simply the categorial form of the determinative strength of values not pressing of its own energy into the realm of the actual. It does not in the least diminish the positive self-determination of the will, rather is it only the adequate expression of the one corresponding part played by values in the moral consciousness of the person.

Hereby the third antinomy of freedom is also solved, so far as it is a factor in this second stage of the problem.[1] The conflict between the solution of the causal antinomy and the meaning of the Ought-antinomy, in so far as it exists in the clash of positive and negative freedom, has been shown to be only an apparent conflict. Actually, on the higher plane, a reciprocal conditioning relation subsists between the two kinds of freedom in one and the same personal volition. And a tearing of the two apart is just as impossible as their unification first appeared to be. The will and with it the person as a bearer of moral acts are at the same time in two senses free— for they are free on two sides, as over against the ontological and the axiological principles. On both sides there is the same self-determination, hence "positive" freedom, but from the side of values there is also in addition "negative" freedom. If then personal freedom be established, the impersonal kind does not thereby fall away. But both stand and fall together.

[1] Cf. Chapter X (c), Vol. III.

## PROBLEMS STILL UNSOLVED

### (a) THE DIFFICULTY CONCERNING INDIVIDUALITY IN MORAL FREEDOM

ALL of the embarrassing puzzles enumerated above[1] may be regarded as solved except the fifth. But even it is practically solved by our elucidation of the antinomy of the autonomies.[2] And what was left there unexplained has been shown in our treatment of the first four intricacies to be only an apparent difficulty. Hence in this respect a special exposition of it is superfluous.

But in one point it surpasses the others in significance. In it we encounter more distinctly than elsewhere the unsolved— and probably insoluble—problem of moral freedom, the presence of which one feels obscurely at every point but which, in the different particular problems that have been treated, crops up in varying degrees of distinctness. Now, as the limit to the solubility of the problem constitutes a special question, from the exposition of which the philosophical value of the foregoing investigations can for the first time be judged, a special ethical interest attaches to this question. It is the last positive task which is laid upon us,—positive because, however negative the treatment of an insoluble problem must be, one can for all that be just as positive and definite as to where the limit of solubility lies.

For this purpose we may take up again the fifth difficulty, which in all essential points has been solved. The question concerns the character of individuality in moral freedom. The freedom of the will must be that of an actual, hence individual person, not that of a universal principle. Otherwise the person cannot be the bearer of responsibility, but the principle must

[1] Chapter X (*b*), Vol. III.          [2] Chapter XVI (*g*), Vol. III.

bear it. Yet in the meaning of the causal antinomy freedom consists in the determination of the will by the moral principle or value. The principle is universal—if we ignore the especial case of the values of personality, which indeed come here into consideration only in a subordinate degree. It is impossible to identify the person with the principle. Now, as freedom of the will must at least be freedom over against the causal nexus also, the radical difficulty is this: How can it be individual, in as much as the determining factor in it, being positively free, is a Universal?

To this difficulty was attached a further problem of the third antinomy. Here also the solution of the causal antinomy came into conflict with the meaning of the Ought-antinomy. The former requires the autonomy of the principle, the latter that of the person. But the question concerns a unitary freedom of a real unitary will. How can the two autonomies coexist in it, not only in so far as they are of different origin and different categorial form (in accordance with the third and fourth difficulty), but also in so far as the independent determinant in them must be at the same time both universal and individual?

### (b) THE POSITIVE RELATION BETWEEN UNIVERSAL AND INDIVIDUAL AUTONOMY

It is necessary now only to be reminded of what has already been said, in order to prove that the conflict has been removed. We have shown it to be a misconception, that according to the causal antinomy freedom must consist in determinedness of the will by the principle or value. Rather is it sufficient, if the determining factor in the will is simply one which is altogether different and is removed from the causal context. Now self-determination on the part of the individual will is such a factor; and at the same time the part played by values has its rightful place, in so far as values are that which presents to the will the alternative, within which self-determination makes its decision. In the part thus played by the counter-authority and counter-condition, the moral principle can very well be a Universal. It may also be Individual, as is the case with the values of personality. This makes no difference as to the autonomy of the will, which decides only for or against the principle and hence always remains in contrast to it. As regards the value, its decision under all circumstances is that of an individual entity, of a particular moral person, even when it is a general decision within the changing variety of its tendencies.

In fact the conflict thereby falls away. The person who wills does not at all need to be identified with the moral principle, since it is he upon whom imputation and responsibility descend, also guilt and merit and, making allowance for circumstances, value and disvalue. All this comes to him, moreover, because reference to the principle is already involved in the individual decision itself. Nor is it true that the one unitary freedom of the will, in so far as it consists of a positive determinant of one's own, must be at the same time universal and individual. Rather does it need to be only individual, namely, the independent determinant of an individual will. The universality of the principle on the other hand does not exist in this determinant but over against it, as something different. The connection of the distinctive determinant of the individual will with the universal principle is not thereby affected in any way, because the will does not determine except in face of the claim of the Ought (of the principle) and in the sensing of it.

Our analysis of the relation between the Ought and the will has taught us, that here two autonomies coexist. Of these the one is universal, the other individual. And since they never coincide, they can never clash with each other. But if it be asked how their coexistence is possible, the answer must be the same as it was in the case of the previous difficulties: they coexist because each is impossible without the other. The universal autonomy of the principle exists as a claim of the Ought only for the individual person, and the individual autonomy of the person exists only with regard to the universal autonomy of the principle as a claim directed toward the person.

And, finally, they coexist because the individual autonomy of the person is itself two-sided: negative and positive freedom at the same time—the former towards the principle alone, the latter towards both the principle and the causal texture.

### (c) The Question as to the Nature of the Individual Determinant

And yet is everything thereby solved which was to be solved? Is it not rather true that with all this the distinctive nature of individual freedom is left untouched? Of course its relation to the causal nexus and to the valuational claim of the Ought has become clear; and this twofold relation is difficult enough and, besides, is so loaded with traditional prejudices that in coping with the confusion one ultimately forgets that the real kernel of the matter, the autonomy of the person himself in all disclosed relations, is already presupposed. But this autonomy is precisely the freedom of the will proper; and all those relations, embedded in which it comes into evidence, are ultimately only the why and the wherefore.

The problem which makes itself felt more distinctly in the fifth difficulty than in the others, is thus still unsolved. What exactly is the determining factor in the person, which constitutes his individual freedom in the positive sense? That it must be positive has become clear from the most diverse sides; even negative freedom towards the principle is only conceivable, provided there stands behind it a real power of self-determination, for which alone it exists.

The question is now no longer concerning the antinomy of the autonomies—which has resolved itself into a complementary relationship—, but so much the more urgent becomes the question: How are we to understand the nature of personal autonomy itself, how is it ontologically possible? The same question of possibility of course applies to the other autonomy, to that of the values. But there it is answered, as far as is possible, by an analysis of the valuational materials and of the categorial structure of value and the Ought. Towards answering it we contributed whatever could be done by our critical treatment of the problem. And if one recalls that there we could lay our finger upon quite a variety of autonomous valuational structures, one must admit that what has been accomplished in this direction is no trifling matter. On the other hand nothing as yet has been done for the clearing up of the personal autonomy, which is confronted by that of the principle. Everything that tended in that direction referred only to external relations.

One must keep vividly in mind that every kind of determination leads back to one or another type of principles. Thus ontological and axiological principles, the two known basic types, correspond to the two kinds of determination, which constitute the habitat of freedom. Now ought one to assume, perhaps, that the specific determinant in the self-determination of the person belongs to one of these two types? Or ought one to assume for it a third, quite differently constituted kind of determination?

If it bears an ontological character, it falls back to the level of natural law and is at best a categorially higher type of those principles which determine by constraint. The freedom of the person would then need to exist over against it, and could not exist in it. If it bears the character of an Ought, it thereby is brought into the series of those principles which of themselves do not determine anything, but always have recourse to a supplementary determinant from some other quarter, which decides for it. But since the nature of personal freedom consists precisely in its playing the part of this determinant from another quarter as regards values, it evidently cannot be an axiological determinant, but would always find itself inadvertibly over against any such—however individualized this might be.

Hence it seems that on all sides the situation points to a

third case: personal self-determination must have a quite unique, a new mode of determining, a genuine categorial *novum* in contrast to both the others. The solution of the first difficulty pointed in the same direction,[1] in that it issued in a threefold stratification of determinational types in the realm of ethical actuality. There also it became clear that for a complete understanding of the matter there must be insight into the nature of the third and categorially highest determinant—an insight which hitherto has always been lacking.

Now this question is insoluble. Not because the relation to the other determinants would be antinomical, but because the new determinant itself does not permit of being conceived. The question: What is it exactly? can never be answered in ultimate terms—for the simple reason that it must be answered in terms of what is already known in other connections; and no such terms can here come into consideration; while what is not known would in turn be subject to the same question. One can only set such a question aside, one cannot settle it. Whether we ask "What are principles?" or "What is Reality?" or "What is a value?" the same barrier always manifests itself and is due to the nature of the question itself.

How could it be otherwise with self-determination! Taken strictly, the two other kinds of determination are almost equally irrational. We know only in part what causality is; and what the Ought is must be still less conceivable—recall our modal analysis of the Ought.[2] Hence one must not be astonished, that the same insurmountable barrier to rationality meets the same question when it is raised concerning the freedom of the will.

Yet an intelligent fixing of this limit is philosophically of the utmost importance. For here the question concerns the mapping out of the essential metaphysical problem of freedom. The various theories have lacked such a demarcation of the boundaries; and on that account they have allowed themselves most startling trespasses beyond bounds. One needs

[1] Cf. Chapter XVII (*b*), Vol. III.      [2] Chapter XXIII, Vol. I.

only to recall such theories as that of Fichte concerning volition anterior to volition, or that of Leibniz in regard to the absolute self-development of monads—not to mention Schopenhauer's "intelligible character"—, in order to understand how seriously such trespassing beyond bounds injures the matter in hand. The common error of these and all similar theories is that in general they intend to solve a metaphysical question by violence. Metaphysical questions do not permit of solution in that way. The assumptions which are then necessary pass beyond all possible control. They constitute an arbitrary maximum of metaphysics. At best they are uncritical assertions, neither verifiable nor capable of being refuted. Precisely of such questions does it hold good that we must proceed with the last degree of critical circumspection. We must in no assumption go beyond the limit of the absolutely required minimum of metaphysics and hypothesis; and, moreover, we must reckon upon an unknown residuum of material as an immovable factor.

Whatever can be learned concerning it we shall discover in this way, by drawing it into connection with the mass of known factors.

(d) PERSONAL TELEOLOGY AS A DETERMINATIONAL MODE OF POSITIVE FREEDOM

If the emphasis of the question be laid upon the How of personal self-determination, a very natural answer, which is not at all metaphysically audacious, forces itself upon one's mind: The determination is finalistic. That there is a teleology of the will—the only actual teleology which we know with certainty—has already been made plain in our categorial analysis of values and the Ought. One need not refer to the conscious acts of the will alone; all inclinations, in so far as they are moral acts, are directed towards persons and aim consciously or unconsciously at something in them, taking sides for or against these. All ethical intention has a teleological character.

The actual conduct of man by no means shares this teleology with the ideal values. Values of course show a tendency to teleological determination, but they do not actually determine of and by themselves; they enhance certain directions of aim on the part of the will, but they have not the power to carry out these aims. The will on the contrary—we may ignore the limits to external achievement—has the power to commit itself to definite ends. Hence it is master of precisely that teleology of which values are not master. So far in the teleology of the will we have presented a peculiarity of its mode of determination, which it shares with neither of the two other kinds of determination. But that, as compared with them, finalistic determination of the will is entirely possible, is to be easily inferred from what has previously been said. If Nature were finalistically determined, the teleology of the will would have no scope; Nature's causal nexus on the other hand is only passive material for possible purposive activity, since it is blind, without direction, without aim, passive. Above it, according to categorial laws, the higher determination of the end has unlimited scope. And concerning values, their tendency is not really finalistic; it is not finalistic determination. The real determination is first brought about by the will.

To this extent an essential feature of the positive determinant which is in question must be recognized in the teleology of the will. Yet one would be greatly deceived, if one thought that the problem was thereby solved. After all, this teleology is only the general type of "positive freedom"—the ability to determine oneself; but it is not the determining factor itself, whence the determination issues. It is not the principle, but only the categorial form or order of its efficacy. Yet here, in this central question of metaphysics, we are seeking for the principle of self-determination as such, for the fundamental capacity of the person in face of values, for the mysterious potency, which is given to persons in preference to all other real entities. Hence a demonstration that the will is teleological not only does not tell us what the unique determinant in the finalistic determination of the will really is, but also misses the meaning of the question.

### (e) THE ONTOLOGICAL DIFFICULTY IN PERSONAL FREEDOM

The question cannot be settled. And when we have once grasped what the question really refers to, every attempt at a solution of it seems to be an impertinence. It stands on a level with the question concerning the origin of the world; indeed, it is a question altogether similar to this, having a parallel aim: the question concerning the origin of moral Being in general. As moral Being exists autonomously together with natural Being, rising above it, so in the nature of the person its origin stands autonomous side by side with that of the person. Over the origins of both lies the same veil of metaphysical enigma, the same irrationality which cannot be set aside.

But another question, closely akin to this, may equally be raised in this connection and pursued a step further: the question as to the ontological possibility of such personal and individual freedom.

If for instance it cannot be the realm of values which is the positive factor in personal freedom but if precisely over against the values a positive element in the actual person gives the decision, and if on his side the actual person, in so far as he is not determined by values, is wholly embedded in ontological determination, how is it possible that there is still contained in him a source of his own, an actual Plus of determination, a positive freedom? On this point our previous elucidations of course give a certain information; and no one who has followed them can be in doubt how this question as to possibility is to be treated. Nevertheless the question has not been proposed in this form and has not been examined. It is parallel to that concerning the causal antinomy, except that now it is on a higher plane. At least the scheme of a solution to it can be given. The root difficulty has the following form.

The question concerns the freedom of the person. Categorially the person is carried by the subject, his freedom is a freedom of consciousness. Now, as we know well enough, consciousness is unfree, wherever we can trace it back to its conditions. It is at all times determined—by outward existence, by preconscious inner Being—, in short it is a convergent point of diverse determinations which do not originate from it. The causal antinomy sets over against it the Ought as a determinant. This, however, showed itself not only to be inadequate for personal freedom, but to be precisely an element of unfreedom. Hence it is here barred out. Is it not rather as if consciousness, and with it the person, sinks back into the universal determination of nature, which at all times includes the person and through him proceeds on its course unchecked? And in that case is not self-determination necessarily a phantasm?

The question may be made still more pointed: Granting that consciousness in all its component parts is ontologically determined, is there still a meaning in freedom of consciousness which may be retained?

It is clear that even the concept of positive freedom does not here offer a solution. Each positive component—it might be axiological and would not be included here—would be already drawn into the texture of ontological determinants. But still less can there be a question of merely negative freedom. Irrespective of the fact that this can exist only over against values, not over against ontological necessity, the merely "empty place" in the texture is contrary to the meaning of positive self-determination.

## (f) The Categorial Structure of the Complex Conditioning-Relationship

The answer apparently must be in the negative. Nevertheless just here the categorial laws of dependence prevail. According to them, above the total determination of each grade of Being there is still always unlimited scope for a higher existential form with its own peculiar and correspondingly higher determination. And over against the whole texture of the lower such a grade is necessarily "free."

The relation between many simple disparate conditions and something complex but unitary that is conditioned, is never a merely one-sided relation of conditionality. Within the complex, the conditions are already different from what they were outside of it; but the complex itself works reactively and conditions them. Yet on its side the complex as such is not contained in them; over against them all there is still a categorial *novum*. Generally one overlooks this basic ontological fact, because one involuntarily judges every conditioning relationship according to the analogy of the causal relation. Now, strictly taken, it is not otherwise even in the causal relation. But the unequivocal irreversible passage from the earlier in time to the later hides from an eye directed to details the structure of the complex effect which was not preformed in the causes as such. If one turns to examples of a really higher but inexplicable complex, such for instance as biological phenomena, the categorial *novum* of the total resultant strikes one immediately.

Accordingly one may say: the complex unitary resultant is always both contained and not contained in the simple but diversified components; contained—in so far as everything in it down to the last detail is conditioned by the components and would itself be changed by the least change in them; not contained—in so far as the unique quality of the complex resultant as such manifests a categorial structure, which in its arrangement is higher than all the components and can in no wise be resolved into them. Now this unique quality is something distinctive, essential—at least in the realm of being of the resultant. It stands upon another plane of existence, a higher one, which is subject to higher categories.

Accordingly in this double relationship there is no antagonism, no antinomy; in it is simply reflected the reciprocity of two categorial laws of dependence.[1] The fact of being contained in the components corresponds to the basic categorial law (the law of strength); the fact of not being contained in them, to the law of freedom (equally of course to the law of material). From the point of view of the former, necessity prevails throughout, proceeding from the lower to the higher forms; the lower are the stronger, against them no higher formation can achieve anything. And thorough-going deterministic necessity means only this bondage in the downward direction, but not entanglement in the conditions. For it is not at the same time bondage in the upward direction. It is this which the other law expresses: there is no bondage of the categorial *novum* as such to the elements which it catches up into itself and upon which it mounts; the peculiar quality of the higher form has the lower forms merely as material, as a passive, neutral foundation. Above them it is, with all that proceeds from it, categorially "free," autonomous. It has its specific determinant in itself.

This is the scheme, according to which the difficulty concerning the ontological possibility of personal freedom is to be solved—at least in principle. It would be a mistake to enter into the details of the ontal complex of conditions. Even if something of these could be explained, the totality of conditions—and this alone is of import—would remain inaccessible to our vision. But there is also no need of this, in order to discern in principle the ontological possibility, the compossibility, of personal freedom and the all-pervasiveness and permanence of existential determinism which is by no means simply causal. On the ground of the universal ontological relation of dependence, the categorial determinant, unifying and independent, in the moral person, above the texture of the components, is unquestionable.

Once more, of course, only "in principle." The unquestionability does not mean that every person at every moment, in every act or even in every line of conduct, would necessarily

[1] Cf. Chapter XXXVIII (*c*), Vol. II, and Chapter VI (*b*), Vol. III.

be free. That would not be in agreement with the moral phenomenon. Ordinarily man is in many directions not accountable and responsible; perhaps he is indeed never wholly responsible, never quite a free being. But he may be so—in principle—and he ought to be so. Moral freedom means standing upon the summit of humanity, and not everyone can attain that height at every moment. And his smallest fragment of real freedom confirms the reality of his freedom; it is already a proof that he is not merely a dependent entity under determining principles, but is at the same time himself a determining principle among other principles—and indeed that each one is for himself a unique individual principle. No difficulty of an ontological nature is to be found here; for to a principle it is a matter of indifference, whether it is determined by one form or many or by none.

## (g) Moral and Categorial Freedom

The ontological relation which we are here considering is by no means unique in kind. Wherever various existential components cross one another in a complex structure, the same relation is found. The separate components merge in the resultant. They are cancelled in it as in a higher equipoise of the constituent elements. The complex structure is of a higher form and order of being. It draws everything into itself, assimilates everything to its nature, and at the same time achieves a total "reflection in itself" of its components. We are using only another metaphor for the same thing, when we say that the higher form is suspended, without weight, above the ontal elements. For in fact it lies in another plane of Being. This simply means that in it an existent of another order is present—an existent of an equally real mode of actuality and in so far also of like mundane weight, but dissimilar in structure and inner constitution.

It is thus with the distinctive categorial nature of the organic in its relation to everything inorganic which, as an existential component with its entire lower (perhaps mechanical or otherwise physical) order and mode of determination, is introduced in its complex. Its peculiar mode of being, vitality, is just as real ontally as that of the components; but structurally it is coincident neither with any one of them nor with their sum total. It is this which constitutes the inadequacies of every mechanical explanation of "life." Herein vitalism is forever right as over against all such theories, but only in so far as it remains fully aware of the impenetrability of its subject-matter and of the irrationality of its own vitalistic principle, and does not in short-sighted fashion seize upon the first best-known higher category (perhaps purpose) as a principle. More impressively than in physiological processes (in assimilation and dissimilation, for instance), this law is manifested in the life of a species, where in the relation of the mortality and reproduction of the individual there is disclosed a quite unique kind of preservation, which is at the disposal of no lower structure. Such preservation of life is not subsistence—for subsistence is the continuation of the lower structure (like the continuity of energy) while the higher changes—, but is a kind of super-existence on the part of the complex and higher structure, while the lower changes. For by virtue of its higher principle the life persists above the passing of the individuals.

It is quite another kind of existential structure which is found in a moral personality. Nevertheless the essential feature in it is also a super-existence *sui generis*. But here it is precisely the individual which has its unique mode of existence above its components. This does not change the situation in principle. Here the point at issue is not preservation but independence. Neither inheres in the components. And in both cases the higher, the more fragile structure is shown to be at the same time the superior, compared with the components. Not indeed as the stronger—that would contradict its categorial superiority—but as the directive structure.

Every higher type of existence with its own categorial formation is *eo ipso* "free," as over the lower. Its mere superiority suffices for this; and all dependence upon the lower structure signifies in the latter only the inevitably greater strength of the elementary, not an admixture with its peculiar quality. This categorial law of freedom is all-pervading. Even in the causal antinomy everything depends upon it. Viewed ontologically, the freedom of the will is only a special case of categorial freedom. But of course it is a very specific case, in content profoundly different from the freedom of a living being in relation to inanimate matter, or from that of consciousness (for instance of thought, of fantasy) in relation to the inflexible necessity of biological processes. It cannot well be doubted that living matter as such has its own inner laws, although we cannot conceive them. The fact has been established ever since Aristotle that thought has its peculiar "logical" principles, to which it is subject, independently of every law of consciousness, upon which it rises as a differently articulated structure—a doctrine which has been the victim of much foolish misinterpretation, but which has never suffered a single serious attack. So must it be accepted as highly reasonable in principle, and in accord with the entire structure of ontological and categorial stratification, that into the disposition, volition and moral conduct of the individual person there enters a distinctive law, which appertains to the person alone, a genuine, positive autonomy of his own, together with all inner and external conditioning, and that his self-determination consists in this autonomy. For the understandable distinctiveness of the structure can here be as little misconceived as in the world of thought. Fundamentally in its ontological structure autonomy is the same, whether in organic, psychological, logical or ethical entities. These autonomies are peculiar only to different stages of being; and they present different problems. The texture of the lower categorial components also, upon which they are built, varies greatly as to the degree to which it can be known. But all this constitutes no fundamental difference, but only a gradation of a subordinate kind. On this account the analogy is convincingly decisive for the question of the freedom of the will.

### (h) THE LIMIT TO THE PROBLEM

Our final word on this subject must mark the boundary, up to which the problem of freedom may be pursued. There are two judgments of different kind and origin which apply here, and together give a picture of the situation. In the first place, freedom of the moral person is ethically necessary, and secondly it is ontologically possible. The first affirms that the factual complexes of the moral life can exist only under the pre-supposition of it; the second, that the entire series of the more general and elementary questions, as they are conceived in the problem of knowledge and Being, contains nothing in the widest outlook, which would seriously contradict such freedom as is required by the ethical problem.

Nothing more can be said on the problem of freedom. As for a proof of ontological necessity, the facts are not adequate. Only the complete series of the conditions could decide whether personal freedom is ontologically necessary or not. And if one reflects that in the strict sense the real existence of freedom would be proved, if its ontological necessity were proved—since, by the laws of modality, possibility and necessity to-gether constitute ontological actuality—, one sees distinctly that here lies the boundary to the problem, beyond which no human insight can penetrate.

A rigid proof of freedom of will cannot be given. It would need to show the ontological necessity of freedom. The coin-cidence of ethical necessity and ontological possibility does not extend so far. On the other hand we ought not to undervalue the philosophical significance of such coincidence as exists. It furnishes a hypothetical certainty of the freedom of the will, and indeed one of a high degree. But here the hypothetical strain can be just as little removed as in the case of the problem of thought and Being.

Afterwards, as before, the door stands open to ethical

scepticism. Should it attempt to step over the threshold, hypothetical arguments could not prevent it from doing so. But precisely in this matter philosophical pessimism would be unjustifiable. For ethical scepticism cannot cross the threshold. The burden of proof falls upon it, it must explain the appearance of freedom, when it challenges the reality of it; for it is scepticism which takes upon itself the contest against the significance of the phenomena. It cannot carry the burden of proof without becoming a positive theory. Thereby it ceases to retain for itself the "nihilistic strength" of the sceptical position and is hurled headlong into those embarrassing difficulties, of which we saw that a solution by the round-about way of forced theories leads back unintentionally but inevitably to the very position which originally was rejected—the freedom of the will.

In respect to this matter the discovery of the limits of the problem is equivalent to an absolutely positive theory. In it there is not only nothing contradictory to personal freedom, to which all the perspectives of ethics unmistakably point, but it is precisely the knowledge of the limits of the problem which makes it certain—and indeed absolutely, not hypothetically—that every conceivable rejection of freedom—be it sceptical or otherwise grounded—necessarily has no foothold in reality, seeing that it can produce neither a factual complex to speak for itself nor any sound ontological argument against freedom.

Thus the door remains open to scepticism. But scepticism stays outside. Of itself it cannot cross the threshold. And if anyone, although dazzled by its jugglery, does not extend his hand to it, he remains within the field of ethics untroubled by it.

*Section VI*

**APPENDIX TO THE DOCTRINE OF FREEDOM**

# CHAPTER XX (LXXXIV)

## APPARENT AND REAL DEFECTS OF THE THEORY

AFTER what has already been said, there is no need to insist further that the arguments, which have been submitted here, are inadequate and that the whole theory of freedom is incomplete. Neither must one allow oneself to be deceived by the display of distant metaphysical vistas, any more than by the solubility of certain difficulties in regard to defects which are still present. Every justification would here be out of place.

Nor is there need of any justification, considering the state of the problem. The problem of freedom, here set forth in sharp outline, is far too new to be ready for final forms of expression. And, lastly, the presentation of the second and higher stage of the problem, as it first appears in the Ought-antinomy, still remains in the first stage of investigation. The work of any one person can have only the character of a preliminary attempt.

Nevertheless not all the defects in the theory which at first glance strike the eye are real defects. Some among them only appear to be such. They make themselves felt as a certain unsatisfactoriness, which is rooted in the fact that the developed concept of freedom does not tally with the preconceived notions with which one starts out. One does not notice that one's expectations themselves perhaps constitute a false standard, so long as one remains emotionally in their grip. The verifiable ethical phenomena, and nothing else, form the only right standard. The theory must be justified only in relation to them. Every other standard is arbitrary.

For instance, the peculiarity that the personal freedom which is here presented is not absolute freedom, is such a seeming defect.

This is proved not only by the fact that, as was indicated above,[1] not every human will is free, but also by the fact that,

[1] Cf. Chapter XIX (f), Vol. III.

together with the free, there also exists an unfree will and that this perhaps is predominant. It is also proved by the fact that even the free will is always only in part free, that is, that there is in it only one independent determinant amidst many that come from outside and are heteronomous. That this fact is not in harmony with the lofty claims of our human sense of independence, one must take on the word of those who proudly delude themselves with philosophical problems. But is this a defect in the theory?

It only seems to be a defect. The very phenomena show that the human will is not absolutely free. Even our psychological knowledge of the encircling conditions and complete dependence must be included in the phenomenon. This dependence, as is well known, goes so far that freedom in the midst of it appears only as something miraculous. Hence it is the concept of a will that is merely in part or only relatively free, which tallies with the phenomenon. If theories demonstrate an absolutely free will, they demonstrate something false. To prove too much, is to prove nothing. What alone corresponds to the phenomenon is simply this: amidst the various heteronomous determinants of the will one determinant is autonomous, and that suffices as a foundation for self-determination, for imputability, responsibility and guilt; it suffices also for the bearing of moral values and disvalues. On that account it does not need to be present always and in every actual volition; for not every will is free, not every man on every occasion is in reality morally responsible.

Hence to this extent the defect is actually not in the theory but in the object, in the imperfection of human freedom itself, and ultimately in the imperfection of the moral existence of man.

\* \* \*

But it becomes still more suspicious, if one puts the question in the form: Which human will is free? Or again, if not every will is free, as long as in principle it can be free and ought to be, wherein does the difference consist? And in any given case what distinguishes the free from the unfree will?

There have been many attempts to answer this question. Even in Kant's distinction between the pure will and the empirical there was such an attempt, in so far as the pure will was to be the free will, while the empirical was to be under complete psychological bondage to heteronomous factors. This conception approaches dangerously near to the familiar confusion of the contrast between the good and the bad will with the contrast between the free and the unfree. But this is a complete denial of the phenomena: if the bad will is not free, how then could guilt be assigned precisely to it, indeed, how would a sense of guilt on the part of the doer himself be possible?

If by "pure" will one understands not the good will but some kind of a "transcendental" will, and under the empirical that which manifests itself psychologically, the distinction is all awry. Evidently the transcendental will is not, as such, that of the actual person; it is in the fictitious sphere of an ethical "subject in general." Guilt then and responsibility would needs fall upon the latter and not upon the actual person. This flagrant blunder has already been refuted, it is the πρῶτον ψεῦδος of "transcendental freedom."[1]

If one keeps the risk of such confusion of concepts clearly in mind, one can well understand how Nietzsche—of course with quite a different object in view—could no longer speak of free and unfree, but only of strong and weak, will. That was at least logical. Nor need it imply a denial (as with Nietzsche) of the freedom of the will. Only, in that case, by the strong will one must not understand one which in action ruthlessly executes its purpose, nor one that is inwardly passionate and stops at nothing, but a will in which the autonomous determinant rules over those which are heteronomous, with decisive energy. Yet in this no distinction is provided, the same thing is affirmed as is contained in the developed concept of moral freedom. Which will is strong can no more be inferred here, than which will is free.

[1] Cf. Chapter VIII (b), Vol. III.

There is also no advantage in meaning by the free will that which is far-seeing and directed to ideas. This also misses the intended distinction. Ideas moreover can be very heteronomously suggested. And on the other hand even the will which misses its distant goals is not blameless in its failure, hence not unfree. In general it is the most erroneous of all traditional notions, that moral freedom increases with the valuational quality of the conduct, that is to say, that the will is so much the freer, the higher it aims in the scale of values. It must be just as free in its badness and degradation, in so far as moral badness is concerned.

The result of all such attempts at finding the distinguishing mark of freedom is that we in fact have no such mark, and that even philosophical thought, so far as it may be able to pursue the problem, nowhere encounters anything of the kind. We can in no wise tell which will is free and which is not. In ethics there is no standard of freedom—as there is a standard of good and bad in the sensing of values. Freedom and unfreedom of the will constitute a standard of another dimension.

This is a defect in the theory. But it also is a defect only from the point of view of exaggerated expectations. Is there then an ethical phenomenon which would counteract the absence of a fixed standard? Is there an emotional certainty in regard to another's responsibility and accountability, which might be compared, let us say, with our certainty of feeling in regard to moral value? Evidently there is not. The injunction "Judge not" by no means refers merely to the popular warning against heartlessness and self-righteousness in condemning; it also expresses the impossibility of knowing whether there is blame or not, that is, whether the volition was free or not. The man of fine moral feeling is the very one who is always dimly conscious of this impossibility. He knows that he has no infallible sign by which to distinguish freedom. For him accordingly every imputation and every confident moral judgment have in them something of the nature of a venture.

What looks like a weakness in the theories and is so, if taken absolutely, proves to be exactly in harmony with the ethical phenomenon and in so far has its justification. It is precisely our ignorance of freedom and unfreedom in the concrete case, which is characteristic of the moral consciousness.

Yet this proposition also must not be pressed too far. We must not forget that freedom also has a valuational character, and on its axiological side is an object of our valuational sense. In the sensing of values there always inheres a standard for what is presented to it. Just at this point of course our ability to appraise is poorly trained. But there is always a possibility of discrimination. And it is perhaps not difficult to show that this sensing of freedom and unfreedom in the conduct of a person is always inherent in every moral judgment.

But to settle this matter would require a special analysis of acts in detail—a task which still awaits the new phenomenology of the moral consciousness.

*   *
 *

The question concerning the knowledge of freedom and unfreedom, which is of such decisive import for the completion of ethics, constitutes only one of very many which still remain unsettled. To enumerate these fully would be a tiresome and thankless work. Instead of doing that, we can here touch upon only two questions, the treatment of which may throw some light upon the fundamental problem.

In the whole of our investigation we have examined only the freedom of the person in his conduct, volition, disposition, and so on. Now the presupposition of this complex of acts is this, that values are somehow or other presented to the moral consciousness—in the feeling for values—, and that always in every act, somehow or other, decision is involved as to the felt values and felt claim of the Ought. But this feeling itself is never adequate; it is always only a section of the valuational realm which is felt or discerned. How is it with the values which are missed?

It is very natural to reply that these are not moral failures, they are not to be imputed to the person, because they do not arise from free decision; a free decision for or against is possible only in regard to a value that is vividly felt. But this reply is highly unsatisfactory when we apply it to cases of elementary badness, like brutality, unscrupulous greed and dishonesty, where it is evident that even in the absence of feeling towards the disvalue (hence also towards the value) there is a moral inferiority. In the life of the soul there exist factors which obscure values, and the person himself is by no means guiltless in regard to such factors. One need only recall the well-known phenomenon of moral callousness due to the person's own repeated transgression, or the very justifiable warning that if you give the devil an inch he will take an ell. Ever since Aristotle, the dictum has often been repeated that a man is himself to blame for not discriminating between good and evil, that it was open to him not to be involved in such ignorance.[1]

Is there then, besides freedom of the will in regard to discerned values, also a freedom of discernment itself? Or at least a freedom of the primal sensing of values?

If one keeps close to the phenomena, one cannot deny that in its scope and acuteness a man's valuational sense is to a certain degree dependent upon the amount of trouble he takes about the good. On the other hand it is undeniable, that the single individual, even by the most strenuous moral discipline, could not at pleasure extend his discernment of values indefinitely. Therefore, in case there be a freedom of the valuational sense, it is at all events limited in a quite different degree from the actual capacity to decide in regard to values discerned. The suspicion arises that freedom of discernment extends only to such values as have already been discerned and could again have vanished out of sight only by one's own fault—only through a hardening of one's heart or some neglect (δι' ἀμέλειαν); but the freedom does not extend to those which the evaluating sense would need to attain by effort.

[1] Cf. *Eth. Nicom.* Γ, Chapter VII, especially the passage 1114a 1 ff: . . . ὡς ἐπ' αὐτοῖς ὄν τὸ μὴ ἀγνοεῖν.

Hence this sort of freedom would relate only to the alternative between preserving and losing values already presented, and not to the fresh acquisition of values as yet not seen or felt.

Here accordingly we encounter a further problem, the inherent difficulties of which evidently would permit of being probed more deeply—a problem which could throw an altogether new light upon the total state of the question of freedom. It would especially be helpful in investigating more exactly the limit of the freedom of valuational discernment and its inner relation to freedom of the will. It is natural to suspect here a deeper interpenetration of the reciprocal conditioning of the two kinds of freedom.

But this subject must be reserved for separate and more specialized exploration.

*   *
*

Another question which is akin to the foregoing is whether a man's development in moral freedom rests in turn upon freedom, whether he bears responsibility for his unfreedom also, as for every other kind of moral inferiority.

That there exists in general a development in moral freedom, as well as a retrogression into unfreedom, there can be no doubt. And if it were not evident in all its concreteness to the man of moral experience, yet it would follow irresistibly from the analysis we have made of the question of freedom, which showed that it is precisely the absolutely free will which never exists; what exists is always one that is only relatively and in part free. Altogether it is only in principle that freedom is demonstrable: a man can be free but is not always and unconditionally so. Accordingly the question arises: Is a person's entrance into moral freedom conditioned by his own cooperation or not? Is his falling back into unfreedom a moral fault or not?

That various external factors influence his development is certain before any investigation at all. But naturally such self-evident truths decide nothing. There might be present at the same time an inner determinant of self-determination in the direction of freedom and moral awakening; likewise, one in the direction of unfreedom; at the same time, a tendency to moral inertia.

The decisive factor here is this, that freedom itself has a valuational quality, and indeed that of a basic value conditioning all distinctively moral values.[1] This value is directly felt, wherever there is a question as to a person's capacity to pledge himself, as to his imputability and responsibility. The sensing of this capacity is so common, that our very respect for a person morally—the general basis of personal and moral conduct—appears as a function of it. That this valuational feeling may increase until it becomes a willingness to accept blame is only an extreme case of the general phenomenon; but on that account it is the very strongest of proofs.

If anyone cared to draw the conclusion that all will desires to be free, he would be shooting beyond the mark. As we saw in regard to the value of freedom, there is also the reverse tendency, the craving for deliverance from guilt and responsibility. But the question does not concern such generalizations. It suffices if we are clear as to the fact that there is a tendency toward freedom and that it is evidently not without influence upon the development of the basic moral capacity, that mysterious potency of the human being which is not further analysable. This capacity is established by the well-known fact that man's responsibility and his delight therein—even in youth—can be aroused to a high degree and disciplined; just as in general man grows morally with his larger enterprises.

But the root difficulty which is found here is peculiar and is altogether different from the other difficulties connected with freedom. If for instance there be a tendency to be free, and if this itself is again free, apparently the very same thing which it makes its aim is presupposed as its condition. Man must already be free, in order to will to be free. So long as it is here

[1] Cf. Chapter XI (f), Vol. II.

only a question as to the mere augmenting of a freedom already present in germ, there is of course nothing contrary to sense in it. But perhaps that is not the whole of the question. There might very well be a lower limit to actual freedom, a limit below which no one could rise even to a sense of freedom or even to a consciousness of his own moral worthlessness. An abundance of facts corresponds to the existence of such a limit—facts ranging all the way from mere moral indifference and inertia to complete stupefaction of conscience and of the sense of responsibility.

At this point there must be a real defect in the theory. For it cannot solve the problem. To-day the investigation of the matter halts even at its beginning and is in need of a fundamental clearing up, before any definite conclusions can be drawn.

## ETHICAL AND RELIGIOUS FREEDOM

THERE are more difficulties than those which have been mentioned. We have not yet even touched upon the gravest defects of the theory—defects not only apparent but real. They disclose themselves, when we look further into the metaphysical side of the problem of freedom. There arises a series of unanswered questions which are alleged to be unanswerable, and which exist independently of the problem of remainders which was set forth in Chapter XIX of this volume. From this they are distinguished by the fact that they no longer belong to ethics itself and need not be treated at all in it. They are problems concerning the boundary line between ethics and religion.

Ethics is not the whole of philosophy. And as philosophy, in order to be sure of its foundations, must find its bearings in the ethical field, so in the field of religion it must needs find not only its ontological and ethical but perhaps many other bearings. Accordingly in ethics we can very well avoid religio-philosophical questions, but in the philosophy of religion we cannot avoid ethical questions.

Hence in the questions as to the boundary line, which are here under discussion, we are consciously transcending the domain of ethics. Here accordingly these questions cannot be treated in detail, but only touched upon, at most formulated. But since there is a deep inward connection between the two domains, the outlook of ethics leads us beyond its own proper problems directly into those of religion. It is not as though there followed from its problems anything concerning the existence of God or anything related thereto; it is not as though even a mere doctrine of postulates, in Kant's sense, could be joined to ethical questions. The contrary is the case: granted that the existence of God and the factors of religious experience were firmly established on other grounds, it is the propositions of ethics which, as regards their contents, are shown to be at the same time in the highest degree relevant to religion.

This is a fact so well known that no argument is needed to defend it. Upon it rests the claim which religion has always made, to speak the final word in ethics. Whether this be a metaphysical encroachment on the part of religion—like its claim to speak the last word in the domain of ontological theory,—this is not the place to decide. Perhaps it is a question which transcends the limits of human insight. At all events philosophy has needed to struggle hard enough, to secure freedom of action for itself over against these claims. The service rendered by "critical" philosophy, in so far as it has set up barriers against the dictatorial aggression of religious thought, cannot be estimated too highly. But since critical philosophy by its very nature at the same time secures thereby the independence of religion within its own boundaries—and this means naturally not "within the limits of pure reason," but precisely beyond those limits,—we must in the interest of ethics itself take up the task of subjecting those limits to investigation at that point where ethical problems go beyond them.

At the same time and independently of their purely ethical significance, the majority of ethical problems fall also under the point of view of religion—precisely therefore under the point of view which it has been necessary to exclude from the entire series of our investigations. Good-bad, value-disvalue, commandment-prohibition, will, disposition, guilt, responsibility, freedom, unfreedom, are just as much religious as ethical problems. Before philosophical ethics became the independent master of these, which are its own problems, and long afterwards, it was religion which dealt with them, and it has continued to do so.

But because in religion they come ultimately under a different point of view, they cannot be the same to it as to ethics. This in itself is no occasion for conflict; indeed it might be that religion simply constitutes a higher stratum of the problem, a stratum in which, because it is higher, the old contents show themselves in a new and more significant aspect. That in Idea such a relationship may hold good, we may quietly assume without doing violence to one or the other domain, so long at least as we keep in mind that it is only an assumption. Moreover, the circumstances are by no means such, that the mere emergence of contradictions destroys the value of such an assumption. Antinomies prove nothing against the coexistence of what is antinomically divided, even though they should be proved to be genuine antinomies, that is, should be insoluble. They only prove the inability of thought to comprehend the coexistence.

But to be assured of such antinomies when they emerge, is so much the more important. For in them, if anywhere at all, the great problems of metaphysical remainders can be more exactly outlined at least in respect to their boundaries. The one task which in this particular falls within our ethical survey—the last which we are to consider—is therefore the elaboration of these antinomies between ethics and religion, in so far as ethics and religion have the same subject-matter.

* * *

It would be easy to enumerate a whole series of such antinomies. But here we can select only five, which lie more or less at the base of all the more specific ones and are besides sufficient to enable us to survey, in principle, the whole situation. The first three of these constitute a smaller group, they refer to divergences as to contents; the last two on the other hand are concerned with the problem of freedom in that peculiar displacement, which it undergoes in the transition from ethics to religion.

The first antinomy concerns the tendency towards this world or towards the Beyond. All genuine religion tends to look from our present existence to a "better" world. The extreme emphasis which has sometimes been laid upon this distinction, and which after all is only logical, reaches a point at which our mundane sphere has no values whatever of its own—is heard of only as a preparation for the other world. All the values which are of inherent worth lie in the Beyond. The true life is another life, not the so-called "real" life in which we have our being. Hence the demand that this world with its apparent values be sacrificed for the sake of that true existence and its values; since no one can serve two masters. To seek the values of this world for their own sake is bad; within this world only that is good which tends beyond it. The consequence is a depreciation of our present existence, a turning away of man from the life that now is and—in idea at least—a complete escape from the world.

Ethics has exactly the reverse tendency. It is wholly committed to this life. The contents of all the moral values bear upon a man's concrete conduct in this world towards men of this world. Even the most far-seeing moral ideals look to this world as their place of fulfilment. From the ethical point of view, the tendency toward the Beyond is just as contrary to value as, from the religious point of view, is the tendency toward this world. It is a waste of moral energy and a diversion of it away from true values and their actualization, and on that account is not moral. Moral striving regards everything which transcends this life as a deceitful phantom. And even where the two tendencies could in substance agree—as in regard to self-abnegation and delight in sacrifice—, still the tendency itself loses its ethical worth, as soon as it casts longing glances towards a better lot in the Beyond.

By no compromise can this antinomy be solved. That the two tendencies are seldom presented in all their baldness is only a proof of human inconsequence. At bottom they are strictly contradictory to each other. Each denies the other. One of them must necessarily be illusory. Were the conflict to be settled, it would not in any case be settled for reason, but only beyond it—in the irrational.

The second antinomy carries the conflict over into the relation between man and Divinity, as the ultimate substratum of values. It does not coincide with the first antinomy but intersects it. Ethics is always concerned finally with man, religious thought with God. His power, his action, his will, set the standard, in this world as in the next. Man has only a subordinate place; for him the good is what God wills. Compared with God's will, his own is good or bad, according as it recognizes God's will and humbly places that above his own or does not.

This also is a complete, genuine antinomy, which for Reason is insoluble. The very constitution of man is such that of all the objects which come within his range of vision, man is ethically the most momentous, the most real and at the same time the highest and in responsibility the richest. Of course not man in any individual's own personality, but the personal element in every human being. That anything whatsoever in heaven or on the earth, even though it be God himself, should take precedence of Man, would be ethically perverted; it would not be moral; it would be treason to mankind, which must rely upon itself alone. Many religious teachers have acknowledged this essential law, in that they have presented devotion to God as the true concern of man in his own interest —for the salvation of his soul. But this is a compromise, even from the point of view of religion. For it is inherent in the nature of God, that only he, and nothing outside of him, can be the aim of all aims, the most important and real for every finite being whom he has created, and that as compared with God everything, even man, is nothing.

The third antinomy is connected with the first two and yet is distinct from them. Like them it also is at heart axiological. But it is concerned not with the content but with the origin of values.

The proposition that ethical values are autonomous, that is, that they are of worth not for the sake of anything else but purely from their own nature and for their own sake, is a necessary foundation (as has been shown) for every system of ethics that deserves the name. The concrete meaning of the proposition is this, that no authority nor any fiat of power nor any will—not to mention man's sanction—stands behind ethical values—for otherwise their evidence would not be absolute and aprioristic—; on the contrary, the meaning is that in ethical values themselves, there is something which to our sense of values proves their irreducible nature.

Against this proposition religion sets up the antithesis: every moral claim of the Ought is at bottom a commandment of God, an expression of his will, and only on this account does man, towards whom the commandment is directed, feel its content to be a moral value. For morality consists in a life according to the law of God. Hereby the moral values lose their self-dependence and become heteronomous. They are simply given by the fiat of divine power. It is a matter of indifference, into what form one casts this notion. Whether one says "God commands what is good," or "God is the good," or "all moral values are based upon the value of God (the holy one) as the absolutely supreme value," makes no difference as to the heteronomy of values. In the last mentioned case they would still be axiological, although their axiological foundation would not be ethical; in the first two cases they would be altogether super-axiological, for neither God himself nor the fiat of his power is contained in the ideal mode of Being peculiar to values. Hence as regards the fundamental meaning of the antinomy one may ignore all further interpretations.

No one who grasps the problem can entertain any doubt that this antinomy, even if not so urgent as the first two, goes just as close as they to the root of the matter. And that it is equally a genuine and insoluble antinomy, can be seen in this, that the thesis and the antithesis bar each other out at the point where, as regards their contents, there is no occasion for opposition. It is inherent in the nature of God that, in a world which is his thought and his value, nothing can be of value on any other ground, except that he wills it, that he commands it, or that it in some other way issues from his essence; only thus does it have the power of an Ought-to-Be. And if besides these there were values existing in themselves, God needs must either repudiate them or first sanction them by his will.

But it is inherent in the essence of moral values, that they have convincing power in themselves—and are self-evident and are applicable to men, only as an imperturbable Ought, in so far as their content itself, as such, bears the characteristics alleged to be derived from outside authority; hence no one could make them self-evident in their claim—even by the most powerful *fiat*—unless he were already supported therein by their own power or self-evidence. But in this case all commending of them by any person would be superfluous. Accordingly to values, which apart from him have strength of validity, God might lend a prestige among men by his power and authority; but he could not prescribe values as a law-giver. For if he dictated what did not harmonize with self-existent values, his dictation could be carried out only as a commandment but could never be sensed as a value.

Here there is a radical and rigid contradiction, which spurns every compromise that one might suggest. By over-refined reconciliation one only obscures and falsifies the opposing claims of God and man. And for both sides the falsification is equally ominous.

*   *   *

The most marked antinomies, however, become manifest only in reference to the problem of freedom. They are correctly called "the antinomies of freedom"; without a break they unite with the causal antinomy and that of the Ought, except that they themselves are no longer of an ethical character. The first of them we might name the "antinomy of providence," the second that of "salvation."

We have previously pointed out, in how far religious differs from moral freedom, although in both the question in regard to freedom concerns the same claims of the Ought. In ethics the will only stands over against the law of nature on the one side and the moral law (values) on the other. Both allow scope to the will, because the uniformity of nature determines only causally, while values in themselves do not determine at all. On the other hand, in the religious conception of the world the will has, besides all this, to cope with the providence of God.

Here is an authoritative factor of quite a different ascendency. The course of nature also, it is true, is preponderant, but it is blind; it points to no goals to which it binds man: accordingly if man has the capacity to set up ends for himself, he finds the course of nature neutral towards them and within the limits of possible adjustment entirely dirigible. Altogether different is divine providence. It is teleologic, a finalistic determinism. Its ultimate ends are the determinants. And because their determining power is infinite and almighty and moreover permeates every event in the world—even in the little spiritual world of man—, over against it man with his teleology is impotent. He finds here no more scope for his self-determination; more correctly, what to him appears to be his self-determination is in fact the power of divine providence, working onward through him and above him.

At this point it is only necessary to be reminded of what was previously said, in order to see in what bold antithesis these consequences of divine providence stand to the ethical demand for freedom. By them the foresight of man is simply annulled, his self-determination is reduced to a phantom; his ethos is annihilated, his will paralysed.[1] All initiative, all setting up and pursuit of ends is transferred to God. But the foundation of this general paralysis is an inversion of the basic categorial law: the higher form of determination is made the stronger form, the finalistic nexus alone dominates.

In this way the finalistic determinism of divine providence abolishes ethical freedom. But if we grant validity to personal freedom, it inevitably abolishes the finalistic determinism of divine providence. Each stands in contradiction to the other, as thesis to antithesis. That this is no longer an ethical antinomy

[1] Cf. Chapter VI (g), Vol. III.

of freedom, we have already seen; for ethics does not affirm the existence of divine providence. Just as little do any of the extra-ethical presuppositions implied in ethics affirm divine providence. That affirmation is contained only in religious thought, towards which ethics throughout its entire series of problems stands in absolute neutrality—it stands on this side both of theism and atheism. And the antinomy first arises with these.

Nevertheless this antinomy is in a different position from the first three between ethics and religion. It is found for example not only in the opposition between the two spheres of the problem, but also within the domain of religion itself. Even religion cannot do without man's freedom of will. For it is pre-eminently religion which takes into account responsibility, imputability and human guilt, as is proved by the central position assigned to the concept of sin. Hence not only the ethical but also the religious interpretation of man imperatively requires man's self-determination. Together with ethical freedom of will there is a no less necessary religious freedom of will. But the latter is wholly different from the former. For in the ethical domain the difficulties involved in the freedom of the will are solved, at least in principle. But since thorough-going finalistic determinism is first introduced along with divine providence, an evidently insurmountable obstacle is opposed to divine providence. In no way can the new difficulty involved in religious freedom be solved. Man's religious freedom is no longer freedom as regards natural law or the moral law, but as over against the will of God within the world and in man himself. That is what renders this antinomy insoluble in principle.

And yet, if the religious view of the world is to be at all capable of maintaining itself, this antinomy must be surmounted, even if not for human insight, yet in itself and in opposition to human insight. It is at bottom a false fear of God, if we surrender the ethos of man to the honour of God. In truth we thereby degrade the Creator of the world to the level of a blunderer who does not know what he is producing. With the highest before his eyes, his own Divinity, he must have created a distorted image of the Divine, a world which completely failed to reflect his glory, a glory which could be reflected only in the foresight and self-determination of the creature. And after he had so made the world and had so placed man in it, he was to condemn man on account of "sin," as if God might not rather have withheld entirely from man the capacity to sin.

It is no accident that such reasoning sounds like blasphemy. In all ages it has been felt to be such. And on that account again and again, precisely by men of deepest religious insight—contrary to all reason and all understanding—, religious freedom, the freedom of man before God himself, has been affirmed. Of course only affirmed, not proved; for a proof is not here conceivable. One cannot assume religious freedom without *sacrificium intellectus.*

There has been no lack of attempts to prove religious freedom. The dialectical thinkers have gone furthest in this direction, in that here—whether to justify God or for the moral rehabilitation of man—they have tried to bring to their assistance an "identity" of freedom and providential necessity. That was a radical procedure; for what was here set up as identical is nothing short of an absolute contradiction. It was like an act of despair on the part of human reason; and yet, as such, it would have been honourable evidence of philosophical earnestness, except that it called forth the appearance of a solution which it by no means achieved, and which thereby proved itself to be a sophism.

All such attempts have failed and must necessarily fail. Neither real identity nor any other kind of dialectical synthesis can be demonstrated. What is contradictory remains contradictory. All such dialectic begins by inverting the basic categorial law, upon which alone freedom can rest.

Hereby of course neither freedom nor divine providence is refuted. A demonstration of the falsity of proofs and theories is never as such a refutation of any proposition. The proposition can very well be true; but it persists as something absolutely irrational. If one looks closer, one sees that religious thinking all along the line of its problems has to do with nothing but such irrationalities. The existence of God can in no way be either demonstrated or refuted. All that matters here is philosophical clearness as to the absoluteness of the limit to rationality, that is, as to the fact that nothing either positive or negative can be settled by any theory of religious freedom.

* * *

The reverse side of the antinomy of providence is the antinomy of salvation. It is somewhat more closely akin to the axiological antinomies—for in it the "value" of freedom plays a part—, but it is still at bottom a genuine antinomy of freedom.

The religious relation of man to God is not contained wholly either in his dependence upon God's providence or in his sinfulness before God; it culminates in man's deliverance by God from "sin." Sin is the same moral guilt of which ethics speaks, yet not conceived as moral, that is, not as guilt before the tribunal of conscience and of values, but as guilt before God.

It inheres in the essence of moral guilt that it is a burden, and that man must take this load upon himself and carry it, or else must be weighed down by it. But, in the religious conception of sin, still a second factor is added: the burden makes the man bad, makes him incapable of good, blocks his way to moral advancement. Thus it becomes to man only a curse, an evil fate. And here is the point where salvation, the work of God, impinges upon man.

Sin is thereby stamped as something substantial, something which cannot be blotted out by man or by his conduct. For salvation—however in other aspects one may understand it, with whatever symbolism one may drape it—is precisely a taking away of sin, a disburdening of man as regards sin, a freeing, a purification, a restoration of man. Hence, from the point of view of religion, evil is properly not at all the bad deed or the bad will—for these cannot be retracted; even through salvation they ought not to be wiped out, rather are they merely "forgiven"—; the real evil is the burden, the necessity of carrying it, the moral state of being impeded by the load. The state of being guilty on account of the bad deed cannot be taken away from anyone, since it is inseparable from the guilty man—one would need to deny his guiltiness and impugn his accountability. But in contrast to the moral meaning of guilt, sin, in so far as it is understood to be separable, can be taken away.

Ethics has no such conception of sin, having no room for it. In moral guilt there is nothing which could be separated from the person of the guilty man, nothing existing substantially for itself. There is indeed a burden of guilt, just as there is on the part of the guilty one a yearning to be able to throw it off. There are also a limit to the capacity to endure and a moral collapse under the load. But on the man's part there is, in principle, no incapacity to be good, due to his guilt. Fundamentally the possibility of moral betterment always exists— and it is rooted in that very yearning and grows with it. The yearning for the good is never and under no circumstance sheer impotence. It is the most positive power that makes for goodness.

The permanence and insuppressibility of guilt are necessarily connected with moral freedom. Guilt inevitably lasts as long as the values exist which condemn it. It survives the person, just as moral merit also survives him. No one can rid himself of his guilt, if he has at all the capacity to feel it. The evil in which it may materially exist is an axiological quality of his own conduct; and this can no longer be changed, either by a change of disposition and improvement on the part of the guilty or through a genuine forgiveness on the part of another. Forgiveness is indeed simply a moral act on the part of him who forgives and solely concerns his conduct toward the guilty; it is due to his moral superiority, or to his humble sense of the fact that he himself is no better. Forgiveness may very well take from the guilty that special sting of guilt which inheres in the deserved contempt and hostility of the man who has been wronged; and it may give back to the guilty the outward peace which he had spurned; but it can never remove the moral guilt itself. Morally there is indeed such a thing as the triumph of good over evil, always at first of course through an inner conversion; but there is no annulment of guilt as such.

It is then a mistake to regard guilt in itself, in so far as it weighs a man down and must be borne, as the distinctive moral evil. Its load may indeed cause deep misery, pain, spiritual anguish, even punishment—and, more often than one supposes, punishment of a terrible kind. But one sees that precisely in this punishment there is no moral evil. In the proper sense only an act, a will, a disposition can be morally evil, just as only these can be morally good. In comparison with them guilt on the other hand is only a consequence, an incurred destiny. But in so far as it is incurred, it is at the same time a factor in freedom and in its distinctive moral value. An abrogation of guilt would be a violation of freedom and, thereby, of the person in his fundamental capacity.

Hence it should be said: morally there is no taking away of guilt. This does not clash with the fact that to the religious sense there is a taking away of guilt, since God might be able to do what a man cannot do; but from the ethical point of view the taking away of guilt is false, preposterous; it is not a thing which a man may will or, as a moral being, can will. Even if it were possible—and through the grace of God it may be so— it would be an evil and indeed, in comparison with the necessity of bearing the guilt, the greater evil; for it would really be a moral evil, the disfranchisement and degradation of man, the avowal of his unfreedom. Morally it is a thing which ought not to be. The free Being who is moral cannot will it. Against it he must set his Will-to-Guilt, the justifiable moral pride of self-determination.[1]

[1] Cf. Chapter XI (f), Vol. II.

Now if one recalls that it is precisely this complete degradation, involved in the surrender of freedom, this slavishness and prostration on man's part, which is said to have value in the sight of God, one sees without more ado that here a fundamental antinomy is involved, in which thesis and antithesis once more are strictly contradictory to each other. Salvation itself is ethically contrary to value, quite irrespective of the fact that it is also ethically impossible. Yet, from the religious point of view, it is not only possible but is even the most important and valuable benefit which can accrue to man. Ethically it is a degradation of man; religiously, an elevation. From the religious point of view, that freedom which deliverance from guilt violates is an indifferent side-issue, which was necessary only in order that man might become good or bad in the sight of God, but which should be gladly surrendered, as soon as the higher freedom becomes a possibility; for, if once sin has been committed, the one object is to destroy it and to restore purity before God. On the other hand, from the point of view of ethics, freedom for or against is the chief concern—of course not as being the highest but as being the "strongest" basic value of personality, with which every higher moral state of being stands or falls.

The most varied forms may be given to this antinomy, if we carry it to its extreme. In popular language it may be expressed in the form of two injunctions. The first says: "Never mind what you do, let happen what will, if only you do not have to bear the guilt of it; for before God guilt is the offence." And the other says: "However guilty you may be, bear the guilt honourably, only take care that the good triumphs."

One may also characterize the conflict as that between guilt and sin, or as that between the preservation and the surrender of freedom, between the will to deliverance from guilt and the will to protection against deliverance from it,— between the will to bear responsibility and the will to escape it.

With each of these conceptions the thesis as well as the antithesis is substantiated by well-known facts, on the one side by the phenomena of the ethical life, on the other by those of the religious life. Whoever takes his stand on one of them, to him the opposite will always seem unnatural, violent, preposterous. But precisely such preposterousness is characteristic of the whole problem. In it inheres the essence of the antinomy of deliverance from guilt.

Overwhelming historical materials might be cited in proof. In closing we may refer only to two very familiar formulations by religious thinkers. Above the attitude expressed in the phrase: *posse peccare et non peccare*, by which is clearly meant the moral freedom of the person even in face of the commandment of God, Augustine set up as a higher attitude, to which man must rise, that which is expressed in the words: *non posse peccare*. This higher attitude is evidently no longer moral, even in its supreme perfection. For it is no longer the position of freedom. And similarly Fichte speaks of a "higher morality," to which man must raise himself by surrender of his freedom, a condition in which he no longer can sin, because he has once for all chosen the good and, therefore, has no more need of freedom. This higher morality, however, is in truth no longer morality—for the simple reason that the values which then attach to the person are no longer based upon freedom. For a foundation in freedom is the condition of moral goodness and badness.

This antinomy is as insoluble as are all the others. In them all that human insight can here see is only an irreconcilable antithesis. But ethics is not called upon to remove the antagonism, as it is not ethics but the philosophy of religion, which conjures up these antinomies. In truth the philosophy of religion is itself confronted here with what is forever insoluble, an enigma, an irrationality which can never be removed.

# INDEX FOR VOLUMES I-III

Lightning Source UK Ltd.
Milton Keynes UK
UKOW02f2217260215

246979UK00005B/372/P